DARK
FAITH

DARK

FAITH

New Essays on Flannery O'Connor's
The Violent Bear It Away

edited by

SUSAN SRIGLEY

University of Notre Dame Press

Notre Dame, Indiana

Library of Congress Cataloging-in-Publication Data

Dark faith : new essays on Flannery O'Connor's The violent bear it away /
edited by Susan Srigley.
p.   cm.
Includes bibliographical references and index.
ISBN 978-0-268-04138-0 (pbk. : alk. paper)
ISBN 0-268-04138-5 (pbk. : alk. paper)
E-ISBN 978-0-268-09279-5
1. O'Connor, Flannery Violent bear it away. 2. O'Connor,
Flannery—Religion. 3. Violence in literature. 4. Faith in literature.
5. Christianity in literature.   I. Srigley, Susan, 1967–   II. Title:
Flannery O'Connor's The violent bear it away.
PS3565.C57V5633   2012
813'.54—dc23
2012006672

for Jill

CONTENTS

ACKNOWLEDGMENTS

A collected volume such as this requires the work of many fine people. First, I would like to thank my colleagues for sharing their essays with me for this book. It has been a pleasure to work with everyone. A special thank you to Richard Giannone, who has been a mentor to me and to this project. I am grateful for his abiding presence in my life.

I would like to thank Hank Edmondson and Father John Wauck for inviting me to the Flannery O'Connor conference in Rome, where I presented my essay in this volume. My brother Ron Srigley read and edited an earlier version of my paper when I began working through some new ideas about asceticism and abundance. Irwin Streight also offered many helpful suggestions for my paper after reading one of the later drafts.

At Nipissing University, I would like to thank my dean, Craig Cooper, for his assistance with the indexing costs, and Colette Cousineau, who, as the Religions and Cultures research assistant, did valuable work editing and formatting all of the essays for me. Thanks also to my friend and colleague James Abbott, for his unfailing support and kindness.

At the University of Notre Dame Press, I am grateful to Stephen Little for carrying this book forward expeditiously after some long delays, Rebecca DeBoer, the managing editor, and our copy editor, Katie Lehman, for her careful attention to the fine tuning of the manuscript.

My personal thanks always to my family for their love and support.

This book is dedicated to Jill DesRoches, who shares a wooded corner of the world with me and a host of creatures, Nurtchy, Fousse, Fez, and Strider.

ABBREVIATIONS

CS   *The Complete Stories.* New York: Farrar, Straus and Giroux, 1971.

CW   *Collected Works.* Ed. Sally Fitzgerald. New York: Library of America, 1988.

HB   *The Habit of Being: Letters of Flannery O'Connor.* Ed. Sally Fitzgerald. New York: Farrar, Straus and Giroux, 1979.

MM   *Mystery and Manners: Occasional Prose.* Ed. Sally Fitzgerald and Robert Fitzgerald. New York: Farrar, Straus and Giroux, 1969.

VBA   *The Violent Bear It Away.* New York: Farrar, Straus and Giroux, 1960.

Introduction

SUSAN SRIGLEY

The idea for this book began to take shape in my mind at the Flannery O'Connor in an Age of Terrorism conference held at Grand Valley State University in October 2006. As a few of us chatted between sessions, a colleague mentioned that his "desert island" book of choice would be *New Essays on Wise Blood,* edited by Michael Kreyling (Cambridge University Press, 1995). This comment not only spoke to the enduring quality of the collection but also demonstrated how a focused series of essays on one of O'Connor's novels could continue to yield deeper insights and new perspectives into her fiction. I immediately thought to myself, "Why is there no comparable collection on O'Connor's second novel, *The Violent Bear It Away*?" After all, many have regarded this as her best novel, a more mature work, both structurally compelling and scripturally resonant. As it turned out, the next afternoon I went to a panel of papers, titled, remarkably, "New Essays on *The Violent Bear It Away*." After the session, I approached the panel participants and suggested that we had a good start for a collection of essays on the novel. There was enthusiastic agreement and I set to pulling this book together.

The conference in Grand Rapids was on Flannery O'Connor and violence, a topic rendered all the more complex when interpreted in relation to the religious themes pervading *The Violent Bear It Away*. In much of the general discourse on violence in O'Connor's work, religion is held to be either the cause or a force behind the most penetrating critique. Some would argue even further that for O'Connor violence is a necessary outcome of divine justice. In the simplest of terms, the debate is usually divided between those who are critical of religion and those who want to defend or promote it. The difficulty of grasping honestly the question of violence, in human beings, in fiction, and in religion is a more subtle challenge that I believe the contributors to this book have met. The essays here resist the either/or characterizations of violence (as positive or negative, religious or nonreligious), instead raising the question in terms of both/and, without the compulsion to provide definitive answers to its meaning. By extending the scope of O'Connor's religious and spiritual landscape further, beyond institutional notions of belief, the authors suggest expressions of faith found in human relationships and experiential rather than doctrinal encounters with the divine.

I was convinced that a new collection on *The Violent Bear It Away* needed to explore and push some of the well-worn assumptions prevalent in existing interpretations of the novel. In this motive, Michael Kreyling and I are on common ground with our collections on O'Connor's two novels. He argues in his introduction to *New Essays on Wise Blood* that one reason "O'Connor's fiction is interpreted with such solid consensus is that almost no one doubts her own testimony as to its Christian meaning" (Kreyling 3). His collection therefore aims to question the seemingly unthinking application of a religious template applied to O'Connor's fiction, based on her own professions of faith: "As Christian tradition interprets the Bible as expressing one Word in each and all of its many parts, so is O'Connor's fiction given a similar unity, wholeness, and transcendental authority." The essays on *Wise Blood* are thus meant to "question this process and accretion" (4). These two points are worth distinguishing: one concerns the choice whether to believe O'Connor's claim that her fiction is informed by her Christian vision; the second is how scholars use that religious claim to proffer a more "authoritative" meaning to O'Connor's fiction.

There have been enough moralistic religious interpretations of O'Connor's fiction to keep this complaint ringing in our ears for some

time. Such a critique, however, remains inadequate when it comes to
religious interpretations that neither use O'Connor's own religious beliefs as a platform nor promote a single "whole" religious ideology as
the hermeneutical key to her fiction. This collection proffers myriad
forms of religious interpretation without resorting to dogmatic asser-
tions. If there is one all too common and problematic approach to reading religion, or, more specifically, the "Christian tradition," it is the
assumption that one can possibly find "one Word" to provide the unity
that Kreyling supposes scholars use for interpreting O'Connor's religious fiction. A kind of rigidity prevails when one makes assumptions
about what O'Connor's religious vision is, and then uncritically applies
it to her fiction. Religious pronouncements will invariably collide with
any interpretation of the violence in her fiction, left only with the
choice of either dismissing or justifying it. Cursory or judgmental explanations fail to account for the nuances in O'Connor's thought and
art. While each essay stands on its own as a reading of violence in the
novel, the collection as a whole considers religion as lived experience,
not ideology.

What the following essays share is a personal and committed approach to religious ideas in their complex incarnations, critically testing different interpretations and always cognizant of the violence that
cuts through O'Connor's whole canon. The title for this collection
comes from the opening essay by Richard Giannone, "Dark Night,
Dark Faith: Hazel Motes, the Misfit, and Francis Marion Tarwater,"
underlining the fact that Flannery O'Connor's art does not shy from
reckoning with the darkness of faith. To this end, a passage from the
Jewish theologian Martin Buber's *Eclipse of God*—read by O'Connor—
illuminates what the present collection seeks to explore regarding
O'Connor's religious sensibilities, seldom affected by the sentimental
or saccharine:

> the crucial religious experiences of man do not take place in a
> sphere in which creative energy exists without contradiction, but
> in a sphere in which evil and good, despair and hope, the power of
> destruction and the power of rebirth, dwell side by side. The divine
> force which man actually encounters in life does not hover above
> the demonic, but penetrates it. To confine God to a producing

function is to remove Him from the world in which we live—a world filled with burning contradictions, and with yearning for salvation. (21)

Giannone's essay is especially representative of an analysis that delves into the darker places of faith, where the deepest uncertainty and hope thrive, in the lives of three of O'Connor's most memorable characters: Hazel Motes, the Misfit, and Francis Tarwater. Each journey is charted as a course of self-discovery for those who are both unbelievers and yet seekers. The meeting point, or symbol of darkness for these explorations, is the pit or the ditch, a literal and metaphorical image used by O'Connor to convey a deeper spiritual chasm.

John F. Desmond's essay, "The Lost Childhood of George Rayber," maps some of the more remote details of the young man's life portrayed in *The Violent Bear It Away*, revealing the complexity of his darkest moments of self-recognition. Quick assumptions about Rayber's rationalism abound in O'Connor scholarship, and Desmond's perceptive insights challenge these treatments of Rayber and offer a compelling side of his character not yet explored. Gary M. Ciuba's essay, "'NOT HIS SON': Violent Kinship and the Spirit of Adoption in *The Violent Bear It Away*," also traces the subtle undertones of the complex familial relationships in the novel, probing O'Connor's appreciation of orphanhood and arguing how O'Connor was "redrawing the boundaries of family life so that they transcend biology and make room for the most unlikely of members." Ciuba looks at the violence in kinship ties from the perspective of the orphaned Francis Tarwater and his search for identity, while engaging current research in adoption studies to deepen the reader's understanding of the psychological and spiritual meaning of affiliation.

Jason Peters' essay, "Abstraction and Intimacy in Flannery O'Connor's *The Violent Bear It Away*," demonstrates how the "threatened intimacy of creation" in the novel dramatizes the tension between Mason and Rayber, outlining the theological implications of their choices. Peters also expands his analysis beyond the novel to consider the way in which O'Connor's insights into Manicheanism reflect an increasingly disembodied world. Peters evaluates the violence of abstraction, an idea that ultimately distances human beings from themselves, each other, and the land on which they walk. Another example of a study that chooses to push beyond the limits of abstraction and explore "the monstrous struggle precipitated by affliction" is Ruthann Knechel Johansen's essay on Flannery O'Connor and Simone Weil: "Transfiguring Affliction: Simone Weil and Flannery O'Connor." Johansen delves into the darkness of faith in the novel through Weil's analysis of affliction, interpreting the inherited Tarwater bloodline as an experience of affliction and tracing its theological connotations.

Scott Huelin explores the question of *imago Dei* in his essay, "Only Love Overcomes Violence: *The Violent Bear It Away* as Case Studies in Theological Ethics." Huelin offers an interpretation of the novel based on three different responses to the question of what "image" of God inheres in human beings. The dominant ideas in Western theological ethics, he argues, are reason, will, and love, and his study focuses on each of these possibilities as they are lived by the characters of Rayber, Francis Tarwater, and Bishop, respectively. Continuing some of the biblical and ethical themes raised in Huelin's essay, P. Travis Kroeker and Karl E. Martin both undertake a discussion of the novel's primary tropes in light of two different gospels. Travis Kroeker's essay, "'Jesus Is the Bread of Life': Johannine Sign and Deed in *The Violent Bear It Away*" delineates the prophetic thrust of the novel with a reading of Jesus' words and deeds in John's gospel. Kroeker explains how O'Connor's second novel is imbued with a Johannine apocalyptic prophetic pattern, upon which he builds a focused analysis of the tropes of baptism and Jesus' representation as the bread of life. Karl Martin, employing similar themes of prophecy, messianism, and violence, argues for a close relationship between the gospel of Matthew and novel. Martin's essay, "Suffering Violence in the Kingdom of Heaven," suggests that even beyond the title and the epigraph, the gospel of Matthew provides the novel with its primary structure, images, and symbols. He focuses on the child Bishop as key to the transformation that occurs in Francis Tarwater's understanding of the kingdom of heaven. These twinned essays provide a striking comparative account of O'Connor's use of different biblical texts to illumine the novel's central themes. Concluding the collection is my essay, "Asceticism and Abundance: The Communion of Saints in *The Violent Bear It Away*," which augments my previous research on asceticism in the novel with a renewed effort to examine the possibility of divine fulfillment and abundance. Guided by O'Connor's understanding of the communion of saints as a bond between the living and the dead, I trace the idea of hunger in the novel as it signals desire and Francis Tarwater's search for something beyond himself.

My hope is that readers will be opened to a new appreciation for O'Connor's religious vision in *The Violent Bear It Away:* the centrality of love, the struggle with faith, the darkness of uncertainty and its attending violence. *Dark Faith* allows for some critical voices to unravel common assumptions about religion and violence without sacrificing the artistic integrity of O'Connor's novel. Each essay invites the attentive reader into the darker turns of faith, but with a wider perspective: the darkness is only a part of the world in which we live, one that Martin Buber describes as "filled with burning contradictions, and with yearning for salvation." The myriad approaches to the novel gathered here attest to the fullness of O'Connor's legacy as an artist who grappled with the "burning contradictions" in the divine-human experience.

WORKS CITED

Buber, Martin. *Eclipse of God: Studies in the Relation between Religion and Philosophy.* New York: Harper and Brothers, 1952.
Kreyling, Michael. *New Essays on Wise Blood.* Cambridge: Cambridge University Press, 1995.

CHAPTER 1

Dark Night, Dark Faith

Hazel Motes, the Misfit, and Francis Marion Tarwater

RICHARD GIANNONE

Don't expect faith to clear things up for you. It is trust, not certainty.

—Flannery O'Connor, *The Habit of Being*

The people who walked in darkness have seen great light; Those who dwelt in a land of deep darkness, on them has light shined.

—Isaiah 9:2

Citizens of Taulkinham, Tennessee, who ventured to the city's outskirts on a stormy winter night not long after the end of World War II would have quite a shock waiting for them. Amid slashing rain, they might come upon a young blind man of crushed frame, who less than a year before was discharged from military service and who now could be seen slogging beside a road. Wheezing from influenza, the cripple wears a drenched wheat-colored hat and soggy faded blue suit—that attire and nothing more to protect him against the icy gloom, always pushing. His cane pokes the way toward something he cannot see, but wants. The lure is there, in the wind, in the outer dark; it lurks behind neighbors' houses, races down the alley, sweeping onto the wayside out of town, but he can never catch up to it. Were onlookers to follow the blind man all the way to where his strength fails, they would find him, as do two policemen, clumsily feeling his way along "a drainage ditch near an abandoned construction project" (*CW* 130).

Here in the ditch the search of Hazel Motes, the hero of Flannery O'Connor's *Wise Blood* (1952), plays out. The man who said, "I don't believe in anything" (*CW* 43), has reached the end of the line in pursuing what he does not believe. Step by dogged step, the pilgrim has gone the distance. Motes is not the only character to land in a pit. There are many unbelievers in O'Connor's fiction, and all find themselves in a ditch. O'Connor may have been unmoved by European shrines and cathedrals, but the gullies and ravines along the roads of her native Baldwin County in middle Georgia aroused her curiosity. A cavity gapes in every O'Connor story and in both novels. The size and topography of the chasm vary according to the character's predicament, but the frightfulness is constant. Sheppard in "The Lame Shall Enter First" teeters on "the edge of a pit" (*CW* 632) that burrows into the "dank-smelling and empty" (*CW* 693) shaft old Tanner must descend in "Judgment Day" and carves out "the pit of despair" (*CW* 554) engulfing Asbury Porter Fox in "The Enduring Chill," then spills out to the "tide of darkness" inundating the "world of guilt and sorrow" (*CW* 500) awaiting Julian in "Everything That Rises Must Converge," sinking further and spreading wider into the bottomless "hole" quarried out at "the new lakeside" (*CW* 525) by Mark Fortune's greed in "A View of the Woods." All end in the hole they have dug for themselves. Many of the pitfalls awaiting the unwary are tinted by the natural red of the earth; all are stained with human blood, some with sweat and tears.

The ditch, through various representations, condenses O'Connor's essential drama. The empty place marks not only a Georgia or Tennessee locale but also the wandering pit that is life itself. In fact, O'Connor develops a canonical palimpsest of biblical, ancient, medieval, and eschatological hollows. By charging these prototypical images of dark, depressed places with her unbelievers' modern experience of hitting the spirit's bottom and with her own personal struggle, O'Connor gives a profound rendering of our empty age. There is much to say about the mental divagations that drive the characters to the ditch; and there is a great deal to excavate in the void itself, for the ditch leads to obscurities more uncharted than Dante's hell, which I believe O'Connor had in mind. Like's Dante's dark pit, O'Connor's inky ditch is filled with judgment and meaning. Unlike the shades going down to the medieval place of no return, however, O'Connor's pit-dwellers do not march inexorably to their doom. For all of O'Connor's preoccupation with sin, her modern abyss is not devoid of hope but filled with a self-understanding that holds the possibility of belief for unbelievers such as Motes.

One way into this complex topic of belief and unbelief is through a comment by Jean-Paul Sartre, who articulated the philosophical position holding sway after World War II when O'Connor was writing. "Atheism is a cruel and long-range affair," Sartre wrote. "I think I've carried it through" (253). The Frenchman has accurately caught the grim mood and determination of Hazel Motes in *Wise Blood,* O'Connor's requiem for World War II. In carrying through his atheistic task all the way to death at twenty-two, Motes deals with the same historical forces of warfare and uncertainty besieging Sartre. Surrounded by the horrors of bloodshed, Sartre along with Albert Camus, another shaper of the modern mind, saw a world without ultimate meaning and felt the need to create meaning for themselves. Suffering, they saw, imposes a solemn obligation to rebel against the evil torturing humankind. Sartre—and, even more, Camus—argued that Christians are held back from responding to the anguish of this world by placing their hope in the world to come. Camus' and Sartre's ethical grappling with doubt and suffering influentially challenged Christianity at its core. Their reasoned opposition to her faith resonated with O'Connor. It was her recognition of religion's moral responsibility being rubbed by theirs.

O'Connor, I suggest, accepts the challenge that existentialism issues. Suffering is her subject too. Her reply incorporates the theoretical framework of existential philosophy that assumes people are, above all, driven to find meaning in their lives. In responding to the pain of our age, she is, moreover, as a Christian as morally engaged with those who do not believe as Sartre and Camus are with those who consent to Christianity. One feature of O'Connor's witness is her concern for the ordeals undergone by those without faith. She recognizes that unbelievers experience life as deeply as do believers, but differently. This sympathy comes through poignantly in an undated letter of 1959 to Louise Abbot, a young Georgia writer who became a valued friend. "I think there is no suffering greater than what is caused by the doubts of those who want to believe. I know what torment this is, but I can only see it, in myself anyway, as the process by which faith is deepened" (*HB* 353–54). The deeper sounding of faith does not dispel the gloom of enigma or contradiction enveloping those struggling to believe. Both believer and unbeliever must trudge on through the dimness that is the human condition. Far from making light of the ordeal, O'Connor uses doubt as Motes relies on his cane—and to progress through the very same haziness. "You arrive at enough certainty to be able to make your way," O'Connor encouragingly remarks to Abbot; and then from grounded calm she delivers a sober adversative, "but it is making it in darkness" (354). The night does not lift. Nor does the hope of day, the day without end, wane.

O'Connor's aim in her stories and novels is not to dismiss the unbelief of her time but to understand its strife and build on its authentic conscience. We need look no farther than the neglected construction site at the end of *Wise Blood* to see where O'Connor's self-appointed job of reconstruction lies. Like Buford Munson in *The Violent Bear It Away* (1960), O'Connor picks up the work others leave behind. Her project is to sift through the remains of war to find ground on which spiritually to build anew.

The sinkhole in the vacant lot hardly presents itself as worthy of religious interest, but that is what the construction site holds for O'Connor. To understand how she endows the forsaken place with sacred properties the reader needs an eye of hope. This way of seeing comes not through the lens of dogma, institutional guidance, or intelligence. The power inheres in the darkness itself. In this deep opacity we have the presentiment of the mystery of faith. One enters interiorly by the heart into a movement of revelation. What this dark uncovers is not a new area of knowledge so much as something disturbing about ourselves. A light shines in the unbeliever's dark. This light is beyond the light we are used to. By blinks and dazed glances, eyes averted and riveted, the stunned unbeliever, like an owl blinded by the sun, catches a gleam. This ray signals the entrance into the dark of a faith.

The experience in the night of unbelief, as I see it, is a three-stage process. It begins with a devastating awareness of culpability. That initial sense of guilt generates the sense of a need for mercy. And an experienced need for mercy points the way to a relationship with God. In effect, O'Connor's ditch combines the geography of Dante's descending hell with the psychology of his rising Mount Purgatory. The stages could be summarized as knowledge, forgiveness, and divine kinship. The stress that O'Connor lays upon each phase in any given work varies according to the unbelieving protagonist's moral needs and temperament. Wherever the emphasis falls, however, the pit into which the unbeliever tumbles proves to be a place to encounter the source of life, which is God Godself.

Here I want to glimpse into the empty place where O'Connor's unbelievers find themselves to consider the moral outcome of their adventure. This exploration requires a brief statement about the darkness in which O'Connor locates modern life. Then the discussion considers three unbelievers who chart the progression of O'Connor's treatment of unbelief: Hazel Motes, the war veteran in *Wise Blood,* the Misfit, the escaped convict in "A Good Man Is Hard to Find," and Francis Marion Tarwater, the reluctant prophet-elect in *The Violent Bear It Away.* All three are cut from the same modern, incredulous cloth. They differ in age and intellectual grasp of unbelief, but all are ardent, even principled, exponents of nihilism. If pure or single-minded of heart, they are not clean of hands. They are killers. Strikingly, they are also seekers. As seekers, they draw God's compassion. On the immense poverty of their unbelief O'Connor founds the immensity of hope. After marking their new relation to God, I consciously move away in my final observations from the cool detachment expected of literary commentary to participate in O'Connor's presentation of a dark faith that sustains one in present grief and allows one to face whatever is to come.

THE AGE OF ENDARKENMENT

For O'Connor darkness is the condition of the modern age. "Right now," O'Connor says in a letter of 6 September 1955, "the whole world seems to be going through a dark night of the soul" (*HB* 100). In the mystical life-process from which O'Connor makes her observation, darkness results from the loss of the divine light that the soul has previously experienced. God is absent. This vacuum, O'Connor notes, "is what Nietzsche meant when he said God was dead" (90). In fairness to the positive thrust of his stark declaration, Nietzsche also put forward the possibility of intellectual enlargement, for he saw in the death of God the freedom for humankind to seek a new foundation of morality beyond that of failed Christian institutions.

In aligning the mystic's dark night with Nietzsche's death of God, O'Connor theologizes divine absence. God's disappearance for her leaves a void in which the person roams in falsehood and illusion. Deprived of clarity and moral direction, the soul is exposed to trials of many kinds, interior and exterior. Impotence, blankness, and aridity take hold. Negation blankets consciousness. O'Connor's stance is the mystic's view. "The soul," says John of the Cross, "is conscious of a profound emptiness in itself, a cruel destitution. . . . It sees itself in the midst of . . . miserable imperfections, dryness and emptiness of the understanding, and abandonment of the spirit in darkness" (Underhill 391). With the loss of the light of divine companionship comes the loss of self-control that renders the soul unable to progress on its own. Nevertheless, the questing soul must keep struggling. Perseverance gains relief from deprivation. The torments and desolations of the dark night strengthen the soul through purgation of doubt. The dark night, then, from the standpoint of mystical desire, is a necessary stage in the growth of spiritual awareness. In the end, the soul surrenders as the crisis passes; the dark night fades; and the spirit moves toward union with God.

O'Connor's use of the mystical experience is selective. The ecstasy of illumination with its rapturous levitation that precedes the dark night does not appear in her writing. Although the stories in her posthumous collection *Everything That Rises Must Converge* (1965) do flash hints of the characters drawing close to God, the bliss attending union with God lies outside O'Connor's writing. O'Connor deals primarily with the intermediate dark state of the Godward journey. She locates the moral sphere of all her art when describing "the loss of faith" as "the underlying subject" of *Wise Blood* (*HB* 130). For those seeking God, thrashing in the dark is the cost of living in the modern world.

Hazel Motes exemplifies life in the dark night of the spirit at mid-twentieth century. The war showed Motes on a massive scale that governments and societies believe in nothing. Entire cities exist to be sent up in vapors. Weapons and death camps are built to slaughter over sixty million people. Millions more are displaced from their homeland. To the army, Motes himself is little more than cannon fodder, shipped halfway around the world, injured, and forgotten. Getting home, then, is more than usually urgent. Wounded by shrapnel, O'Connor's soldier seeks a sanctuary from bloodshed. Crippled from having meaning taken from him, he needs something to sustain him. The promises of American liberal democracy are as empty as the construction pit. Postwar America affords neither safety nor meaning. Far from belonging here, Motes is as much an exile in the volunteer state, from which he was dragooned, as he is in North Africa, where he fought.

Trained by his grandfather to trust in God, Motes naturally looks to religion to count as a person. What he finds in Taulkinham, instead, are imaginary Christs, pseudo-religions, and religious unbelief that compete with secular unbelief for followers. Kitchen gadgets are marketed alongside scripture. False prophets proliferate to the degree that a believer must fake unbelief to get attention. The bogus and counterfeit prevail. Having internalized deceit and brutality, people take emotional and physical violence as normative. Inevitably, human relationships suffer because people use one another. Death is a national sport. The knowing boardinghouse owner Mrs. Flood, "who had had a hard life" (*CW* 130), sums it up perfectly: "'Mr. Motes, there's nobody to help us,' she said. 'Nobody. The world is a empty place'" (128), one big ditch. One finds disquieting echoes of the landlady's plaint throughout O'Connor's short stories and novels. What Motes basically encounters upon his return is entrenched nihilism, the total rejection of law and decency that caused the terrible armed carnage that still plagues his shrapnel-ridden body and shredded spirit. In narrating the final months of Motes's life, O'Connor reaches deep into modern nightmares.

This soldier's search is short and bitter. In less than a year, after a crash course in homegrown disbelief, he ends up groping "along the edge of the ditch" fumbling for something to hold on to (*CW* 131). By the time the police find Motes, it is daylight; but for the blind seeker the hour has always been nighttime. Sightless, goalless, and godless, the man lies waiting a destiny that lies beyond his grasp. But not beyond O'Connor's moral gaze. She sees the nihilist's fate, the soldier's destiny, the human end all as part of the creative movement of divine life.

O'Connor's regard for the unbeliever brings us to the perplexing intersection of belief and unbelief. There is not a trace of uncertainty about Motes's incredulity. Motes considers his not believing in anything to be true. Whether or not he can supply intellectual reasons for his inner conviction, Motes upholds negation (not unjustly) as accurate to his experience of the world. The whole of his life is based on this trustful unbelief. It determines his relations with others. His disbelief goes so deep that he kills for his truth and blinds himself to atone for its trickery. Such a principled and committed conscience, though not his violence, wins O'Connor's respect. She calls Motes, as many think of Camus, "a kind of saint" (*HB* 89).

Motes's sanctity arises from confrontation and resistance. He fights against religious smugness and deceit. His instincts revved for combat, Motes's opening conversation on the homebound train with the righteous Mrs. Wally Bee Hitchcock pulls the reader directly into the O'Connor battlefield. He brazenly assails his fellow passenger with the sanctimonious assumption behind her prim manners: "I reckon you think you been redeemed" (*CW* 6). He seeks a truth to live by but does not see truth in Christians. Later, he snarls, "You ain't true" (88) to one of several prophets hawking pseudo-Christianity. The accusation applies to others in the novel, many of whom profess Christianity. Whereas Jesus was a man for others, the Christians Motes encounters look out only for themselves. Because Christians do not live by their belief, Motes rejects the god they worship. His attack is as much cultural as it is theological.

Motes's withholding belief in the God of Christian revelation may invite O'Connor's fascination but not her condemnation. Unbelief is not, in her writing, a term of denunciation. Rather, it is a descriptive term characterizing the mental position of one who does not believe in the Christian God who is the center of O'Connor's personal faith. In her 1962 note to *Wise Blood*, O'Connor three times goes out of her way to honor Hazel Motes as a man of "integrity" (*CW* 1265). Belief in Christ for O'Connor is personally "a matter of life and death" (1265), and the measure of her faith is the degree to which she, who numbers herself among a believing community, concerns herself with those persons outside the community of belief. Unbelief too is so much a matter of life and death that the struggle of unbelievers and the discoveries they make are concomitant, I suggest, with belief. O'Connor's deniers all try seriously to take their bearings in the outside world in their relation to people, to things, and to the earth and universe.

In O'Connor's novels and stories, unbelief is no single attitude of mind. True unbelievers come in a wide array. They range from insouciant Christians who do not believe a word of Christianity to aggressive despisers. In between lie the garden variety of passive amoralists, missionary secularists, zealous agnostics, raging heathens, and combative atheists whose lively political and racial rigidities enrich the drama of everyday life in modern America. Empathetic engagement with the varieties of unbelievers accounts for much of O'Connor's distinctive theology, not to mention her artistic brilliance and comedy.

If these narratives do not portray a Julian of Norwich taking succor in Mother Jesus or a Catherine of Siena betrothed to her divine bridegroom or a Meister Eckhart hovering in irresistible trance, O'Connor's fiction does give us glimpses of the mystical talent in common people. To readers' continual amazement, each of O'Connor's disbelieving protagonists manifests a slight hidden talent, some greater, some lesser, for intimacy with God. This spark of spirit abides in the neglected construction site and its adjacent barrens of the characters' soul that is their dark night.

When the policeman destroys Motes's car, Motes sees that he has placed his belief in a material vessel that cannot hold it. The experience of nothingness that overtakes Motes in the ditch proves to be a fruitful starting place for his moral and ethical inquiry. By taking unbelief all the way to its inevitable results, Motes comes to new knowledge of himself. With his inner eye he recognizes that he has invented a false self out of a lifeless doctrine that leaves him without power. Seeing the shards of his constructed self opens the way to a new self, a true self that will not be lied to. In the dark of physical blindness he strikes the true unseen ground of being. On these dark grounds, God begins to be.

Although the former combatant is blind and cannot take up physical work on the halted project, we sense that he is onto a plan to reform his inner life. The blueprint is there in the starry sky on the night he arrives in Taulkinham. A hidden power presses him in a certain direction and molds him to the certain design set by the "long silver streaks" in the "black sky" (*CW* 19). This new mission consumes him. Every sinew of his body, the fragile token of his humanness, is swept up into the last leg of his search. Paradoxically, as his body weakens, his spirit strengthens; and his seeking leads him to the source of life that is his true home in the darkness of faith.

Darkness encompasses the drama of *Wise Blood* from the opening scene on the train speeding south past the deep red sun on the edge of remote woods to the final deathbed vigil in Taulkinham. O'Connor focuses relentlessly on Hazel Motes as he moves from the oncoming darkness of twilight to the faceless dark of death. Death's dark leads to a deeper dark. With her eyes shut, the landlady Mrs. Flood at the end stares into the dead Motes's eyes to see him receding "farther and farther into the darkness" (*CW* 131). This unfathomable darkness has "the pin point of light" (131) that at once holds and illumes the dark mystery of faith. "Faith is blindness," O'Connor writes to Betty Hester, a troubled correspondent whose theological dilemmas elicited provocative responses that invariably go to the heart of the matter at hand, "and now you can see" (*HB* 455).

And at the end of *Wise Blood* the benighted Mrs. Flood gains some of that sightless trust. First, she must "shut her eyes" (*CW* 131). Then, by the sight in her soul, the landlady senses things in Motes that we, the near-blind readers, can try to discern. Trained by O'Connor's resolute view, we can overcome our incredulity to see the integrity in Motes's nihilism. Unbelief is his truth, and he obeys that truth to the end. In loyalty to his truth lies danger and dignity. When Motes hits bottom, he comes to a hard understanding of himself. Near death, he knows that he has no faith, and he knows that he must have faith. The man who founded the Church Without Christ to justify his belief that "Nobody with a good car needs to be justified" (64) learns that his own cause does not win out. Motes lies in the ditch judged wrong before his personal experience of life. He trusted his will, and it failed him. He, not Jesus, is the liar. Having relied on words to blaspheme, Motes remains silent about his terrible repentance with quicklime that extends his course into blindness. His last words, uttered to the arresting policemen, simply state his resolve to soldier on. "I want to go on where I'm going" (131). He has made headway. And he is in a hurry not to rush.

It comes as no surprise that Motes, the Green Beret of the Church Without Christ, cannot win the battle to be justified either in his mind or in God's sight. The wonder is that humankind can even conceive the idea of being right before the Absolute, which is to say before life and before God. The added marvel is that O'Connor shows that modern unbelievers do not see this unattainable supposition as preposterous. But then O'Connor knows when to smile. In the end, the absurdity of Motes's claims elicits her warm humor. After all, he obeys his truth. For Motes to obey truth is to be free from the illusion of self-sufficiency and to be free at last from nothingness. The good soldier has fought the good fight.

In death, Motes's "composed" (*CW* 131) face suggests his coming into full being. Advent, the season of arrival or coming into being, is very much in the winter air. Mrs. Flood associates the point of light with the star of Bethlehem on Christmas cards that signals O'Connor's calm reconfiguring of the Christmas Night Office. The evening prayer in the Liturgy of the Hours, which O'Connor would have known, promises that "the darkness that covered the earth" gives way "to the bright dawn" of Jesus' incarnate Logos. That nocturnal trust occasions the diurnal petition, "Make us a people of this light" (*Hours* 420). As Hazel Motes ebbs into the pin or pure point of light, the outcast seeker joins the people of this light in the silence that is their homeland.

SELF-KNOWLEDGE

Freedom is the state of being the Misfit seeks as he skulks the Georgia back roads in "A Good Man Is Hard to Find," and with good reason. His is a lifetime of confinements, in and out of jail. The most recent lockup was in the Federal Penitentiary from which he has just escaped. Being out of prison provides no release. He carries within him a lockup from which he cannot slip away. The warden is life itself. The unfairness of the world defies his understanding. That one person "is punished a heap and another ain't punished at all" (*CW* 151) offends his absolute sense of justice. The inequity of life, as though anything human can be perfectly just, bedevils the moral purist because it makes life absurd, intolerable. The Misfit does not realize that if life were just, there would be no need for God. Like the positivist who disparages both faith and speculation and insists on hard facts for assurance, the Misfit in actuality seeks a rational fiction.

For all of his mental rigidities, the Misfit is on to a truth about the world. The anguish with which he seethes over the plight of humankind rings with the authenticity of a prophet's exhausted rage. The Misfit does not sugarcoat the unfairness around him. To his credit, he owns up to the malice in himself. Good human blood spills for no reason, so why not shed more? There is little gore that he has not seen. His eye can bear the sight of any cruelty, but his mind cannot put up with the disparity between all the punishments that seem to outweigh their crimes. The Misfit is a tough moralist, not to say rigorist. He is at once O'Connor's most tender malefactor in recognizing suffering and the most brutal in meting it out.

The Misfit's fierce sense of justice sensitizes him to a truth about Jesus' sacrifice that many Christians pass over. The Misfit understands that Jesus is totally innocent and mercilessly punished. Such a miscarriage of justice affronts reason, which for the Misfit is the only basis for action, event, and fact. Since life must be rational and logical, the Misfit needs to know why things are out of whack. His need to know becomes his reason not to believe. Unbelief born of pure reason boxes him in. To numb the pain of self-entombment, the inmate tortures himself like a caged animal. "'Turn to the right, it was a wall,' The Misfit said. . . . 'Turn to the left, it was a wall. Looking up it was a ceiling, look down it was a floor'" (150). This description of the federal slammer doubles as a snapshot of his mind that shuts the door to what he cannot grasp by reason. All the while he laments being trapped, he is looking up at "the cloudless sky" (150) that reveals a vast horizon of experience he says *no* to. Nature, people, and Jesus have no meaning, offer no contentment.

"Nobody had nothing I wanted" (150), he boasts. A world he cannot understand is a world without pleasure. Although the Misfit rebuffs the world, he still seeks to know Jesus, a desire not found in all Christians. Here he is, wracked in pain and seeking satisfaction, and yet refusing to heed the feelings in and around him to move beyond a maddening, disabling rationality.

Fittingly, we encounter the morbid jailbird on the lam as he gets out of a stolen black hearselike car along a dirt road and ever so carefully steps down ten feet of an embankment into a ditch. In the ditch, the Misfit meets the grandmother. In a ditch, the Misfit confesses the pain of his life sentence. In the ditch, he encounters a true penitential opportunity to atone. In the ditch, mercy comes, as it always does, abruptly and without reason. As the grandmother experiences the methodical slaughter of her son, daughter-in-law, and three grandchildren, she hears the Misfit plead to know by direct experience Jesus' raising the dead. This demand for immediate, certain contact with God makes faith, the only way to experience Jesus, unnecessary. Thoughts of Jesus smolder in the killer's mind. Manacled to unbelief, his rage at and desire for Jesus' resurrecting power strikes the grandmother's heart deeper than any logical argument or bullet could reach. She does not think about what to do. The woman certainly does not pause to analyze the gunman's desire for conclusive, physical interaction with God. She feels the Misfit's burning need and responds to it. She acts. Faith is an event. It comes freely into being as a consequence of her self-donation.

Indifferent to her own dignity and life, but fortified by the plentitude of self-giving, the grandmother draws close to the convict's "face twisted" (*CW* 152) by psychic torment over Jesus. With extraordinary, ladylike courtesy, she touches his bare shoulder to adopt the Misfit as one of her children. This ordinary gesture gives highest expression to the sacrament of the moment. It is a profound and calm act of faith, one that gestures to dispel evil. In effect, the grandmother becomes the estranged Misfit's godmother.

Here as elsewhere in the O'Connor world, the body is a place of God's acting in us, where God's action is revealed. In the ditch, physical dread teaches the grandmother's soul how to be free, free to love. Her hand of mercy points the way out of the walls sealing the Misfit in the dark of self-hatred and unbelief. His excruciating need to know elicits mercy from the grieving grandmother. The widow's mite shakes the Misfit's universe under the impact of loving sacrifice. Her benevolence exposes her captor's inability to say *yes* to her *yes*. Like a horse that rears up at the sight of a rattlesnake, the Misfit is spooked by kindness. He is so ashamed of his spiritually tattered life that he has to demean and destroy the person helping him. He seems possessed by a demon that seeks new ways to hurt him and keep in stir. Too weak to accept love, too proud of estrangement to incur the humble responsibilities of true freedom, the Misfit robotically pumps three rounds through her chest.

As belief in mercy makes the grandmother believe in herself, so unbelief crushes his sense of personal stability and worth. If we trace the Misfit's impulsive hatred back to its source, it takes us to self-hatred. Whereas the grandmother attests to faith by simply acting, the Misfit must go to the extreme of killing to prove himself right. Also, there is something possessive in this unbeliever's attitude. Unconsciously, the outlaw is saying that the grandmother and the world must be like him and he will hammer with bullets her and reality into his limitations. This is self-sabotage.

Nihilism aims to discourage and desolate; mercy, an outpouring of belief, wishes to save the sinner. From the Misfit's preoccupation with Jesus, we sense that for all his self-flagellating rationality he yearns for deliverance. The rescue he seeks is at hand in the flesh, but he cannot understand the need for a savior apart from himself. As a result, isolation and pain please him more than does liberty. The scourge of the Misfit's unbelief is an inability to enjoy life that attends a marked incapacity for intimate human relationships. One of his accomplices exclaims that killing the family is "fun." The very idea of mirth or enjoyment angers the Misfit. In his response, the killer reveals himself to be not only a slayer of the body; he is also an assaulter of the mind. "'Shut up, Bobby Lee [the accomplice],' The Misfit said. 'It's no real pleasure in life'" (*CW* 153). These are the Misfit's last words but not the final word of the moral drama.

I have always felt that there is more to the ending of "A Good Man Is Hard to Find" than I have grasped, that there is more to this richly imagined moment than a disparity between the Misfit's narrative of evil and the grandmother's narrative of good. I would like to try again, this time building on a simple fact that anchors the understory. Plainly, the grandmother, though far from a saint, does not deserve her suffering. Typical of O'Connor, the grandmother's punishment surpasses the cause. Even more exceptional, victims do not usually forgive those who harm them. When they do, we stand before a holy mystery. Belief does not come of itself. The grandmother's heart is torn by the joy of forgiveness and the grief of her family's massacre. Neither edict, nor learning, nor reason, makes the grandmother available to faith to the point of sharing her assailant's anguish. O'Connor wants the reader to respond to the dark cruelty and irrationality in the ditch through awe. In keeping with the gentle motion of the grandmother's hand contacting the Misfit, amazement comes lightly. With Elijah, we learn that the Lord comes not in earthquake, the wind, or lightning, but in the soft whisper of the breeze (1 Kings 19:11–12 and see *HB* 373). The moment the grandmother offers in compassion and fidelity her maternal bosom, an indefinite lightness of heart descends on the merciful woman. Then wonder glitters in the weird and breathtaking light coming from the old woman's "face smiling up at the cloudless sky" (*CW* 152).

The facial glow advances in two directions of self-knowledge. With the grandmother, there is a natural inner lighting toward faith. Although the Misfit's sin is the occasion, the grandmother's instinct enters through pardon yet more deeply into the dark of faith. Her experience of uncertainty is prerequisite for renewal of faith. Such insecurity is the preliminary condition to new life. When the grandmother goes beyond right and wrong to risk all to forgive, fear loses its grip. Her touching the killer's shoulder imprints a spiritual sentiment in him. Her face brightens with a courage radiating outward to affect the Misfit's vulnerability. "Without his glasses, the Misfit's eyes were red-rimmed and pale and defenseless-looking" (*CW* 153). Since the need for positive proof and clarity blinded him to decency and truth, obscurity brought by weeping can only improve the Misfit's vision. Tears can clear away foreign particles of torment and self-deception.

Sorrow and emptiness have brought the Misfit to yet another penitentiary, this one without judicial bars of containment but rather opened by the gate of penance to its unconditional obligations. As the grandmother's horror dissolves into tenderness through the power of mercy, so the Misfit's gruesome violence could disperse through penance. The discipline of penance lies before the murderer "in a puddle of blood with her legs crossed" (*CW* 152). The grandmother's persecuted body offers a lesson in the demand that penance makes, namely that one respond at all costs to our neighbor's need. The Misfit must stop killing people and begin to atone for those he put to death. The remorse filling his bloodshot eyes suggests that his empty soul sues for fulfillment. Although the ferocity of the Misfit's hatred lingers in the air, the incentive to make amends glimmers in the grandmother's smile conveying a pleasure and human acceptance he has not felt in life. At this moment in the ditch, he counts for the grandmother who truly cares about him. Were the Misfit to alleviate rather than increase his neighbor's suffering, he could live by his fervor for justice and zeal for truth. In that interior place that will not be lied to, he could heed the call to "thow away everything and follow Him" (*CW* 152). Given his suppressed desire to follow Jesus, pulling the trigger in the gulch may be the Misfit's last-ditch effort to parry the invasion of God in his life. This "spoiled prophet" (*HB* 465) has in his unbelief the power to be open toward faith and to go on to great things, both to announce doom and to effect return and reconciliation. Probably we have not seen the last of the Misfit. There is new terrain to be discovered.

GOD'S SWIFT MERCY

Moving on from the ditch of new knowledge about oneself to momentous duty is precisely the path Francis Marion Tarwater takes at the end of *The Violent Bear It Away*. The act of accepting his moral responsibility brings the unbeliever-protagonist of O'Connor's second novel to the deepest ditch in her fiction. After a week's rampage of scorning the dead, pyromania, blasphemy, murdering his young cousin, being raped, wandering, hungering, thirsting, and setting a final conflagration to assert ownership of Powderhead, Tennessee, the fourteen-year-old hero arrives at the grave of his great-uncle Mason Tarwater. The warpath of blind anger leads to the clarifying gaze of defeat. The very sight of the newly dug grave stuns Tarwater and crushes his ego. The boy learns that he did not cremate Mason and wipe out the prophetic demand the old man put on the boy. This awareness is a mere preliminary to the self-knowledge to come. The gravesite forces the proud

Tarwater to take in a vast subterranean realm. "Nothing seemed alive about the boy but his eyes and they stared downward at the cross as if they followed below the surface of the earth to where its roots encircled all the dead" (*CW* 477).

The main words in the Hebrew Bible for the abode of the dead are "the Ditch" and "the Pit." The psalms repeatedly ask that one not be given over to Sheol and be forced to "see the Pit" (Psalm 16:10). Being spared "the pit of destruction" occasions Isaiah (38:17) to give thanks for the Lord's show of mercy. The biblical ditch arouses a range of emotions from ordinary apprehension to utter dread caused by imminent danger in the unknown, for the pit is dark, grimly silent, lifeless, and remote, lying beneath roots of mountains. This nethermost region of creation (Numbers 16:30) holds "the secret things" (Deuteronomy 29: 29) belonging to God alone.

There are countless ways into Sheol. One entrance opens in the Tennessee backwoods. The scorched red earth of Powderhead splits asunder for Tarwater with interior sight to descend into life's genesis and consummation. O'Connor's hollow shares crucial features with the biblical crater. Both are repositories of the dead that hold a divine mystery instilling terror. The typical scriptural response sets the abode of the dead against the world of the living. After being healed, the psalmist asks rhetorically, "What profit is there in my life, if I go down to the Pit?" (Psalm 30:9). As we know from the encounter with death that concludes most of O'Connor's narratives, an awareness of mortality can give rise to faith. The ordeal the psalmist seeks to avoid is the trial to which O'Connor submits her teenage nihilist. Jonah, Tarwater's precursor, guides O'Connor. Not only does the great fish swallowing Jonah serve O'Connor as the model for Tarwater's being enveloped in the Detroit-bound auto-transit truck, O'Connor also configures the action according to Jonah's prayer of thanksgiving when he is released from the fish's belly after three days. "I went down to the land whose bars closed upon me for ever; / yet thou didst bring up my life from the Pit" (Jonah 2:6). The pit for the disobedient prophet is a school of remorse. Jonah in the pit learns the lessons of mercy and repentance to become a proclaimer of God's word despite himself. The preposterous little book of Jonah, replete with laughs at the prophet's expense, is very much O'Connor's affair. The reader can find something of Jonah's comedy at the end of *The Violent Bear It Away* in the deflation of the boy's grandiosity before Buford Munson, but for me the boy's reading his own dark heart by the light from Mason's grave solemnly opens an eschatological horizon of divine humor.

Unlike Jonah who rediscovers God's mercy against a background of Hebrew belief, Tarwater experiences God's power for the first time amid the godlessness of the modern age. Tarwater is the dark toxic age writ young and human. Heeding the culture, Tarwater aims to root out God from his life. Because the idea of responsibility to God threatens his human freedom, he must reject God to be free. To get rid of God, he must eradicate Mason's teaching to live by and for God. That prophetic life begins with two duties. Tarwater must give Mason a Christian burial and he must baptize Bishop. Just as Motes's unbelief arises as an attack on religious hypocrisy, and the Misfit's unbelief is a reaction against unreason, Tarwater's unbelief is a proxy for wiping out his great-uncle's influence. For all three deniers, a certain psychology of unbelief supports its theology.

We know from "Good Country People" that mental snobbery and psychological need are more effective than books in educating a person to believe in nothing. This good country boy from Powderhead can skip graduate school and get straight to the job of burning Mason's corpse. Cremation will refute the resurrection, and drowning Bishop will disprove at the source the need of God for new life. Whatever else stands in the way of his private will, Tarwater will obliterate with his trusty matches. A dead old man and a feeble child are surrogates to get at God, the real target. We see vividly in *The Violent Bear It Away* a decisive feature of O'Connor's representation of unbelief. Throughout her fiction, unbelief is not an evolved intellectual position. Rather, unbelief is an event, a reaction against a belief or custom that is untenable, undesirable, or untrue to one's willful experience of the world.

Given the soot and rubble left by Tarwater's weeklong havoc, one expects, in O'Connor's economy, that divine wrath will fall upon Tarwater. It does come but less as devastating a rebuke than as a lamentation. This grieving ritual brings the story to an end with particular emotional vitality. Like the grandmother in "A Good Man Is Hard to Find," Tarwater is in a state of mourning. His spirit's coming to terms with loss over Mason's death softens the heart. Tarwater's belated funerary rite for Mason has none of the demand for vengeance or curse upon the enemy associated with cases of violence. On God's side, the state of misfortune elicits consolation. On Tarwater's part, admission of guilt is followed by acceptance of the need to compensate for not burying his protector-teacher Mason honorably. In this dialogue of lament at the gravesite, the prayer of the people of God is born; it is from here, the raising of the dead, that the hope for new and exalted life springs eternally, never separate from its source.

Nowhere is O'Connor's writing more fully and imaginatively realized than in the final incandescent pages of *The Violent Bear It Away*. As the Powderhead woods burn away, an ardor of obedience ignites in Tarwater, the one who set the fire. Surrender makes each moment an event by virtue of the majestic calling at stake. From sundown to midnight, roughly four hours, a silent exchange ensues between the hidden God and the concealed desire in Tarwater to know Him, soundless voices echoing across time almost before memory. In response, Tarwater throws himself on the grave with his face in the dirt. Here the Lord smites Tarwater with forbearance. Leniency comes as a command heard in the blood of the flattened hero: "GO WARN THE CHILDREN OF GOD OF THE TERRIBLE SPEED OF MERCY" (*CW* 478). Tarwater is called to repent; and, in keeping with the biblical gesture of striking oneself as a pledge to atone, Tarwater smears dirt on his forehead (2 Samuel 1:2). The confession and forgiveness now running through his arteries and sinews embody permanently the message he must deliver with his burning tongue. The violent quality of mercy felt by Tarwater will issue a call to end violence, a message to be received or rejected by each individual liberty. The physical cost of being God's instrument is staggering. Mercy abruptly grabs the soul to conduct the messenger's body in following Him, readying the body to bear marks of suffering imposed on and from others. For all its munificence, the Lord's mercy is challenging, adamant, terrible, and laden with peril. The recipients of divine tenderness are left with secret fissures beneath aching injuries.

Tarwater's repeatedly victimized body, throbbing with tragic self-knowledge, serves as a mentor of his soul to move beyond the role of traumatized victim and to become a servant of the Lord. Pain teaches Tarwater that the world does not fit into the confines of his personal will or rationalizations. In the marrow of his adolescent bones he learns that he has been seeking a god limited by his own limitations. But he has at least been seeking. Again, knowing that he is a sinner puts him in the acknowledged need of clemency. The supremacy of mercy precludes the possibility of seeking a rational understanding of God's dealings with the world. The knowledge of insufficiency gathers force in Tarwater's vision of Mason among the multitude at the messianic banquet. Of all the secrets God embeds in the sloping earth, the greatest is the mystery of the risen dead.

As passing observer of the synagogue of all being, Tarwater gets the answer to the question afflicting the Misfit. Whereas Jesus' returning to life throws "everything off balance" (*CW* 152) for the Misfit, for Tarwater Jesus' raising the dead sets everything right. The dead still live. Jesus' raising the dead is the crucial object of faith. Mason believes that world is made for the dead, and Tarwater's vision illustrates the realization of the yearning for the fullness of life. Artistically, without a hint of coercive apologetics, O'Connor dramatizes the foundation of all human hope. God, Tarwater and the reader see, is always making creation new, unexpectedly new. The resurrection shows the future world and determines its perspective—not to say O'Connor's culminating vision. And as the Misfit reasons, if Jesus raised the dead, "then it's nothing for you to do but thow away everything and follow Him" (152). Tarwater does that. At the end, O'Connor gives us death twice over: Mason's death, which opens into risen life, and the demise of Tarwater's false self. The passing away of Tarwater's old self prepares for the unexpectedly new spiritual reality of inner transformation, a new self within the shell of the old. Having learned to live with death at an early age, the boy henceforth must go by divine appointment even further to convey his vision of the dead being sustained by the bread of the living God.

Tarwater's experience and decision at the end are all about darkness, the dark of his plight, of faith, and its dangers. As Tarwater arrives at Mason's grave, the "encroaching dusk seemed to come softly in deference to some mystery that resided here" (*CW* 476). The scene fades "in the gathering darkness" (478). "By midnight" (478) the "boy's jagged shadow" with eyes "black in their deep sockets" sets out "toward the dark city" (479). He will bring the sleeping children of God the message of mercy pounding in his blood. As only a diamond can cut a diamond, so only the trusting dark of faith can slash Tarwater through the darkness of time and the weight of flesh. It taxes the imagination to consider what his victimized body, already suffering the harms done to and from others, will have to bear. The battered, but by no means diminished, fourteen-year-old must go where Motes first feared and then dared to tread. Both do accept the invitation of the "wild ragged" figure of Jesus to "come off into the dark" (*CW* 11) unsure of their footing. In the dark they might unknowingly walk on water, but "suddenly know it and drown" (11), which is to say that in dark faith one either advances or perishes. The lack of certainty expresses the need for and power of faith. Put another way, mystery for O'Connor is the dark moral of faith and the strength of faith. With Hazel Motes and the Misfit before him, Tarwater's inchoate belief entails endless struggle, especially against the human inclination to put one's personal desire above the needs of others and the will of God. And if we happen to observe Tarwater up close, setting off to his future in the city, as we tracked Motes going to meet his fate out of the city, we would see that there is no wiping away from Tarwater's seared eyes the knowledge of death, as well as the fresh understanding of the risen life that that knowledge gives.

All of these spiritual implications come to the reader unobtrusively. *The Violent Bear It Away* is discreetly orchestrated, as O'Connor is content to have simple action show the theological aura. In calling the ending a lamentation, I want also to suggest the spare liturgical artistry informing her best fiction. Craft this ending has; power it commandingly sends forth. The sorrow occasioning the lamentation lies not only in Tarwater's nihilistic plundering but also in the larger cultural narrative spanning the fourteen years of his life from 1938 to 1952. The period witnessed the slaughter of over sixty million people in World War II, the ravages of nuclear explosions, the satans swarming America instigating the massacre of innocents, scorning the dead and the light, and the helplessness of society and politics to redress these evils. Neither reason nor doctrine helps Tarwater. But concentrated in O'Connor's lament is the conviction that belief springs from the ruins of individual human evil and political annihilation. This grieving belief affirms the responsibility for sin, the disciplinary value of suffering, and the absolute mercy of God for which patience is needed to absorb its deep healing. God's purposes, grounded as they are in dark recesses of his hidden love, may be inscrutable, but in story after story O'Connor shows Him to be reliable. The habits of compassion and worship that O'Connor does not find in daily life can be found in the liturgical practice of her art that expresses the need humankind has of a creator upon whom a person can entirely depend.

CALLED OUT OF DARKNESS INTO GOD'S WONDERFUL LIGHT

For each descender into the dark ditch of unbelief O'Connor provides a lamp to guide the way into God's wonderful light. Dante has stars at the end of each canticle conducting the wayfarer from "the lowest pit of the universe" ("l'infima lacuna de l'universo infin," *Paradiso* 33.22–23) to the unmoved mover's supreme light ("somma etterna," *Paradiso* 33.66). O'Connor, following her master-teacher, unseals a living ray to bid the unbeliever out of the dark cavity of our age. From the tiniest spark to starry pyrotechnics, O'Connor's light shines enjoining the blind, willfully blind, and clueless seeker to look upward. Sightless as he is, Motes ebbs "farther and farther into the darkness until he was the pin point of light" (*CW* 131). This supernatural light acquires plain human form in the radiance of the smiling grandmother's face that directs the Misfit to hope. A lacerating beam suits the flint-hearted teenage prophet. As a lamp, O'Connor provides Tarwater the "diamond-bright" (*CW* 479) companion of the "moon, riding low above the field beside him" (478). I use the word *lamp* deliberately to underscore again the liturgical mode imbuing O'Connor's art. In biblical times the lamp was kept burning, partly because a house had little daylight and mainly because the lamp was hard to light. The poorest home maintained a lamp. Its extinction signaled disaster. By reason of its light, the lamp signified the living presence of humankind and of God. Israel keeps a lamp lit in the sanctuary (Exodus 27:20). God requires still more. The servant of God must let light shine forth in the midst of an evil world.

O'Connor, not one to hide her lamp beneath a bushel (Matthew 5:15), artistically serves as witness to the true light (John 1:7) in our dark night by keeping lit the wick of glory located in the pin point until the end of time. Besides mentioning the lamps lit for the three unbelievers previously discussed, I cannot help taking the sheer pleasure of gazing skyward to revisit the "gigantic white clouds illuminated like lanterns" (*CW* 230) honoring Mr. Head's insupportable agony of feeling love restored with his grandson Nelson in "The Artificial Nigger." There's no telling where, how, and for whom the incandescence will ignite. One would be remiss not to cite the signature O'Connorian transfiguring light flashed by the peacock. Though Mrs. McIntyre's eyesight is deteriorating at the end of "The Displaced Person," the peacock still struts around the empty place—forlorn and neglected as Motes's vacant lot—for all to see its tail lift from the ground out of the blue and fluoresce into a celestial comet emitting a radiant stream "of fierce planets with eyes that were each ringed in green and set against a sun that was gold in one second's light and salmon-colored in the next" (*CW* 290). Like Edward Hopper, with his painterly evocations of transcendence in empty American settings, O'Connor is an artist of light in forlorn native places. Star, sun, moon, bird tail, emblazoned ice, luminous tree line, or enflamed tattoo, wherever O'Connor sees brightness she seems to associate God with the idea of light approaching the mind.

That such a beacon of beauty and being glistens in the age of endarkenment for the unseeing, unfaithful Mrs. McIntyre and even for the most treacherous killers makes a case for O'Connor's distinctive cultural criticism that further argues for the capacious quality of her Christianity. After the war, the United States proudly celebrated its defeat of European fascism and imperial Japanese aggression. Americans commemorated the triumph by embarking on the greatest economic expansion in our history. O'Connor, however, did not mistake victory for peace. Nor did she confuse material prosperity with fulfillment. She knew that the satanic forces driving the war were not overcome by the vaunted American way of life, much less by pious ecclesiastical admonitions. The battle is local, personal, and interior. In *Wise Blood,* she observes the war that many so proudly hailed as just and honorable from a very different angle than that of patriotic zeal. Astute social historian that she is, O'Connor looks at the war and its aftermath from the bottom up. Ignoring treaties, alliances, propaganda, material prosperity, and global politics, she focuses on country people and their culture to see what is happening. They too, the reader finds out, inhabit the jet dark abyss into which World War II plunged the modern world.

Neither geography nor spiritual struggle protects one from the lethal current of the time: "if you live today you breathe in nihilism." The fumes from God's death detected by Nietzsche's keen nose a century earlier flow in the modern century. The toxin not only fuels and emits from the Buchenwald ovens; the vapor trail circulates in religious institutions as well. "In or out of the Church, it's the gas you breathe" (*HB* 97). Religious unbelievers and those for whom God is dead are O'Connor's heroes and heroines. Her readers also inhale the contaminant. "My audience are the people who think God is dead," she explains. "At least these are the people I am conscious of writing for" (92). Her mature, persevering faith accounts for the depth of her identification with those who think God is dead.

O'Connor examines unbelief as she looked at World War II, which is to say from the bottom up. Her church, hierarchy that it is, would typically consider belief and unbelief from the top down, regarding unbelievers as caricatures, misfits. Whereas the institutional mind looks at atheism censoriously through an order of rules, obediences, and chastisements that protects its century-old authority, O'Connor's view is from the dark base of the drainage ditch. The unbeliever is not the enemy to be persuaded or proselytized (certainly not to be burned at the stake). Far from being rigid or dogmatic, she is theologically progressive in date and daring. O'Connor is a religious writer who has the courage to think and feel beyond conventional categories. O'Connor's belief in God confers belief in herself as artist and person and woman of faith. As one might expect of a person who finds her identity in God, O'Connor's self-assurance comes through without smugness. She operates, rather, from a humility that leaves room for the unbeliever to live within her. Embraced as worthy, the unbeliever is the veiled face of the believer's identity. Openhearted, O'Connor enters nonbelievers' experience sympathetically disposed to their authentic motives and to the human integrity driving those who deny God. O'Connor imbues her unbelievers, however perverse or silly, with great humanity, visible even through monstrous evil. As she surrounds the poor and weak with grace, so she encircles unbelievers with divine benevolence. Some enjoy a certain charisma. This is the case with Hazel Motes, the Misfit, and Francis Marion Tarwater.

This nuanced portrayal of unbelievers benefits from O'Connor's familiarity with Thomas Aquinas's writing. "The more I read St. Thomas," she observes on 28 August 1955, "the more flexible he appears to me" (*HB* 97). Thomas's expansive theology encourages believers to respect those who disagree with them about God because nonbelievers are also after the truth concerning the creator. O'Connor does Thomas one better. Seeing herself in the other, O'Connor investigates unbelief as one way to God. In writing from inside the experience, she makes a compelling art of its murky labyrinthine passages. As the Heraclitean way down meets the way up, so unbelief in the O'Connor world functions as one coordinate in the continuum of belief. From that position of rejection and abandonment, her unbelievers are witnesses *malgré eux* to the holiness of creation.

MAKING IT IN DARKNESS

Whether one believes or does not believe, seeking necessitates struggle. Because God is shrouded in mystery, O'Connor can more readily understand how the temptation to distrust confronts believers in a way that can be salutary. Such doubts constitute the dark night for those needing to deepen their faith. This darkness strips the believer's heart bare. It tears away the pretensions and excuses and inevitably flawed images of God. We have only to skim the amusing book of divine figures that the tattoo artist offers O. E. Parker in "Parker's Back" to catch some of the countless imperfect pictures we make of the divine to satisfy callow optimism. The rending of these false images can be beneficial for faith, since it is at the very heart of misery, the dark night, that God's mercy reveals itself.

The dark night benefits unbelief by revealing the denial of God to be a belief. O'Connor's nonbelievers identify themselves with their invalidation of any truth all the while they hold fast to the certainty of their denial. There is no real world, but the denial of it has meaning. God is a pretense, but God's death is actual. By virtue of sharing in "the modern consciousness" (*HB* 90), O'Connor is perhaps in a good position with her sense of the dark night of absence to offer hope in the God who is inaccessible to human concepts. In holding God as mystery, O'Connor sees God as beyond all being. Mystery in her art pertains to God's sovereignty.

The power of O'Connor's treatment of unbelief lies in her ability to infuse her nihilists with the intensity and struggle of her own faith. The validity of spiritual seeking is in the struggle. She avoids spelling out the dogma anchoring her own belief. When she deals with the driest doctrinal considerations, they come to the reader as seen for the first time in the lived experience of dramatic action. The presentation is natural and suffused with the risk of longing for the infinite by the half-light of desire, as is the poignant case of little Harry Ashfield's baptismal drowning in "The River." With the child's heart-smashing suicide, O'Connor gets under our skin to tear us apart and then put us back together. She makes us feel, not analyze, the rush of life in the sacrament of watery immersion. The emotions that belong to religion—terror, consolation, and elation—can be felt in this art. Given the opacity of God and the limited human mind seeking the concealed God, there is, in O'Connor's own words, "no satisfactory answer at all, no assurance at all" (*HB* 92) to the question of faith. How can there be certainty in the pursuit of the hidden God? "I can only say with Peter," O'Connor writes, "Lord I believe, help my unbelief" (92). Clearly, O'Connor's personal doubts worked for her artistically. Darkness of interior trial and fear of suffering are essential to the charisma of her vision and to her work, an art of sacred intent. With her characters, O'Connor struggles in the dark of faith. The violence defining O'Connor's art expresses her understanding that the great effort for faith is not won without keen suffering. Wise or unwise—or in the case of the grandmother, foolish and trusting—the price to pay is the heart's blood.

O'Connor's dark night and dark faith fall under the shadow cast by the cross. In Matthew's account we read that "from the sixth hour there was darkness over all the land until the ninth hour," which is to say from our noon to 3 p.m., at which time Jesus cries in a loud voice, "My God, my God, why hast thou forsaken me?" (Matthew 27:46). Abandoned by the Father, Jesus as he dies is left in the void of nothingness and in the dark night of the spirit. When we realize that these groaning words begin Psalm 22, the experience of nothingness acquires fuller meaning. Psalm 22 cries of trust in the God who protected the psalmist's fathers and has drawn the psalmist from the mother's womb. Deliverance brackets abandonment. An exclamation of joy and hope concludes the psalm: "All the ends of the earth shall remember and turn to the Lord; / and all the families of the nations shall worship before him" (Psalm 22:27).

Emptiness opens the way to fullness. This nothingness is everything. O'Connor, in a letter of 4 February 1961 to Elizabeth Hester, expresses the experience with arresting candor. Her enlightening comment comes with deep simplicity: "I measure God by everything that I am not. I begin with that" (*HB* 430). O'Connor begins where Psalm 22 ends. To gauge God by one's becoming nothing is to rise joyfully to fulfillment. Descent precedes ascent as nothing to everything and death to resurrection. O'Connor finds this motif in Dante and major enlightenments of the mystics. O'Connor's fictions fling us into the ditch to stare into the dark of our insufficiency and dependence wherein lies the injunction calling us out of darkness into God's wonderful light. The power to respond to that directive goes beyond reasoning and thinking. Faith is impervious to the rational mind. In struggling with unreason and doubt we can integrate ourselves. This tension gathers us together to make us whole. We rediscover the movement in O'Connor's stories of faith in our age of endarkenment. All faith is dark. For God, who is incomprehensible, is like the dark to the human spirit.

O'Connor makes us aware of the impenetrable darkness that the object of faith is for our intelligence. We understand nothing; we simply believe. With Motes, the Misfit, and Tarwater, cliffhangers all, we hover over an abyss adhering only to the fine thread of God's promise. Among those suspended in unbelief and dereliction, O'Connor finds her bearings. Through this preoccupation with the themes of pain and hurtling confusion, with difference and reconciliation, she comes to understand much about the soul. Whatever the greatness of O'Connor's art may be called, it is present in her narratives of unbelieving seekers; and as is so often the case, that power lies in concealed spiritual extensions that touch us. Flannery O'Connor is the sister of those who have no faith, who eat the bread of sorrow, who are making it in darkness by yearning for the creator of darkness, and who meet in exile.

NOTE

I am grateful to Joseph Sendry and Susan Srigley for their critical reading of this essay and for their suggestions to improve the argument.

A portion of this essay was given as a lecture on 18 July 2007 at the National Endowment of the Humanities Summer Institute, "Reconsidering Flannery O'Connor," hosted by Georgia College and State University, Milledgeville, Georgia. I thank Bruce Gentry and John Cox, co-directors of the institute, for inviting me to participate as guest faculty.

WORKS CITED

Dante, Alighieri. *The Divine Comedy*. Trans. Charles S. Singleton. 6 vols. Bollingen Ser. 80. Princeton, NJ: Princeton University Press, 1977.

The Liturgy of the Hours. Vol. 1, Advent Season/Christmas Season. New York: Catholic Book Publishing Co., 1975.

O'Connor, Flannery. *Collected Works*. Ed. Sally Fitzgerald. New York: Library of America, 1988.

———. *The Habit of Being: Letters of Flannery O'Connor*. Ed. Sally Fitzgerald. New York: Farrar, Straus and Giroux, 1979.

Sartre, Jean-Paul. *The Words*. New York: George Braziller, 1964.

Underhill, Evelyn. *Mysticism*. New York: E. P. Dutton, 1961.

CHAPTER 2

The Lost Childhood of George Rayber

JOHN F. DESMOND

Many critics of Flannery O'Connor's *The Violent Bear It Away* regard George Rayber as a doctrinaire rationalist and discuss him in terms of the novel's larger thematic debate between modern secular humanism and fundamental Christianity as represented by Rayber and Mason Tarwater, respectively.[1] Other critics argue that the failure by Rayber to feel anything when his nephew, Francis Marion Tarwater, drowns his son Bishop is a sign of his total collapse and spiritual suicide.[2] The case, however, may not be as clear as these interpretations indicate. Close examination of the text reveals that Rayber is truly an irreducible mystery, as O'Connor intended. His rationalism is an intellectual mask he adopts as a defense against the vulnerabilities and needs of his heart and the deprivations and confusion he experienced as a child. Beneath Rayber's intellectual mask lies another guise: that of the pitying romantic who comes to consider all children, including himself, as innocent victims. This romantic guise serves as an additional defense against the losses and bitterness of his actual childhood. Rayber uses both masks— rationalist and romantic—to evade the dark mystery of good and evil at the heart of his personality. In her final view of Rayber in the novel,

O'Connor rips away the masks and leaves him facing the inner void he can no longer ignore—the terrifying knowledge of the consequences of his actions. O'Connor leaves open the question of what Rayber will do with this new knowledge. She leaves him at the nadir of his journey and does not foreclose the possibility that he may yet recover. For her, further life and the possibility of grace obviate any notions of final collapse and spiritual suicide.

To grasp the mystery of Rayber's personality, we must look closely, and imaginatively, at his earliest years. Rayber's childhood from birth to teenager was a complex and confusing period of neglect, affection, longing, abandonment, resentment, and childish guilt. His experience during those years nurtured in him a profound sense of grievance against a hierarchy of fathers—his biological father, his uncle and adoptive father Mason Tarwater, and God—all of whom he has come to believe have wounded and betrayed him. Paradoxically, his early experience also nurtured the romantic counter-myth of innocent childhood he adopts later as an adult. Most critics overlook the first seven years of Rayber's life before his abduction by his uncle Mason, and O'Connor provides few explicit details about those years. But the details she gives are revealing clues into his personality. We learn that Rayber's father is a cynical insurance salesman with little regard for his son. When he comes to retrieve the seven-year-old Rayber from Powderhead, he tells Mason, "For my part you can have him but you know how she is" (*CW* 410). The "she" is Rayber's mother, Mason's sister, whom Mason calls a "drunken whore." Indeed, Rayber's bibulous mother is in bed drinking when the young boy disappears and does not even notice his absence for three days, at which point she sends her husband to retrieve him. And on the day Mason came to abduct Rayber, he found him alone in the backyard, "digging holes and lining them with glass" (370). The image is telling—that of a child, playing alone, rearranging nature into some kind of brutal pit or trap. Later, Mason reveals that prior to the abduction, Rayber's "parents never taught him anything . . . except not to wet the bed" (370).

From these few details it is not difficult to imagine Rayber's childhood before he is taken to Powderhead at age seven and baptized. His home life is a loveless and lonely existence in a parental world where, like Harry Ashfield in O'Connor's story "The River," Rayber does not "count." In *The Violent Bear It Away*, O'Connor registers the effects of this neglect indirectly by showing Rayber's immediate, joyful response to the loving care showered on him by Mason: in four days his "sallow face had become bright" (*CW* 371). Given his early home life, it is tempting to regard the child Rayber as an innocent victim of his uncaring parents. But such a reading is only superficially true. In O'Connor's theology, and indeed as any child psychologist or parent knows, children under seven are not "innocent" except in terms of moral responsibility. They feel and act out rage, fear, jealousy, envy, guilt, loneliness, and longing for love—in short, the complex range of emotional experiences. Full responsibility for action only comes with understanding and self-control in the process of maturation. Nevertheless, those early experiences are crucially important for character development.

Though Rayber did not yet understand the full meaning of his home life, he is an intelligent, sensitive child who clearly felt the neglect and indifference of his parents, and it left an indelible mark on his personality. It is the original "blood knowledge" in his life, the first "seed" that becomes as influential in his adult life as the seed of Christian belief Mason Tarwater plants in him. Throughout the novel, Mason, Rayber, and young Tarwater all refer to the blood knowledge as the seed of baptism and the knowledge of Christian redemption sown in Rayber and Tarwater as children under Mason's tutelage. But O'Connor was aware from reading the work of depth psychologists such as Carl Jung and Josef Goldbrunner that the notion of blood knowledge also refers more generally to the natural intuitive, unconscious knowledge embedded in the human psyche, as distinct from conscious knowledge or supernatural revelation.[3]

When he is taken to Powderhead, Rayber is innocent in terms of full moral responsibility, but he is already burdened with the blood knowledge of his loveless home life. By setting Rayber's age at seven, O'Connor emphasizes this threshold year in his development—the awakening to greater self-awareness, to the new knowledge of divine revelation, to mystery, and to an increased capacity for moral judgment and responsible choice. In his four days at Powderhead, Rayber is rebaptized by Mason (he was first baptized by his guilt-ridden alcoholic mother) and instructed that the Lord Jesus is his "true Father" and not "that simpleton in town," as Mason tells him (*CW* 371). This baptism initiates Rayber into the supernatural life of grace. He learns that the purpose of his existence and his destiny is to "rise in glory" with Jesus on the last day (371). Responding to Mason's love, care, and commanding presence, Rayber joyfully accepts baptism and the Christian vision of his eternal destiny. He now learns that he "counts" in the redemptive scheme, but he has not yet experienced the cost of that knowledge.

The effects of this new life and new knowledge are complicated and far-reaching. As he responded so warmly to Mason's love, Rayber would also have realized intuitively that his parents had failed him badly. A sense of alienation from his parents would have followed from this realization and, no doubt, a festering resentment against them for their betrayal of his inchoate but real longing for affection. Mason's love sharpens Rayber's sense of what he would already have felt through his original blood knowledge—that his parents consider him an unwanted burden. Now burdened himself with baptism and the knowledge of his place in the redemptive scheme of things, he must face the difficult choice of which "father" to follow in his heart and deeds—the same choice his nephew Francis Tarwater will face later—and be responsible for the choice he makes. Though at age seven he is powerless, the seeds of rebellion against his parents are already sown. And such resentment will come at a price, nurturing in him a grievance coupled with an irrational guilt for rejecting his parents in favor of Mason and the Lord Jesus as his new "fathers." Rayber's biological link to his parents alone would have provoked such guilt, now complicated by the stark opposition between their values and the values of Mason. Given these circumstances, the mixture of love, longing, resentment, false guilt, and impending responsibility propels young Rayber into a state of moral and psychological confusion. At Powderhead Rayber would have learned the story of Adam and Eve, the main points of biblical history, and the message of salvation in the idyllic circumstances of a remote setting and Mason's loving tutelage. But his "conversion" by rebaptism and his new knowledge have yet to be tested. When they are tested, Rayber's confusion becomes evident.

O'Connor makes his confusion and ambivalence clear when his father comes to Powderhead to reclaim him. Rayber initially thinks of escaping him by running away to the river where he was baptized, but he hesitates to act, a foreshadowing of the indecisiveness that will paralyze him at crucial times as an adult. Compounding his confusion is that his adoptive loving father, Mason, fails to prevent Rayber's father from taking him back to town. Neither of course does his acclaimed "true Father," the Lord Jesus, intervene to prevent his return. At age seven, Rayber's sense of failure on the part of his parents, his adoptive father Mason, and his divine Father Jesus, coupled with his own powerlessness, only reinforces his isolation and abandonment. It sows the seed of his mistrust and even contempt for the world, as well as of the cold intellectual detachment and drive for solitary self-sufficiency that will characterize his adult life. Equally important, since Rayber will come to see himself as a child victimized at age seven, it sows the seed of the myth of childhood innocence, of children victimized by adults and especially by God the Father, that Rayber later adopts. Rayber attempts to return to Powderhead a week after being returned to town, but fails. And although Mason tries to abduct him again, the old man is unsuccessful, leaving the boy to make his own way in the loveless world of his drunken mother and cynical father. Nevertheless, the seed of baptism, the supernatural life, and the message of redemption are now indelibly mixed with his intuitive blood knowledge. But his initiation under Mason is too brief. Rayber is raised in his parents' unloving world, only returning to Powderhead once at age fourteen to denounce Mason and his teachings as "insane."

O'Connor does not present any of Rayber's life from teenager to adult. The key question to consider is how Rayber's childhood experiences, the confusing mixture of longing and abandonment, guilt and betrayal, knowledge and mystery, help determine the adult he later becomes and the choices he makes. After Powderhead, he is no longer the "innocent" child digging holes in the yard. His baptism by Mason, his new knowledge and awareness of his situation, preclude a return to that state. What he must deal with now is the baffling mystery of his own identity, his conflicting thoughts and urges, his desire for affection and his sense of powerlessness, and the heavy burden of allegiance and choice. Faced with this complicated reality, and weakened by the circumstances of his upbringing, Rayber tries to evade the challenge of that mystery and the painful struggle it entails. Although he is returned to his parents at age seven, Rayber does not succumb to the decadence of his mother or the cynicism of his father. Rayber is too intelligent to follow them. Though he returns to Powderhead as a teenager to shout his father's charge that Mason is insane and that belief in redemption is worthless in "the real world" (*CW* 376), Mason is surely correct when he tells Tarwater that Rayber was merely parroting words that did not reflect his true feelings (372). Mason senses a deeper truth about Rayber: "he loved me like a daddy and was ashamed of it" (375).

At fourteen Rayber seemingly renounces his adoptive father Mason's vision of a world transfigured, its mysterious promise of eternal salvation, its call for unconditional love and for obedience to God's will. But the fact that he would even bother to return to Powderhead at all indicates the blood-hold Mason has on him. As an adult, Rayber tries to solidify his rejection of Mason, as well as his rejection of his parents. Against both influences he forges a willful, self-reliant identity encased in stoic isolation. This contrived identity is a suit of armor designed to protect him from the mystery of his own conflicted heart. But the old wounds of resentment, his anger over abandonment, and his longing for love and to love, remain inside him. Since he is unable to truly confront or heal his anguish, Rayber's stoic mask is a deep self-betrayal. Self-analysis alone is fruitless, a fact revealed whenever his wall of emotional self-sufficiency breaks down and he is left prey to the mysterious forces in his blood he cannot control. Ironically, Rayber the outwardly mature adult lives in a state of "arrested development" as he attempts to retreat into the "innocence" of intellectual detachment and ruthless self-control.

Blinded by his coldly analytic reason, Rayber sees himself as divided into "a violent and a rational self" (417). His self-analysis is wrong. The truth is that he is a mystery he cannot fathom because of the rationalistic and, later, romantic masks he adopts. Both masks hide the deepest mystery of his being.[4] The "rational," or rationalistic, component in Rayber's personality is obvious and has been fully discussed by several O'Connor scholars.[5] Rayber's rationalism is a reductive parody of genuine knowledge. It attempts to exclude or reduce to human intelligibility the whole dimension of mystery so crucial to self-understanding, personal freedom, and development. But Rayber fails to grasp his mysterious self. Moreover, Rayber's rationalism is truly demonic because he uses his crafty intelligence as a weapon to manipulate those around him, particularly the sister he maneuvers into a loveless marriage that ends in death and suicide (366–67). Yet he cannot successfully manipulate his handicapped son Bishop, or Mason or, finally, young Tarwater. Like Walker Percy, O'Connor recognized modern rationalists like Rayber as in thrall to a form of demonic possession.[6]

Since Rayber's rationalism is a tool he uses to dissociate himself from the complicated reality of his childhood, his intelligence also becomes an instrument of revenge. He knows that neither father nor mother loved him (which may partly explain his zeal to "develop" young Tarwater), and he sees himself as having been neglected as a child by his parents. He is glad to be rid of his drunken mother, his cynical father, and his wayward sister, the mother of Tarwater. When they are killed in a car wreck, "no one was gladder than he was" (372). Once they are dead, he purges the house of any traces of them (373). As well, he "got rid of his wife," Bernice Bishop, when she deserted him, leaving him to care for Bishop alone, although the "problem of Bishop" he had not "conquered" (400). Indeed, marriage for Rayber was solely a means to father a son he could raise in his own image, a plan confounded when Bishop turns out to be handicapped. Now he would transfer that plan to young Tarwater (392), in great part to justify his rebellion at fourteen and extract revenge against the "fathers"—Mason and God—whom he believes have also exploited him even more than his neglectful parents. Rayber now uses Tarwater to defy Mason, the father who "corrupted" him with love, baptism, knowledge of redemption, and responsibility. But deep inside, he seeks revenge against a mysterious God who did nothing to protect him as an "innocent" child, and nothing to assuage his deep longing for love except send him a handicapped son who embodies the mystery and challenge of unconditional love.

Like the prototypically evil Iago, Hawthorne's Roger Chillingsworth, and Melville's John Claggart, Rayber's revenge is fueled by envy, ultimately envy of God. And like these classic villains, his revenge is also self-inflicted, as we see in the puritanical parody of asceticism he adopts. Genuine asceticism is self-discipline aimed at uncovering the deepest mystery of the self in relation to transcendent Being. Rayber's asceticism is a sterile form aimed at suppressing the mystery of his inner self. Through it he tries to reject "the way things are" and who he truly is. Iron self-control and intellectual detachment are Rayber's way to control his deepest urge to love by renouncing a world for which he has a large measure of contempt. Rayber is the antithesis of the hermaphrodite in O'Connor's "A Temple of the Holy Ghost," who accepts her/his condition just because "God made me thisaways" and who says "I don't dispute hit" (*CW* 206). In contrast, through self-discipline Rayber attempts to control his heart's longing for love, as well as the violent forces of resentment, anger, and despair that he has harbored since childhood. Ascetic self-denial is his way to overcome and outdo the "fathers," Mason and the Lord Jesus, by creating his own rational order where they, in his view, have failed him. But his asceticism cuts him off from the inner dynamism of his soul, leaving him a prey to the eruptions of violent emotions. Ironically, his steely will, the instrument of his contrived ascetic self, often becomes paralyzed when his "irrational" self erupts. Control degenerates into rage, leaving him exhausted.

Before young Tarwater arrives at his house, Rayber's dilemmas are centered on his son Bishop. Paradoxically, Bishop is the focal point of both his longing to love and his resentment; he uses his handicapped son as a way to subdue the longing and exercise his resentment. To his credit, Rayber does give Bishop care and training, unlike the mother who abandoned him. He does not place his son in an institution, though he does tell Tarwater, approvingly, that in a hundred years children like Bishop will be euthanized (435). However, his motive to care for his son is partly self-serving, since Bishop is useful as a way to control his urge to love. Yet Bishop's effect on Rayber is not entirely within his power, and at times he is threatened by an irrational love for his son that might overwhelm him. As the narrator states,

> it was love without reason, love for something futureless, love that appeared to exist only to be itself, imperious and all-demanding, the kind that would cause him to make a fool of himself in an instant. And it only began with Bishop. It began with Bishop and then like an avalanche covered everything his reason hated. He always felt it with a rush of longing to have the old man's eyes—insane, fish-colored, violent with their impossible vision of a world transfigured—turned on him. The longing was like an undertow in his blood dragging him backward to what he knew to be madness. (401)

The source of Rayber's longing—the impossible dream of a world transfigured—is supernatural. It is an effect of the baptism he cannot eradicate. Even Rayber recognizes the urge to love as being "of a different order entirely" (401). O'Connor states in a letter to Elizabeth Hester: "Rayber's love for Bishop is the purest love I have ever dealt with. It is because of its terrifying purity that Rayber has to destroy it. Very interesting" (*HB* 379). Rayber's love for Bishop is pure because, given Bishop's handicap, he demands unconditional love, that is, to love him and all creation as it is, absolutely, for its own sake.[7] But Rayber resents this demand—the seed of love in his own blood—with its insistent call to the heart.

Deeply ambivalent toward his son, Rayber at times rationalizes Bishop as being "an *x* signifying the general hideousness of Fate" (*CW* 401). This cruel abstraction of his son into a cold symbol of Fate reveals that the schoolteacher's resentment is really aimed at the mysterious God. When Mason tries unsuccessfully to baptize Bishop, Rayber shouts: "Ask the Lord why He made him an idiot in the first place, tell Him I want to know why!" (351). Rayber's outburst at Bishop's handicap exposes his romantic view of childhood as well. When the doctor first informs him of Bishop's disability and tells him he should be grateful that his son is not more afflicted, Rayber hisses, "How can I be grateful . . . when just one—just one—is born with a heart outside?" (416). Rayber's protest universalizes his personal trial and, like Ivan Karamazov, he rejects a God who permits even one child to suffer affliction.[8]

Behind Rayber's protest lies the central question posed by theodicy: How is it possible to vindicate a loving God and divine justice in the face of the existence of evil? Rayber's implicit answer is simple: given the fact of evil, the idea of an omnipotent, loving God is a cruel joke. Rayber's position is that of a typical theodicist. Walter Brueggemann explains the central issue:

> The conventional idea of theodicy concerns God in relation to evil. If God is *powerful* and *good*, how can there be evil in the world? If the question is posed in this way, religion can offer no adequate response. Logically one must compromise either God's power or God's love, either saying that evil exists because God is

not powerful enough to overrule it, or because God is not loving enough to use God's power in this way. To compromise in either direction is religiously inadequate and offers no satisfying response. (169, qtd. in Hauerwas 42)

As Stanley Hauerwas and Kenneth Surin have pointed out, the theodicists' concern is a product of Enlightenment rationalism, when "the problem of evil" was abstracted from its historical-theological context by rationalists who attempted to know or prove God on strictly philosophical grounds. Prior to the Enlightenment, the existence of evil vis-à-vis a loving God was not seen as a *problem* to be understood or solved but as an experience within "the Christian community's narratives, which are inextricably bound up with the redeeming reality of the triune God" (Surin qtd. in Hauerwas 49). In contrast, the theodicist's approach to the question is a strictly intellectual, theoretical enterprise. As Surin notes in *Theology and the Problem of Evil*, the theodicist is "the putatively rational and autonomous individual who confines herself (or himself) to the entire *worldly* discipline of 'evidencing' and 'justifying' cognitive formations, formations which, moreover, are restrictively derived from reason and sense experience" (qtd. in Hauerwas 52).[9] Rayber is such a theodicist; he separates the issue of evil vis-à-vis a loving God from Christ's redemption, that is, from what O'Connor calls the "sweat and stink" of the cross (*CW* 334).

Nevertheless, Rayber's protest against God is not to be dismissed lightly. It expresses *his* deep suffering; and it reveals his tormented relation to a God he finds incomprehensible and therefore rages against. Though he intellectually condemns such a God, he cannot escape the pull of his own conflicted "blood," and the powerful though consciously denied longing to be a loved child of the Father once again. Viewed in this light, Rayber can be seen as both Job and his comforters. Like the comforters, Rayber seeks a logical explanation for gratuitous suffering. But like Job, his heart cries out for some vindication of his suffering as father of his handicapped son, and his own suffering as a child. Deep within, Rayber feels himself the victim of divine injustice. As Brueggemann has shown, in the Hebrew scriptures, especially in Psalms 13, 35, and 86, complaint against God is a legitimate expression within the covenant relationship to Yahweh (169, qtd. in Hauerwas 42–43).

Though Rayber has intellectually rejected that community, the intensity of his anguish and rage against God reveals his insoluble, albeit parasitic, relationship to it. To regard Rayber in any other light is to discount his real suffering and make the mistake of reducing him to a stereotypical rationalist.

When O'Connor claims that Rayber's love for Bishop is "the purest form of love," she is pointing to the fact that, despite his handicap, Bishop is "precious in the sight of the Lord" (*CW* 350), as Mason said. In the eyes of God, Bishop's handicap means nothing because the child has a sacred soul with an eternal destiny. But his handicap is a direct affront to Rayber's humanist anthropology, so he refuses to allow Bishop's baptism as "a gesture of human dignity" (351). Thus Rayber's love for Bishop, "pure" in its demand for unconditional love, turns perversely into a "hated love" that must either be controlled or destroyed. Through a strong effort of will, Rayber is mostly able to contain the "irrational" urge to love Bishop. But the urge is greater, beyond Bishop. Rayber's perverse willpower has already transformed the urge and longing into a demonic instrument to control and manipulate others. Underlying this demonic will is the resentment, envy, and desire for revenge that have festered in him since his youth. Control of Bishop cannot salve those wounds. For that, Rayber plans to use young Tarwater. His nephew's sudden arrival gives Rayber the opportunity to act the dutiful father to a new would-be son, and so redress the loss and exploitation he suffered in childhood. But *only* if young Tarwater does his will and accepts indoctrination into his view of the "real world."

Once Tarwater arrives at Rayber's house, Bishop is reduced to being a pawn in the power struggle between Rayber and Tarwater. In Rayber's mind, Tarwater can replace Bishop as the intelligent, independent son re-created in the schoolteacher's rationalistic image. Rayber claims to want to help Tarwater overcome his fixation with the "mad" Mason and his obsession to baptize Bishop (*CW* 421). But his motives are more complex and, since he depends solely on his intelligence, largely hidden from him. Beneath his humanistic "concern" for Tarwater is Rayber's inner drive to avenge his youthful "seduction" into belief at the hands of Mason (408). Curing Tarwater would help clean the slate. It would destroy the seed of belief in his nephew and by extension, vindicate Rayber's own attempt to eliminate the seed Mason planted in him. Moreover, it would give credence to his belief in the childhood innocence he feels was taken from him at age seven. But, again, his real target of revenge is the "fathers," especially the God-Father Jesus, whom he believes abandons innocent children to their destruction. But Tarwater proves intractable, igniting Rayber's rage against an "evil" order of creation that confounds his romantic vision of childhood innocence.

O'Connor makes Rayber's romantic vision of childhood innocence clear in chapter 5. In the scene at the tabernacle church she focuses his encounter with Lucette Carmody on the father-child relationship at the heart of his conflicted soul. The sight of the child-preacher stirs bitter, threatening memories in the schoolteacher:

> Another child exploited, Rayber thought furiously. It was the thought of a child's mind warped, of a child led away from reality that always enraged him, bringing back to him his own seduction. Glaring at the spotlight, he saw the man there as a blur which he looked through, down the length of his life until what he confronted were the old man's fish-colored eyes. He saw himself taking the offered hand and innocently walking out of his own yard, innocently walking into six or seven years of unreality. Any other child would have thrown off the spell in a week. He could not have. He had analyzed his case and closed it. (408)

Rayber's unacknowledged love for Mason, the "father" who planted the seed of belief in him, makes Rayber unable to "throw off the spell" as he thinks any other child might have. Rayber began to blossom in this love and in his new life as a baptized, redeemed child of God. But life in town with his feckless parents eventually undermined his nascent faith. Rayber's early years are thus marked by a double disillusionment and sense of betrayal by the "fathers." Given this background, we can understand how as an adult he adopts a brittle rationalism while at the same time holding to a romantic myth of childhood innocence. Rayber rejects belief in the Fall and Christ's redemption and instead affirms the innocence of children, who must be saved from the brutish, disillusioning world and from "illusory" beliefs. Rayber's intuitive religious impulse, his sacralized blood knowledge, becomes paganized and sentimentalized as pity for innocent child "victims." O'Connor, Jung, Girard, and others have well described this devolution.[10] Rayber typifies what Girard sees as a neo-paganism that "presents itself as the liberator of humanity" by trying "to usurp the place of Christ in its concern for victims" (179). Typical of the avenger who believes he has been wronged by Fate or by God, Rayber sees his suffering as heroic, and himself as a righteous defender of justice and savior of others he considers victims. A parody of Christ, he would be a secular "man for others" (Girard 179). Driven by this romantic impulse, Rayber tries to fashion himself into a would-be savior of innocent children to correct the "injustice" done to him and all other children. But as Ernest Becker points out in *The Structure of Evil,* "the rebel who wishes to replace [the] world with a new just world must himself replace God" (qtd. in Hauerwas 61).

The sermon delivered by the child-preacher Lucette recapitulates the pattern of disillusionment, rejection, resentment, and revenge that Rayber experienced after his brief stay at Powderhead, but now projected on a universal scale. Lucette recounts the disappointment felt by "the world" when the coming of the promised savior does not fulfill their romantic expectations for a powerful worldly king who will establish an earthly kingdom. "The world," she proclaims, "wanted as much as God had . . . wanted God's own breath," that is, wanted to *be* God. When God promised to send a king, "the world thought, a golden fleece will do for his bed. Silver and gold peacock tails, a thousand suns in a peacock's tail will do for His sash. His mother will ride on a four-horned white beast and let the world pull it to pieces, a new one every evening" (*CW* 412). O'Connor's use of apocalyptic imagery here reveals "the world's" fantastic expectation for a dazzling display of majesty and power, a king who would at once establish a new heaven on earth. What is omitted from this romantic view, of course, is the cost of Christian redemption, the loving sacrifice of the Son who suffers rejection, abandonment, and death in order to fulfill the Father's will to redeem all. Jesus' unanswered cry of abandonment on the cross—"My God, my God, why have you abandoned me?"—is the ultimate expression of human grief voiced by an innocent, and yet this Son accepts the cost and fulfills the Father's will to the bitter end.[11]

As Lucette proclaims, instead of a dazzling king of power come to create an earthly kingdom, the world savior comes as a "blue cold" child of winter. The reality is profoundly disillusioning, so "the world" asks: "who is this blue-cold child and this woman, plain as the winter? Is this the word of God, this blue-cold child? Is this His will, this plain winter-woman?" Shocked when its expectations are dashed, "the world" protests: "Where is the summer will of God? Where are the green seasons of God's will? Where is the spring and summer of God's will?" (413). The seasonal metaphors encompass the whole of God's mysterious will, the warmth of love, and the "cold" demand for faith, repentance, and obedience to the Father who is known only through the crucified Son. But "the world" resents such demands and will not give up the romantic dream of easy paradise.

In this confrontation between Rayber and the child-preacher, O'Connor dramatizes the opposition between romantic vision and Christian realism in the starkest possible terms. Lucette's view of childhood is set within a vision of the Fall, redemption through faith in Christ, and resurrection of the dead. But "the world" rejects this vision. "The world hoped old Herod would slay the right child, the world hoped old Herod wouldn't waste those children, but he wasted them. He didn't get the right one. Jesus grew up and raised the dead" (413). As I noted, post-Enlightenment theodicists abstract from this episode to discuss the philosophical "problem of evil." But as Hauerwas, Surin, and Alasdair MacIntyre have shown, such extrapolation ignores the historical-theological context of the episode. That is, the mystery of God's will can only be understood within the narrative of His plan for the redemption of all mankind.[12] O'Connor likewise viewed the episode in light of the larger biblical narrative. Thus she told Elizabeth Hester that God has forgotten Tarwater's murder of Bishop, since in the redemption narrative Bishop and the victims of Herod now count among the risen (*HB* 343).

For the romantic Rayber, the slaughter of the Innocents is a supreme test of vision. His reaction of seeing all children as exploited victims is predictable because it mirrors his own self-concept: Rayber assumes that he was an innocent child. That the adult Rayber would pity *all* children reveals how he abstracts and theorizes in order to evade the truth of "what is." Beneath his pity is contempt for actual children, a denial of their capacity for trust and belief, and not simply for "exploitation." Ironically, Rayber's contempt, like his revenge, is also self-inflicted. He hates his own capacity for trust and love, hates the child in him that was duped into belief, which now intensifies his anger and frustration. Rayber refuses to love the "child" in himself. Bishop embodies that trusting child. Rayber's failed attempt to drown him was, in effect, an attempt to destroy the trusting, loving child in himself. But having failed, he is now left with only his "hated love." Blind to these deeper realities, as he watches Lucette from his window perch, Rayber's "pity encompassed all exploited children—himself when he was a child, Tarwater exploited by the old man, this child exploited by parents, Bishop exploited by the very fact that he was alive" (*CW* 412). When Lucette mentions the slaughtered children and Jesus' raising of the dead, Rayber's anger explodes: "But not those dead! he cried, not the innocent children, not you, not me when I was a child, not Bishop, not Frank! and he had a vision of himself moving like an avenging angel through the world, gathering up all the children that the Lord, not Herod, had slain" (413).

Rayber blames Jesus, not Herod, for the murder of the Innocents, just as he blames God for Bishop and Mason for his own and young Tarwater's lost "innocence" and exploitation by belief. Opposing the God of mystery, Rayber chooses romantic self-deification, fantasizing himself as a savior who would flee "with the child to some garden where he would teach her the truth, where he would gather all the exploited children of the world and let the sunshine flood their minds" (414). Behind this benign mask of savior is the disillusioned child Rayber, filled with rage against the God-Father(s) who did not do *his* will. In his delusion and self-pity Lucette becomes a mirror image through which Rayber tries to recover what he mythologizes as his own lost innocence.[13] "He felt some miraculous communion between them. The child alone in the world was meant to understand him. He felt in the space between them, their spirits had broken the bonds of age and ignorance and were mingling in some unheard of knowledge of each other" (414).

But Rayber's Gnostic vision of a communion of child-spirits is immediately shattered by Lucette's fierce judgment of him. "I see a damned soul before my eyes! I see a dead man Jesus hasn't raised. His head is in the window but his ear is deaf to the Holy Word!" (414). Rayber scrambles to turn off his hearing aid and silence the child's burning words. Fleeing the young preacher's condemnation, Rayber now only longs for silence and peace. But he cannot silence the old rages churning in his stricken heart. What afflicts him, paradoxically—and here O'Connor shows her considered empathy—is what Eudora Welty calls "love's deep anger" (174), an anger that reveals his unquenchable longing for unconditional love for and from a loving Father who transcends all earthly pain and disillusionment. That Rayber will not accept the divine, mysterious source of love *and* pain, or the truth that love and suffering are inextricably mixed, is for O'Connor his real tragedy and the only reason to pity him.

Rayber's encounter with the child preacher reveals that beneath his mask of reason lies a romantic sentimentalist at heart. But rather than acknowledge and accept his own need both to love and be loved, he continues his now flagging efforts to control himself, Bishop, and Tarwater. Through Bishop he had hoped to suppress his "hated love." He believes that "he could control his terrifying love as long as it has its focus in Bishop, but if anything happened to Bishop, he would have to face it in himself. Then the whole world would become his idiot child" (*CW* 442). But Rayber's control of Bishop weakens as the child becomes more fascinated with his cousin Tarwater. Loss of Bishop threatens to collapse Rayber's defense against love, as he is now trapped in his deep ambivalence toward his son. Rayber insists that "if anyone controlled Bishop, it would be himself," but he recognizes Tarwater's new power over the child and is jealous. In truth, Rayber has already effectively abandoned his son by his plan to displace him in his attention with the more promising Tarwater. But when the fiercely independent Tarwater firmly resists Rayber's attempts to adopt him as his son, Rayber concludes that his nephew is beyond "rational" persuasion, that only the psychic shock of a return to Powderhead will help Tarwater overcome his "compulsion" to baptize Bishop. In his deepest self, Rayber now "hates" Tarwater and wants to be rid of him (452–53). At the Cherokee Lodge, Rayber dreams of escaping with his son and abandoning his nephew to his own devices (454). Rayber's conflicted love/hate relationship now extends to both boys. Having lost the battle to indoctrinate Tarwater, Rayber would content himself with a life with

Bishop, whom he can manipulate and through whom he can try to control his hated love, though at the cost of a full life. He would return to his stoically sterile, yet "sane" life. But the death of Bishop shatters that possibility altogether.

The final view of Rayber presented in the novel is fraught with ambiguity, as O'Connor clearly intended. Many critics have been too quick to sum up and judge the schoolteacher's final spiritual state in ways not completely justified by the text. For example, in his fine Girardian analysis of the novel, Gary Ciuba argues that Rayber and Tarwater "unite to kill a substitute as a way of achieving personal peace. . . . *letting Bishop be killed* will enable Rayber to be freed at last from the child that threatens his hardened heart as well as from the young rival-disciple who would never leave as long as Bishop was around." Ciuba points out that the narrator "emphasizes the collusion of Tarwater and Rayber in killing Bishop" and that Rayber's "silent acquiescence in the murder makes him as culpable as Tarwater." Finally, he argues that "Rayber virtually kills himself in allowing Bishop to be killed. . . . By petrifying himself to the murder of his son, the father has committed the ultimate act of self-violence" (Ciuba 145–52, emphasis mine).

In his Bakhtinian reading of the novel, Robert H. Brinkmeyer, Jr. discusses Rayber in terms of a conflict between the "monologic" fundamentalism of Mason (and the narrator) and the rationalist secularism of Rayber. He sees Rayber's rationalism and asceticism as finally defeated by the narrator's "fundamentalist imperative" because Rayber has so withdrawn himself from life that he is left with nothing, not even pain, when Bishop is drowned. Brinkmeyer concludes that even "if Rayber defeats old Tarwater and his fundamentalism," in the narrative perspective, he is, as a result, "reduced to nothing, a man who has lost his soul" (126–27). For his part, George A. Kilcourse, Jr. credits O'Connor for having created a complex, human character in Rayber, a man of free will who refuses offered grace and lives "totally in his head" in a parody of Christian asceticism. Kilcourse emphasizes Rayber's corruption and the irony of his failure to feel anything at Bishop's death as the logical outcome of his sin. He concludes that O'Connor "has masterfully made sin believable through the paralysis of his stony heart. The truth of his *damnation* is earned through his human, sinful character" (Kilcourse 234, emphasis mine).

The problem with each of these representative interpretations is that they impose a closure on O'Connor's treatment of Rayber. Her presentation of Rayber's last days with Bishop and Tarwater is more nuanced than these interpretations suggest. O'Connor remarks in a letter to Elizabeth Hester that she "would have liked for [Rayber] to be saved, and it is ambiguous whether he may be or not" (*HB* 357). O'Connor's statements about her own stories are sometimes misleading, but even without her comment to Hester, the text reveals that O'Connor resisted the kind of formulaic "death" and "damnation" of Rayber imposed by some critics on the ending, just as she resisted the formulaic stereotype of him as rationalist or demonic villain.

Through her use of complicated patterns of doubling characters and actions, O'Connor makes clear that Rayber is complicit in Bishop's murder. Tarwater's drowning of Bishop parallels and reverses Rayber's earlier failed attempt to drown his son. In addition, the drowning ironically underscores Rayber's sometimes paralysis when dealing with the Tarwaters, his failure "to act" decisively. Coupled with these elements is his exhaustion from his struggle with his rebellious nephew and his latent and fateful longing to escape from crises both outside and within himself—all of which point to his complicity. However, complicity does not mean that Rayber knowingly sends Bishop to his death. Such an interpretation would make Rayber a moral monster and undercut the human complexity O'Connor worked so hard and long to create in him. Rather, Rayber's complicity in his son's death is the culmination of his most grievous sin—his abandonment of Bishop and the demand for unconditional love he represents—in favor of the nephew he would raise up in his own godless image. The sin against Bishop (and Tarwater) is also like all sin, self-inflicted. Since childhood Rayber has suffered the need for and the need to give unconditional love, a need he tried to objectify and control through Bishop, or mask with a romantic myth of innocent, exploited childhood that is essentially escapist. With Bishop dead, Rayber will sooner or later have to face this deepest truth about himself.

O'Connor carefully dramatizes this complexity at the end of chapter 9. Just before the fatal boat trip, Rayber is exhausted from his final violent argument with Tarwater, after which he admits that "the only feeling he had for this boy was hate. He loathed the very sight of him" (*CW* 452). The narrator notes that Rayber, wishing to escape the tension, "wanted nothing so much as a half hour to himself, without sight of either of them." Still, he twice cautions Tarwater to "be careful" with Bishop in the boat and to "look after him" (453). His warnings can hardly be read as disingenuous. Once back in his room, Rayber realizes that his only wish now is to be rid of Tarwater and, just before he hears Bishop's death-howl, he dreams of escaping with Bishop and leaving Tarwater behind (454).

O'Connor makes clear Rayber's complicity in Bishop's death, but she also preserves the mystery of the action, in part by having Rayber tell Tarwater to watch over Bishop in the boat. Moreover, in typically contradictory fashion, Rayber checks his earlier impulse to be rid of Tarwater (453) and instead decides to offer an ultimatum to his nephew when he returns: either conform to Rayber's plans for him or leave. Rayber now prides himself on having finally reached a state of "indifference" about whether Tarwater leaves or stays, and so believes he has regained his intellectual control (454). But these contradictory reactions just before he hears Bishop's howl reveal how little he knows his own heart and that he has never truly confronted the mystery of his own personality. When he hears Bishop's bellow, he knows what has happened "as if he were in the boat," and as the silence descends again Rayber waits for the "raging pain, the intolerable hurt that was his due, to begin." But in the end he feels nothing. "He stood light-headed at the window and it was not until he realized there would be no pain that he collapsed" (455).

The final view of Rayber that O'Connor presents is open-ended and does not necessarily infer "damnation" or "spiritual suicide." Her ending is not marked by the closure of neat allegory. She preserves the limits of fiction and avoids any dogmatic conclusion. What the death of Bishop destroys is Rayber's plan to control his "hated love" through his son. Moreover, since he knows Tarwater has baptized Bishop and will not return, it is the end of his dream of avenging himself against "the fathers"—Mason and God—whom he blames for his "warped" life and whom he hoped to defeat by re-creating Tarwater in his own image. Bishop's death also shatters the rationalistic and romantic personae contrived by Rayber to escape the painful need to love and be loved, a need against which he has struggled his whole life. Rayber must now face the void within himself, the cold realization of his desolate spiritual state. But his tormented heart will surely quicken again. To what end, O'Connor does not say. It may awaken to intensified bitterness, rage, despair, and perhaps suicide. Or it may be that, paradoxically, losing Bishop and, along with him, his own illusions, will force Rayber at last to confront the mystery of his own heart. If that happens, losing Bishop may be the second best thing that has happened to him. The whole world might yet become his idiot child.

NOTES

1. See, for example, discussions of Rayber in Asals 165–84; Kilcourse 221–34; and Brinkmeyer, 117–31.

2. See especially Kilcourse 234; and Ciuba 151–52.

3. The best discussion of this theme can be found in Goldbrunner's study of Jung's depth psychology, *Individuation* (146–56).

4. Rayber often speaks of freedom and of freeing young Tarwater from his "compulsion," but his notion of freedom is entirely circumscribed by his rationalistic perspective. Since Rayber denies the spiritual realm, he rejects any concept of metaphysical freedom or the Christian notion of freedom from sin and death.

5. Asals and Kilcourse, cited in note 1 above, offer representative discussions of Rayber's rationalistic viewpoint.

6. See especially Percy's discussion of the "demoniac self" in *Lost in the Cosmos* (175–98).

7. In his discussion of the *skandalon* (stumbling stone), Ciuba argues that Bishop "lives by the Johannine Logos of love rather than the logos of violence" (148). While in comparison to Rayber and the Tarwaters, Bishop's affections are untinged by violence, it seems difficult, given his mental handicap, to equate those visceral affections with St. John's "Logos of love."

8. O'Connor's critique of Ivan Karamazov's argument against the goodness of God is well known: "Ivan Karamazov cannot believe, as long as one child is in torment; Camus' hero cannot accept the divinity of Christ, because of the massacre of the Innocents. In this popular pity, we mark our gain in sensibility and our loss in vision" (*MM* 227).

9. In *Whose Justice? Which Rationality?* Alasdair MacIntyre writes, "It was a central aspiration of the Enlightenment . . . to provide for debate in the public realm standards and methods of rational justification by which alterna-

tive courses of action in every phase of life could be adjudged just or unjust, rational or irrational, enlightened or unenlightened. So, it was hoped, reason would displace authority and tradition. Rational justification was to appeal to principles undeniable by any rational person and therefore independent of all those social and cultural particularities which the Enlightenment thinkers took to be the mere accidental clothing of reason in particular times and places" (qtd. in Hauerwas 53n23).

10. See Girard's chapter titled "The Modern Concern for Victims" in *I See Satan Fall Like Lightning*, 161–70. See also Jung's chapter titled "The Spiritual Problem of Modern Man," in *Modern Man in Search of a Soul*, 196–220.

11. Jesus' cry of abandonment is recorded in the gospels of Matthew and Mark. See Brueggemann (51–53) for an insightful discussion of the theme of abandonment vis-à-vis a loving God who redeems (cited in Hauerwas 78–84).

12. See Hauerwas 39–58.

13. Discussing the rape of young Tarwater, Ciuba points out that, according to some theorists, child molestation is "the attempt of the victimizer to seize the idealized childhood victim" (154). Although Rayber does not propose to rape the child preacher Lucette, his fantasy of spiriting her away to an idealized "garden" where he can be her savior and defender certainly suggests a perverse seduction of the girl, which may reflect his own wish for an idealized childhood.

WORKS CITED

Asals, Frederick. *Flannery O'Connor: The Imagination of Extremity*. Athens: University of Georgia Press, 1982.

Brinkmeyer, Robert H., Jr. *The Art and Vision of Flannery O'Connor*. Baton Rouge: Louisiana State University Press, 1989.

Brueggemann, Walter. *The Message of the Psalms: A Theological Commentary*. Minneapolis: Augsburg, 1984.

Ciuba, Gary M. *Desire, Violence and Divinity in Modern Southern Fiction*. Baton Rouge: Louisiana State University Press, 2007.

Girard, René. *I See Satan Fall Like Lightning*. Maryknoll, NY: Orbis Books, 2001.

Goldbrunner, Josef. *Individuation: A Study of the Depth Psychology of Carl Gustav Jung*. Notre Dame, IN: University of Notre Dame Press, 1964.

Hauerwas, Stanley. *God, Medicine, and Suffering*. Grand Rapids, MI: Eerdmans, 1990.

Jung, Carl Gustav. *Modern Man in Search of a Soul*. New York: Harcourt, Brace and Co., 1933.

Kilcourse, George A., Jr. *Flannery O'Connor's Religious Imagination*. Mahwah, NJ: Paulist Press, 2001.

O'Connor, Flannery. *Collected Works*. Ed. Sally Fitzgerald. New York: Library of America, 1988.

———. *The Habit of Being: Letters of Flannery O'Connor*. Ed. Sally Fitzgerald. New York: Farrar, Straus and Giroux, 1979.

———. *Mystery and Manners: Occasional Prose*. Ed. Sally Fitzgerald and Robert Fitzgerald. New York: Farrar, Straus and Giroux, 1961.

Percy, Walker. *Lost in the Cosmos: The Last Self-Help Book*. New York: Farrar, Straus and Giroux, 1983.

Welty, Eudora. *The Optimist's Daughter*. Greenwich, CT: Fawcett, 1969.

CHAPTER 3

"NOT HIS SON"

Violent Kinship and the Spirit of Adoption
in *The Violent Bear It Away*

GARY M. CIUBA

I thought you would call me "Father"
and not run away from following me.

—Jeremiah 3:19

When the young Mary Flannery O'Connor visited the Catholic orphanage for girls in her hometown of Savannah, she beheld what she
would describe in a 1957 letter as "the ultimate horror." St. Mary's
Home was founded in 1875 by the Sisters of Mercy to care for homeless
girls in the aftermath of the Civil War; it moved to its second site, on
Habersham Street, in 1883.[1] At this "creaking house on a dreary street,"
O'Connor spent time with "the Sisters or some orphan distant-cousins";
sometimes, the children were permitted to spend a day with her—
"miserable occasions for me, as they were not other children, they were
Orphans. I don't know if they enjoyed coming or not; probably not"

(*HB* 244). Although O'Connor recognized that "there was doubtless plenty of love there," St. Mary's seemed like a children's asylum out of Dickens by way of Dante because the love was "official, and you wouldn't have got yours from your own God-given source." She reflected, "[T]hat was probably my first view of hell. Children know by instinct that hell is an absence of love, and they can pick out theirs without missing" (*HB* 244).

The disturbing visits to St. Mary's shadowed O'Connor's life and fiction. Although neither Regina Cline O'Connor nor Edward O'Connor, her parents, listed themselves on the Roll of the Female Orphanage Society in 1936, there on the roster of contributors is the name of the eleven-year-old Mary Flannery (Cash 4; Gooch 27). Her father's death from lupus in 1941 must have later made the near-sixteen-year-old feel more acutely how bereft were the orphans that she had visited. In her 1957 letter about St. Mary's to her friend Elizabeth Hester, O'Connor recalled how every Christmas her mother would ask for her three-dollar donation to the Savannah orphanage, and O'Connor would dutifully write out the check.[2] She speculated that her visits there as a youngster were intended "probably as a salutary lesson. 'See what you have to be thankful for. Suppose you were, etc.'—a lesson my imagination played on exhaustively." For if the young Mary Flannery recoiled at the desolation of these orphans, she also discovered a mysterious kinship with them. As O'Connor wrote to Hester, "Anyway, I have been at least an Imaginary Orphan" (*HB* 244).

Since O'Connor believed that the child gathers most of the experience that the future writer will use in her art (*HB* 204), her early visits to St. Mary's might point toward a corresponding way to read the fiction of this "Imaginary Orphan." Orphan and adoption studies were just beginning when O'Connor was writing; the emergent field would bring together law, memoir, history, religion, psychiatry, psychology, sociology, and literary criticism. Yet if taking this interdisciplinary approach seems to grow out of O'Connor's orphan imagination, it also risks interpreting her work at obviously cross-purposes to her artistic creed. Orphan and adoption studies partly rely on the social sciences, whose aims, O'Connor insisted, were quite different from those of her fiction. Her essays repeatedly emphasized that a story should not be imagined out of a poll, survey, case study, or statistic. Whereas these data-gathering tools turn the specific into the typical and the abstract, O'Connor yearned to see so deeply into the dense particularity that it disclosed what was freakish, eternal, and mysterious. However, O'Connor recognized that even such disciplines might inform the novelist's work, especially if they did not limit the writer's ability to see beyond them (*MM* 163–65). Reading O'Connor by way of orphanhood and adoption demonstrates how she intuited much about the complex world of blood relations and fictive kinship in her violent South. And reading orphanhood and adoption by way of O'Connor reveals how she might contribute to the reconception of family bonds.

O'Connor's identification with orphans might be understood by Betty Jean Lifton, a leading activist in the adoption rights movement. In *Lost and Found* Lifton writes of discovering "that all people, if they dare to think at all, think of themselves in some sense as orphans— foundlings—who are struggling with problems around alienation. Everyone has some feeling of having been deprived, of playing the impostor because they're not supposed to be here" (5). The solitude to which O'Connor gravitated by illness, vocation, temperament, and spirituality made her live out on a daily basis the strangeness and separation that she detected in the children at St. Mary's. Always writing out of the recognition that "[w]e are all rather blessed in our deprivation if we let ourselves be" (*HB* 169), O'Connor adopted orphanhood as a sign of the ongoing loss out of which she created her fiction. Indeed, such bereavement might be the stance of every writer because orphanhood, according to Derrida, is the filial status of writing itself. Whereas the oral word has a father in the speaker, the written word lives in the absence of the paternal voice. Since writing actually displaces and replaces the speakerly father, the orphan script is associated with all that is contradictory, subversive, and patricidal (Derrida 77). O'Connor imagined this radical kind of affiliation as particularly her own. Writing as an orphan, O'Connor had the detachment to look askance at the postwar cheerfulness that concealed a violent and materialistic fatherland in which she never felt at home and to depict the one deprivation that bore no blessing—the hellish lovelessness of her country people who lack what should have come from their "own God-given source."

Although most of O'Connor's characters suffer from a homelessness that belies the domestic settings of her farmhouses and city residences, her orphan imagination made that plight especially evident in the unattached children that wander the landscape of her fiction. O'Connor's stories were always completing the hypothetical lesson about orphanhood that her parents might have been trying to teach her, "Suppose you were, etc." Some of the children that she "supposed" into life, like Enoch in *Wise Blood*, Harry in "The River," and young Rayber in *The Violent Bear It Away*, have parents who are indifferent or neglectful; others, like Powell in "A Circle in the Fire," Nelson in "The Artificial Nigger," and Rufus in "The Lame Shall Enter First," have parents who are absent or dead. Imagining such forsaken children directly shaped O'Connor's narrative art. As Carol Singley notes about orphan fiction, the youngsters' freedom from the constraints of family life opens the action to unpredictable exploits outside the home (51–52). O'Connor's stories about quasi-orphans enjoy the wayward liberty of such wanderers' tales.

Despite the writer's bloodlines in Catholicism, her young adventurers do not follow anything like the reassuringly pious path of Cardinal Spellman's *The Foundling*, the 1951 best seller about an infant left at St. Patrick's Cathedral. The infant boy is brought to an orphanage because the devoted man who finds him thinks it better for this child of a Catholic mother to be raised in a Catholic setting than to be adopted by a Protestant like himself. O'Connor appreciated that the profits from the prelate's book would be used to help orphans, yet she thought that the mediocre tome might well serve the buyer as a doorstop (*MM* 175). O'Connor's homeless kids are more like the orphaned and errant Huck Finn than Spellman's hero of high Catholicism. They travel deep into misery as they sometimes seek quasi-adoptive relationships and sometimes find themselves part of a family despite their resistance to such threatening bonds.

Although during O'Connor's lifetime the orphans at St. Mary's were usually raised there, adoption had been increasingly promoted since before the Civil War as an alternative to such extended and institutionalized care. In 1938, the year of Francis Marion Tarwater's birth in *The Violent Bear It Away*, the Child Welfare League of America issued its first set of adoption guidelines, designed to protect the interests of the child, the adoptive parents, and the state. Its first provision emphasized the need to preserve the bonds with the child's birth family (Carp, "Introduction" 11). By the time that O'Connor was writing in the 1950s, adoption was flourishing in America, for it had been spurred by the postwar baby boom, affluence, and desire to conform to the image of the family as a mother, father, and children (Pertman 40–41). The number of formal adoptions increased from 16,000 in 1937 to 72,000 in 1951, a year before the present action of *The Violent Bear It Away* (Stolley 29–30). Such placements were typically founded on a belief in confidentiality, the importance of environment over heredity, the similarities between birth and adoptive families, and the greatest possible resemblance between the adoptive child and parents (Melosh 219–20). Indeed, couples were carefully screened for their suitability to adopt, and children were sought who might match their new parents in race, appearance, disposition, intelligence, and religion (Gill 168–74).

As an "Imaginary Orphan," O'Connor considered how the stray, the outcast, and the disconnected in her fiction might find a home. They reach that destination with none of the "Leapin' lizards!" glee of Little Orphan Annie, who finds a home with the prosperous Daddy Warbucks. O'Connor wrote in 1949 that she did not read Harold Gray's comic strip about the red-haired moppet that first appeared in print a year before the writer was born, but she then wondered, "Am I missing something significant?" (*HB* 19).[3] Closer to the anguished discovery of home in O'Connor's fiction than the upbeat Annie, who was first found at an orphanage and then found again and again as the paternal Warbucks rescued her, is the wretched "foundling" in a Liverpool workhouse that O'Connor knew by way of Hawthorne's notebook. As she recalls in her "Introduction to *A Memoir of Mary Ann*," the sexless and scurvy-eyed child reached out its hands to the wary Hawthorne, who felt as if "out of all human kind it chose me to be its father!" (qtd. in *MM* 219). O'Connor reported feeling "more of a kinship with [Hawthorne] than with any other American" (*HB* 457). Having adopted the brooding writer of romances as one of her fictional ancestors, O'Connor likewise looks toward redrawing the boundaries of family life so that they transcend biology and make room for the most unlikely of members.

The grandmother in "A Good Man Is Hard to Find" heralds the wider embrace in the house of O'Connor when she recognizes that the serial-killer Misfit actually fits into a revelatory understanding of her own family. As O'Connor comments, the grandmother is "joined to him by ties of kinship which have their roots deep in the mystery she has been merely prattling about so far" (*MM* 112). However, when, like Hawthorne's foundling, the old lady reaches out to touch her distant relative, the Misfit recoils from such sonship by shooting his would-be adoptive mother three times in the chest. This signature moment in O'Connor's fiction dramatizes how the antithesis of adoption is an explosion of violence. It often climaxes prolonged struggles in which seemingly irreproachable adults repeatedly feel shamed by the young vagrants who take up residence with them. In "The Lame Shall Enter First" violence bears away Norton, the son of an egotistical do-gooder who opens his house to an admittedly hell-bound fourteen-year-old while neglecting the needs of his child who is as love-starved as any orphan at St. Mary's. In "A Circle in the Fire" violence bears away the woods of the fearful and possessive Mrs. Cope, who cannot understand the anguish of Powell as the trespassing teen pines for a place on the farm that he recalls as a paradisal home.

Commenting on "A Circle in the Fire," O'Connor wrote that children are capable "of committing the most monstrous crimes out of the urge to destroy and humiliate" (*HB* 120). To endure such mortification is to live at the intersection of the physical and psychological devastation that psychiatrist James Gilligan has explored in *Violence: Reflections on a National Epidemic*. Gilligan's work with psychiatric patients in Massachusetts prison hospitals convinced him that violence must be understood as a "symbolic language." It expresses the "logic of shame" (61, 65). Those who resort to violence have typically been so humiliated in the past through violence that they seem dulled to all feelings except shame. Hence, when these walking dead feel threatened, they may lash out to assert their pride and to protect themselves from being overwhelmed again by their own worthlessness. The violent "literally prefer death to dishonor" (110). Such violence is more likely to occur if the victimizers find no other means to ward off shame and if they lack the love, guilt, or fear that may restrain their aggression (110–15). In

Gilligan's cyclic explanation, violence begets shame, and shame begets further violence.

Gilligan's work seems especially relevant to O'Connor's fictional world because public esteem was so highly valued in the South, long regarded as the most murderous region of the country. Bertram Wyatt-Brown has exhaustively shown how honor in the Old South was often gained by violence, and violence was used to preserve honor. For example, Tennessean Andrew Jackson, perhaps the most famous son of Tarwater's home state, killed the scoundrel who offended his wife and was seriously hurt in various duels and brawls; it is not surprising, then, that he became the seventh president of the United States (Lane 86–87). This view of selfhood as socially mediated has hardly gone with the wind. Psychologists Richard Nisbett and Dov Cohen have demonstrated through surveys and experiments that regard for honor still remains a significant cause of aggressive behavior among contemporary southerners (chaps. 3 and 4).[4]

Set in a country as honor-obsessed as Huck Finn's Mississippi River precincts, *The Violent Bear It Away* follows an orphan's search for home amid a family raised in the culture of shame. Although O'Connor has sometimes been portrayed as upholding the patriarchy (Prown 75–76), she writes out of the female tradition in southern literature that uses "orphaning as resistance." Joan Schulz has discussed how fictional southern women adopt this detachment as a way of rejecting the confinement of traditionally male-dominated family life. O'Connor, the "Imaginary Orphan," is just as critical. She shows how the virtually all-male world of *The Violent Bear It Away*—nephews and uncles, would-be fathers and would-be sons—pursues the cult of honor until it ends in murder. Her orphan-hero must bear away the shame and violence of such family life if he wants to achieve a gentler heart and receive what Paul has called "the spirit of adoption" (Romans 8:15).

Fourteen-year-old Tarwater engages in the psychosocial task that Erik Erikson, who was adopted by his mother's second husband, found characteristic of adolescence—the struggle between identity and identity diffusion (Erikson 94–100).[5] Teens typically face the challenge of achieving selfhood without succumbing to impersonation and conformity, but gaining a sense of identity is particularly complicated for teens who are adopted. Such kinship, as Judith Butler recognizes, "enters into the language of the law to disrupt its univocal workings . . . . a child might say 'father' and might mean both the absent phantasm she never knew as well as the one who assumes that place in living memory" (69). Resolving the identity crisis as the child of such ambiguous fathers is yet even more complicated for Tarwater. The youth defines himself through and against his birth parents as well as two quasi-adoptive parents—one, a member of the living dead; the other, a dead old man who lives in memory—before discovering the possibility of a more ancient lineage. O'Connor's orphan is not simply once-born via his biological parents nor even "twice born," as the adopted Lifton titled her memoir about searching for her birth parents. Rather, Tarwater is thrice born.[6]

"BORN IN A WRECK"

Tarwater's beginnings left him "very proud that he had been born in a wreck" (*CW* 355), a distinction that the fourteen-year-old does not hesitate to recall (397, 460). His maternal grandparents were killed in the car accident, and his "mother (unmarried and shameless) had lived just long enough after the crash for him to be born" (355). Tarwater learned of his disastrous origins from the at least weekly retelling of the story by the old man who was "Tarwater's great-uncle, or *said he was*" (331, emphasis mine). Adoptees would be familiar with tales of such accidents, for the loss of parents in a car wreck was a frequently employed fiction to explain why such children were not living with their birth fathers and mothers (Lifton, *Lost and Found* 25). To complete this nativity story, Mason Tarwater also relayed how the boy's father, an aspiring preacher, shot himself after he learned about the fatal crash.

The story of the wreck has dinned into the illegitimate Tarwater that he was born amid shame and violence. Mason denounces both Tarwater's mother and grandmother as "whores" and likens the chastisement of the accident to the punishment of the biblical Jezebel (*CW* 355), the byword for hussydom, whose scattered limbs were found after dogs ate her flesh (2 Kings 9:33–37). Born shortly after the Civil War ended, Mason would have had it bred into him that whereas men gained honor in the Old South through valor, women achieved it through sexual purity. Mason's sister and niece not only transgressed the moral code of the region but also violated the spiritual discipline of a Christian. Although the elderly prophet once waited in vain for God to punish the whole sinful world, the crash at least punished those family members of whom he was so ashamed.

The prophet's censure is harsh, but it would have been widely understood in O'Connor's time. As early as 1917, adoption records were sealed to protect parents and children from the taint of illegitimacy (Carp, "Introduction" 8). Unwed mothers in the 1950s and 1960s have recalled how they hid their pregnancy by dieting, using slimming underclothes, or staying in maternity homes (Melosh 232). Whereas the car wreck that killed Tarwater's mother might be interpreted by Mason as divine fury upon the shameless, the subsequent suicide of Tarwater's father ended the agony of the intolerably shameful. The would-be evangelizer internalized his shame as guilt. Since his remorse was so great that even his repentance could not assuage it, he directed his violence not at another but at the self that despised itself. The young father, whose countenance already seemed scorched with contrition, shot himself to save face.

The chastening auto accident bears Tarwater into the world as a child of traumatic violence. His psychic damage might be felt by way of Nancy Newton Verrier's theory of "the primal wound," the grievous "separation of the child from his biological mother, the connection to whom seems mystical, mysterious, spiritual and everlasting" (xvi). Developing insights that Florence Clothier first proposed in 1943, Verrier contends that this wound opens when the baby loses the uterine intimacy known for months and then gapes further if the child loses the nurturing presence of the birth mother through death or relinquishment. Since this rupture occurs when the baby's identity is still intimately connected with that of the absent mother, the child may experience a loss of self that leads to anger, depression, and an ongoing search for the maternal connection that was broken.[7] Some children who were adopted after their parents' deaths even feel guilty for having survived and responsible for the loss (Melina 73). The deaths that accompany Tarwater's birth haunt the life of this surly and restless teen, particularly in the way that he is preoccupied with mortality. He denies the resurrection of the dead, regards the deceased Mason as a mere body to be burned, and proclaims that he and his kin will all "rot like hogs" (*CW* 403). Born into violence, Tarwater can only conceive of the wreckage of all flesh.

Tarwater's primal wound goes deeper than the death of his mother, for its source is earlier than his birth. Verrier suggests its primordial origin when she notes that adoptees often struggle spiritually because their severance from the birth mother "violates their sense of order in the universe, replacing order and meaning with chaos and terror" (197). Although Mason lacks charity in his judgments upon Tarwater's parents and grandparents, he locates Tarwater's early losses in the context of a larger story that begins with Adam's loss of Paradise. If the shelter of the womb resembles Adam and Eve's intimacy with God in the Garden (Stevenson-Moessner 93), Tarwater's dead mother leaves him an orphan not just in body but in his very soul. She births him into the wrecked dream of freedom from history, obligation, and God that Brian Abel Ragen traces in O'Connor's fiction about failed American Adams and their deceptively promising automobiles (55–57). The road to perdition runs right through O'Connor's country of shame and violence.

Far from rejecting his origins in family disgrace, Tarwater finds his identity by such opprobrium. As if proclaiming a royal birth, he boasts, "I'm out of the womb of a whore" (*CW* 397). Tarwater never feels the humiliation of what Lifton calls the Bastard Moment, the illegitimate child's recognition of "the shameful social reality of one's birth" (*Journey* 177). Instead, he proudly lives out a peculiar variation on the Freudian family romance. Some adoptees deal with their conflicted feelings toward their new mothers and fathers by simply glorifying their birth parents and denigrating their adopted parents (Melina 92–94). So, Tarwater scorns the paternal Mason and identifies with the shameful parents who were only a few years older than himself when they died. Whereas adoption was often used as a way to hide the birthmark of illegitimacy, Tarwater adopts the stain as his own and flaunts the legacy from his unmarried parents. He is no Oliver Twist, no Esther Summerson in *Bleak House,* orphan heroes whose resilient virtue amid adversity undermined the stigma of their births outside marriage (Novy 94–97, 100–109). Rather, like a member of Bastard Nation, a

radical movement for adoption rights, several decades before its found-
ing, the impudent Tarwater finds no shame in his illegitimacy.

Tarwater's bravado about being misbegotten makes him sound like
an early 1950s rebel against stifling social conventions. However, such
brashness also justifies his increasingly violent egotism, for it appeals to
the popular tradition that bastards were simply born bad. The eugenics
movement of the early twentieth century offered another version of
this folk wisdom that further diminished the prospects of some children waiting for adoption: it claimed that illegitimate offspring inherited the low intelligence of their unmarried mothers (Carp "Introduction" 9). Although the adoption community in O'Connor's time
placed more emphasis on nurture rather than nature, the specter of
tainted heredity, even in a child who was not illegitimate, was connected specifically to adoption through *The Bad Seed*, the 1954 novel
by Alabama-born William March. The National Book Award nominee
quickly became a successful Broadway play by Maxwell Anderson
(1954) and then a movie with Oscar-nominated performances in 1956.
Set in a vaguely southern town, the melodrama focused on an adoptee's
young daughter, whose murders, like drowning a classmate, make her
seem to have inherited the sociopathic tendency of her serial-killer
birth grandmother. In O'Connor's "A Circle in the Fire" Mrs. Pritchard
voices a similar suspicion that hidden evil might take root by way of
adopted children. Seeking to provoke Mrs. Cope's anxiety about the
three juvenile delinquents lingering on her farm, Mrs. Pritchard sagely
remembers, "I known a man oncet that his wife was poisoned by a
child she had adopted out of pure kindness" (*CW* 246). In a novel rife
with images of nature's growth—from the corn that is planted four
feet from the great-uncle's porch to the kernel of the gospel that the
teen and his uncle accuse each other of cultivating more faithfully—
Tarwater seeks to be the bad seed of his parents' sin.

Yet if Tarwater views his origins in a wreck as the mark of inborn
corruption, he understands these same beginnings as a sign of election. The delivery of his birth was also a miraculous deliverance from
death. The orphan believes that the conjunction "set his existence apart
from the ordinary one and . . . that the plans of God for him were
special" (*CW* 355). Indeed, when Tarwater would walk in the woods
and spy a solitary bush, the aspiring Moses would wait for it to start

burning, as if he were the most famously chosen of biblical adoptees. Such an aura of destiny may easily loom over adoptees, who are often told that whereas other children were products of biological chance, they have been specially selected by their new parents. *The Chosen Baby,* a favorite book for explaining to adoptees their unique place in their second families, was published when Tarwater would have been one-year old. Its title might aptly describe the newborn who survived the car wreck. Mason further inculcated in Tarwater a sense of having been blessed by ordaining the youth his prophetic successor "even though he was a bastard" (*CW* 356). Later in the novel, Tarwater recognizes the figure of this vocation, "a gaunt stranger, the ghost who had been born in the wreck and who had fancied himself destined at that moment to the torture of prophecy" (465), but he rejects this second self, this blessed child of catastrophe, as merely deluded. Only after Tarwater is wrecked following a ride in a stranger's car at the end of the novel will he discover that his election is not for violent self-glorification but for generous—and even shameful—service.

"I AIN'T AST FOR NO FATHER"

Having lost his parents in the car accident and its suicidal aftermath, Tarwater continued to feel the desertion and disruptions of family life that often trouble the childhood of boys who later become violent (Garbarino 44–47). The orphan became the object of an informal custody battle between two competing relatives. Like Godfrey Cass and Silas Marner in George Eliot's famous adoption novel (Novy 125–31), Mason Tarwater and George Rayber represent the choice of a different way of life. The rift between the religious Mason and the secular Rayber makes vivid how adoptees report that they often feel divided between heaven and earth, divinity and humanity, because of their uncertain origins and dual sets of parents (Lifton, *Journey* 19, 123–24). Yet, whereas the conflict in *Silas Marner* and in such twentieth-century high-profile cases as those involving Baby Jessica and Baby Richard positions biological against adoptive parents, the contest is more ambiguous in the novel that O'Connor dedicated to her own father. Mason and

Rayber, both blood relatives, wage combat to be the quasi-adoptive father of Tarwater.

Neither the great-uncle nor the uncle seeks a legal adoption. Although Massachusetts enacted the first comprehensive adoption law in 1851, and every state had such laws by 1929 (Pertman 21–22), Mason and Rayber rely on a far earlier tradition of informal adoption. Since colonial America, parentless children had often been raised within the extended birth family without any legal sanction. In O'Connor's novel such kinship care seems especially justified by the southern regard for blood relations. Mason takes comfort that because Rayber's mother was a Tarwater, "Good blood flows in his veins." Recalling how he came to be raised by his great-uncle, Tarwater claims that Mason "grabbed me away from this other uncle, my only blood connection now" (*CW* 368, 381).[8] It was not unusual to entrust a dependent child to such relatives as a way to maintain ties with the birth family and to minimize upheaval after a traumatic loss; however, this kind of custody always risked leaving children with adults who lacked the skills and resources to care for them (Berrick 114). Mason and Rayber may be Tarwater's blood kin, but they are also problematic fathers. Both relatives illustrate Sarah Gordon's claim that "the denigration of human relationships is more the rule than the exception in O'Connor's fiction" (226). The great-uncle and uncle turn the boy into the focal point for their mutual antagonism and humiliation.

Although Mason still refers to his father as "daddy," his own parenting is not always as endearing. When the apoplectic old man reviles Tarwater's mother as a whore, he is insensitive to the way that adopted children may hear such maligning of their parents as a maligning of themselves (Melina 71). The fierce Mason shouts, hisses, roars, and hollers; he slams his hand for emphasis, kicks a door, and grabs Tarwater by his overalls. The great-uncle gained custody of the boy by just such violence. The baby born in a wreck was initially entrusted to the care of his uncle. However, Mason kidnapped the child after Rayber dishonored the aged prophet. While the old man was once staying in Rayber's house, his nephew secretly turned Mason into an object for study and reduced the zealot to a journal article for academics. Mason concluded about such betrayal, "It shames me" (*CW* 344). In response to such disgrace, the elderly kinsman bore the "orphan boy" away and raised the child until he was fourteen (332). Lifton might be describing the whirligig of being caught in the rivalry between Rayber and Mason when she writes that "[b]efuddled adopted children often wonder whether they have been stolen by one set of parents and might be stolen right back by the other" (*Journey* 44). In fact, when Rayber tried once to recapture his seven-year-old nephew by going to Powderhead with the official representative of child welfare Bernice Bishop, Mason defended his fatherhood by shooting Rayber in his leg and ear, as if the very embodiment of the violent fundamentalism that Robert Brinkmeyer views as bearing the novel away (131). The schoolteacher retreated from the field of honor, disgraced before his foe and before the lady that he would later marry. Between Mason and Rayber, shame keeps leading to violence, and violence keeps leading back to shame.

The unforgiving Tarwater has learned the bloody lesson of Mason toward trespassers. The youth asserts that if his uncle ever tries to evict him from Powderhead, he will kill Rayber. Tarwater's imitative violence reveals how he is actually attracted by his great-uncle's rage. The disciple most wants to follow Mason's prophetic calling when the old man returns from the woods in a furious glory after having "thrashed out his peace with the Lord" (*CW* 334). However, Tarwater seeks not simply to be like his pugilistic kinsman but to surpass him. When Mason charges Tarwater to make sure that Bishop, his mentally challenged cousin, is baptized, the upstart sneers at this purported mission from God, "He don't mean for me to finish up your leavings" (335). Mason, the baptist manqué, is simply contemptible to his grandiose nephew. Tarwater seeks not so much to escape being a prophet but to realize his vocation in a less shameful and more violent way.

As God's messenger and Tarwater's adopted parent, Mason overlooks the way that the prophets, according to Paul Ricoeur, modified the biblical conception of God as Father. They viewed God not simply as the Lord of Origins (whether of Creation in Genesis or of Israel in Exodus) but as the Lord of the Future, of a new creation and an eschatological banquet. Jesus spoke even more audaciously out of this prophetic tradition when he addressed God with a term of childlike affection ("Abba") as he memorably taught his followers to pray for the coming of the Kingdom and the giving of every day's bread—precisely the holy repast that Tarwater will behold at the end of the novel. "Fatherhood is thus placed in the realm of a theology of hope," Ricoeur writes,

> It does not look backward, toward a great ancestor, but forward, in the direction of a new intimacy on the model of the knowledge of the son. In the exegesis of Paul, it is because the Spirit witnesses our sonship (Romans 8:16) that we can cry *Abba,* Father. Far, therefore, from the religion of the father being that of a distant and hostile transcendence, there is fatherhood because there is sonship, and there is sonship because there is community of spirit. (490–91)

Mason sometimes seems like the remote and menacing forefather who holds Tarwater in thralldom rather than the harbinger of God's tender closeness to those who are sons and daughters of the Spirit. Mason would be a better prophet and parent if he understood the implications of fatherhood for God and of God for fatherhood.

Although Mason does not always witness to the "spirit of adoption" (Romans 8:15), this would-be father does care for and care about Tarwater. In contrast to the unappealing restaurant fare and home-cooked fiascos that Rayber later offers the boy, Mason provides Tarwater with the abundant and substantial meals that the ever-hungry adolescent always remembers fondly. Mason also sustains Tarwater with the sense of family history that many adoptees lack because it was kept secret by or was simply unavailable to their second parents. The old man constructs what professionals have come to call the "adoption story," an ever-evolving narrative about the child's birth and birth parents, the reasons that the child was available for adoption, and the process that brought the child and adoptive parents together (Hartman and Laird 231–34). Although Mason's version of the story omits and overemphasizes details in order to disparage the Raybers, the veteran chronicler regularly repairs what Lifton describes as the "broken narrative" of the orphan's life by locating Tarwater in the story that began even before he was born in a wreck (*Journey* 36–47). And Mason expands that history even further by placing Tarwater's life on a timeline that extends back from Herbert Hoover to the Fall and forward to the Second Coming.

Despite all of Mason's angry apocalypticism his Jesus is not the herald of cosmic judgment, as he once seemed to have expected. Rather, the savior is a figure stripped of might and shorn of violence, the victim who endured "the sweat and stink of the cross" (*CW* 334). As the likewise-humiliated preacher turns the isolation of the Tennessee backwoods into a retreat for teaching his young charge about imitating Jesus, Mason's parenthood is akin to that of the desert fathers in late antiquity, those spiritual mentors and heirs of the prophetic tradition whom Richard Giannone envisions as seminal to O'Connor's fiction (112). However, Tarwater disdains to be the son of any such *abba*. The scornful teen would never understand O'Connor's claim that the Catholic novelist in the South will feel "more kinship" with prophets like Mason than "with those politer elements for whom the supernatural is an embarrassment" (*MM* 207).

Since Tarwater finds kinship with Mason nothing but embarrassing, he decides to burn the body of the old man who has just died from a stroke. And he sets out on his own "orphan voyage," as Jean Paton titled her pioneering book about searching for birth parents, to locate the man who first cared for him after his birth in a wreck but who later seemed to have abandoned him to Mason. Fleeing the scandal of the supernatural, Tarwater gets a ride to the city from T. Fawcett Meeks, the copper flue salesman who offers the rube guidance on the way to wealth. If the fatherless lad accepts apprenticeship with Meeks, he might easily become like one of Horatio Alger's fictional orphans who gain worldly success by sheer luck and pluck (Nelson 46–47). However, Tarwater seeks a less mercenary form of sonship than the indenture that sometimes blurred into adoption in early America. He wants the rationalist Rayber as a father who will foster his reasons for rejecting the shameful Mason.

Rayber longs to adopt Tarwater but entirely on his own terms. His motivation might have been revealed by any caseworker who studied Dorothy Hutchinson's *In Quest of Foster Parents,* a widely influential 1943 text on placing children who were in need of care. In language that reflects how women rather than O'Connor's men were viewed as the impetus for adoption, the manual urged caseworkers to consider such questions as "How does she wish to use a child? How does she wish to incorporate him into her life? What need must he fulfill?" (9). Rayber's need is for a son who will not shame his father. He feels disgraced by Bishop, a boy whom social workers would probably have never even placed in Rayber's home for adoption because the child's disabilities violated the aesthetic ideal of the homogeneous family that was popular in O'Connor's lifetime (Gill 166–68). But Bishop is not adopted: he is Rayber's flesh in a family that values blood connections, and he is a palpable embarrassment. Whereas the schoolteacher makes his home in his head, Bishop is so inferior in intelligence that he will always think like a five-year-old. And whereas Rayber holds himself proudly aloof from loving intimacy, his offensive son lives to be held and to be helped, to be touched and, simply, to be touching. Although no orphan—at least, literally, Bishop is O'Connor's version of the repulsive and slow-witted foundling that reached out for Hawthorne's fatherly embrace at the Liverpool workhouse (*MM* 219).

Bishop's father was not raised with or for such affection. Parented by a neglectful mother and indifferent father, young George never received the love that would have enabled him to develop an appropriate sense of self. Hence, Rayber now lives in perpetual shame, what Gilligan views as the opposite of the healthy self-affirmation that enables one to endure discomfiture (47). To protect himself from the threat of emotions, Rayber tries to withdraw from all contact, especially with Bishop. For if this daddy ever yields to the fierce affection that bears down upon him, he will behave like his delighted but outrageous son, making a "fool of himself" or throwing himself "to the ground in an act of idiot praise" (*CW* 401). Rayber even tries to drown Bishop so that he can live without such ignominy in his purely cerebral world. Although he fails to carry out his sacrifice on the altar of honor, Rayber speculates of Bishop's kind, "In a hundred years people may have learned enough to put them to sleep when they're born" (435).

Much as parents have sometimes sought to adopt a child as a substitute for one that has died (Lifton, *Journey* 46), Rayber seeks Tarwater to replace the son that should have never been born. The schoolteacher longs to "lavish on him everything he would have lavished on his own child if he had had one who would have known the difference" (*CW* 392). Rayber starts by sitting beside Tarwater's bed on the night that the orphan comes to his house, pleased that "at last he had a son with a future" (455). Just as adoptive parents may scrutinize the features of their children in the hope of detecting some surprising resemblances (Melina 3), Rayber discovers gratifying physical similarities in Tarwater that evening. The next morning the paternal Rayber tells Tarwater that the boy is no longer alone. "'You have a friend. You have more than a friend now.' He swallowed. 'You have a father'" (CW 396–97). Like Mr. Brownlow in *Oliver Twist,* the benevolent patron resolves to give the familiar-looking waif a respectable home. Rayber extends such hospitality because he views his nephew as having sprung from his own head. The intellectual virtually masterminded Tarwater's conception by facilitating the liaison between his sister, who supposedly needed self-affirmation through sex, and the hick who needed to be wooed away from his naive religiosity. Rayber was so eager to claim the child of his mind as his own that he found it "a relief" when Tarwater's father shot himself (CW 366). Now that Rayber has been reunited with his quasi-son, the schoolteacher sets about educating the lad by introducing him to all the wonders of the City of Man. As they explore movies and stores, the post office and city hall, Rayber lives by the faith that adoptive parents typically place in environment over heredity (Melina 87–88). The pedagogue will undo the wreckage of Tarwater's birth and upbringing by nurturing him into sonship.

Tarwater rather glumly follows his avuncular father even during their first four days together. Whereas such turn-of-the-century adoption fiction as *Little Lord Fauntleroy, Sara Crewe, Rebecca of Sunnybrook Farm, Anne of Green Gables,* and *Pollyanna* focuses on how the adopted child brings emotional regeneration to once-deadened adoptive parents and caretakers (Nelson 12), O'Connor writes no story about the orphan as domestic savior of the Rayber household. Even the honeymoon period that adoptive parents and children often enjoy when they first live as a family quickly becomes contested (Melina 22). The struggle can be heard whenever the father tries to rename his son. While Rayber serves Tarwater breakfast in bed on their first morning together, the uncle speaks "in a voice so full of feeling that it was barely balanced, 'Listen, listen Frankie. . . . you're not alone any more.'" An outraged Tarwater replies to the paternal term of endearment, "I ain't ast for no father . . . . And my name ain't Frankie. I go by Tarwater . . ."

(*CW* 396, 397). Rejecting the misnomer, the dismissive son views his bond with Rayber as if it were a mere fiction. It is the kind of pretense that Lifton denounces when she calls adoption the "Game of As If," a charade in which the family by decree tries to imitate all the characteristics of the family by birth (*Lost and Found* 14). The youth may have earlier imagined himself as the professional-sounding "F. M. Tarwater," who shakes hands with each of the 75,000 in the big city (*CW* 346), but such impersonation was merely part of his adolescent experimentation with roles. Rayber ignores the correction of the child who disowns him. As Tarwater's uncle later listens to Lucette Carmody preach about how Jesus escaped Herod's slaughter of the infants and grew up to raise the dead, the ecstatic parent gushes with another name for his son: "But not those dead! he cried, not the innocent children, not you, not me when I was a child, not Bishop, not Frank!" (413).

Much as the adopted family is constructed by designation rather than by biology, Rayber seeks to confirm Tarwater's filial status through language. Melina cautions about such renaming, especially for school-age children who have come to identify themselves with how they have been called. Although adoptive parents may change a child's name as "a way of claiming a child—of signifying that the child belongs," it should never be done as a way of denying the child's past (Melina 12). Betty Jean Lifton, whose own birth name was "Blanche," writes pointedly that "[t]he birth name is a confirmation that you were born and that you exist" (*Journey* 268). In calling his nephew "Frank" or "Frankie" rather than the favored "Tarwater," Rayber assumes a false intimacy by using a nickname and linguistically arrogates the child as entirely his own. Tarwater balks at what his uncle considers a parental prerogative. The teen refuses to beget Rayber as father by living up to the name of son. When Rayber registers his two children at the Cherokee Lodge, the would-be father carries this private christening to its radical conclusion by ascribing his own last name to his nephew. "Frank and Bishop Rayber," he writes on the card after the desk clerk wonders, "That boy there—is yours too?" Tarwater seizes the paper out of her hand, crosses out "Frank," and forcefully disavows the surname by inscribing, "Francis Marion Tarwater . . . Powderhead, Tennessee. NOT HIS SON" (*CW* 425, 428).[9] The youth does not bear the family name of his mother and uncle—Rayber—but of the prophet who raised him as a Tarwater. As if living out Derrida's comparison between the subversions of writing and orphanhood, the brazen Tarwater pens his preferred name and home address as a violent way of writing off this attempt at adoption.

If Tarwater never adopts Rayber as his father, Rayber likewise never adopts Tarwater as the son of his heart. Instead, the pair becomes enmeshed in the same cycle of asserting superiority and avoiding shame that ensnared Tarwater with Mason. Like the adopted Oedipus, the tragic king who fascinated O'Connor (*HB* 68), Tarwater is caught in a deadly contest with his father, but he contends with his adopted rather than with his birth parent.[10] Rayber is a grim adversary. Although the youth is initially attracted to the schoolteacher as a rational alternative to the violent faith of Mason, Tarwater's uncle is actually no less violent than his great-uncle. Rayber has occasional outbursts of rage, as when he slams his wife almost halfway across the room for suggesting that Bishop be institutionalized or when he wants to swing his chair at the teens in the Cherokee Lodge for being appalled by Bishop. Such fierce love resembles Mason's truculent efforts to follow his heart, but Rayber pursues a more pernicious form of violence that is completely interior. Deep in his mind, the schoolteacher eviscerates and annihilates by abstracting. Bishop becomes just a genetic anomaly; Mason, an insecure and deluded fanatic; Tarwater's mother, a woman needing sex for self-confidence; and Tarwater, a teen in the grip of a fixation. Tarwater senses that his uncle does not really want to make him a son but to remake him as a child of his own intellect. When Rayber looks at Tarwater, he "gazed through the actual insignificant boy before him to an image of him that he held fully developed in his mind" (*CW* 388). Like the parents in adoptee Edward Albee's *The American Dream* (1960) that actually cut off the offending hands and tongue of the child delivered from Mrs. Barker's Adoption Agency, Rayber would cut Tarwater down to manageable size by severing him from his heart, body, and soul.[11] To be adopted by the schoolteacher is merely to be coopted into his world of pure ideas.

As Rayber and Tarwater contend with each other, the focus of all their swaggering and belittling is the other father figure, Mason himself. Despite all of Rayber's denials, Pa Mason lives hidden in his nephew's begrudging heart. The old kinsman boasted of Rayber's bond to him, "He loved me like a daddy," before adding the reason for Rayber's violent rejection of him, "and he was ashamed of it!" (*CW* 375). Tarwater is similarly conflicted. If adoptees carry around with them a ghost family from which they have been separated (Lifton, *Journey* 57), Mason is the inescapable specter from Tarwater's childhood home. The prophet has bequeathed to his ambivalent disciple a dissatisfaction with merely being the offspring of his uncle's intelligence. So, Rayber and Tarwater contend over who is less in servitude to the relative that fostered both of them. Tarwater claims that unlike Rayber who merely talks, he *does;* he burned the dead codger's body while Rayber only threatened to do it. Rayber claims that he has freed himself from Mason's hypnotic influence but that Tarwater longs to carry out Mason's order to baptize Bishop. As nephew and uncle hurl accusations and recriminations, each seeks to shame the other and to avert being shamed himself.

Such shame, exacerbated by the inescapable bonds of family life, leads to violence. By the time that Rayber takes Tarwater and Bishop to the Cherokee Lodge, the uncle has discovered what many adoptive parents eventually confront: the child they had imagined is not the child they have adopted (Melina 5, 89–90). The disillusioned Rayber critiques his foolishly indulgent parenting over the past five days: "His indecision, his uncertainty, his eagerness up to now appeared shameful and absurd to him" (*CW* 455). He boldly resolves that Tarwater will reform, or the twice-failed father will seek the equivalent of the "disruption" that ends adoptive relationships even before any court has officially dissolved them. Yet Rayber stumbles upon a more violent solution because Tarwater also seeks to escape his shame.

Although Tarwater's training to be a prophet should dispose him, according to John Desmond, to proclaim the good news of nonviolence (143–44), the cult of honor demands that the youth make a sacrificial offering. Those who have been shamed, as Gilligan explains, may direct their outrage at a scapegoat as a way of eliminating their discomfort (66–69). The victim is Bishop. Tarwater will kill Rayber's biological son to prove that he is not Rayber's adopted son. Bishop himself feels no shame, whether he is eating messily in a restaurant, wearing ill-fitting and mismatched clothes, or supplicating for his shoes to be tied. However, the humble child inspires shame in both his father and cousin. Just as Rayber considers his son an intellectual embarrassment, Tarwater sneers that while humans can calculate, Bishop is really no different from a dumb hog. And just as Rayber feels his overwhelming love for Bishop a disgrace to his pursuit of emotional self-denial, Tarwater fears that his sporadic tenderness toward Bishop will keep him from becoming independent and invulnerable. He cannot even bear to look directly into his cousin's eyes, for shame lives in that part of the face, and the arrogantly virtuous Tarwater does not want to see or let be seen in himself what is proper to be kept out of sight (Gilligan 64–65).

Rayber and Tarwater thus place the burden of their shame on Bishop. As Rayber remains aloof in his room at the Cherokee Lodge, he passively acquiesces in the drowning that he mysteriously hears Tarwater carrying out on the lake. The father's only response is to steel himself even further so that he feels no trace of unseemly emotion while his son is being killed by his nephew. Influenced by Gilligan's theory about shame and by working with violent youths, psychologist James Garbarino explains that boys kill when they seek to redress what is perceived as an intolerable sense of injustice. Taking another's life thus becomes not random and meaningless but perversely moral in their eyes (128–29). Tarwater drowns Bishop because he hopes to free himself from the bondage that he has endured at the hands of his kin. He is proving that he is not Mason's son and not Rayber's son. Rather, Tarwater is *filius nullius,* the Latin legal term for an illegitimate child, "no one's son." However, after Bishop's shameful murder neither of the conspirators finds the relief that he expected through violence. Rayber so anesthetizes himself in order to become silently complicit with his son's drowning that he falls prostrate like one of the "living dead" whom Gilligan met while working as a psychiatrist in prison. Such men cannot only not feel shame; they can feel nothing at all (32–33). Because Tarwater baptized Bishop even as he drowned him, the youth feels shame at having lost his face-off with Mason, and he feels guilt, just as did his own birth father after the wreck, at having killed Rayber's son. Still at least capable of feeling, Tarwater learns in his own flesh how shame bears the violent away.

The sire of such disgrace waits in the lavender and cream-colored car that stops for the homeward-bound Tarwater. The nameless benefactor is just a no one, a stranger, who gives a ride to no one's son, and drives him straight into the abyss of shame. The false friend is the last of Tarwater's adoptive parents. Whereas Meeks at the beginning had called Tarwater "Son" and advised him, "I'm not going to tell you not to lie. . . . All I'm going to tell you is this: don't lie when you don't have to" (*CW* 380), the stranger at the end is the father of lies himself. Just as adoption involves taking in and taking care of the child who was once a stranger, the driver takes the unknown sonny into his car and proffers such teen-age enticements as strange-tasting cigarettes and alcohol. Tarwater's latest patron then ravishes the fourteen-year-old, as if the incarnation of the specter that once made adoptions by single men so rare—the father as child abuser. Gilligan explains that a man's rape of another man is meant as a profoundly symbolic act of shame. Insecure about his own manhood, the predator views sexual violence as a way to assert his power and unsex his victim (179–81). The pedophile's assault is so devastating that Leonard Shengold considers such violence a form of "soul murder." "The victims of soul murder," Shengold writes, "remain in large part possessed by another, their souls in bondage to someone else" (2). The psychiatrist's language accords with O'Connor's portrayal of the stranger as demonic to suggest how the driver takes hold of his prey in body, psyche, and spirit.

Yet if Tarwater is a victim of such degradation and violation, he is also his own victimizer. The stranger seems strangely familiar because he belongs to Tarwater's own family. As the most intimate of relatives, he embodies the nexus of shame and violence that has bedeviled these uncles and nephews throughout the novel. Tarwater actually encountered this stranger on the day Mason died. Sitting across from his dead great-uncle, the boy felt "a kind of sullen embarrassment as if he were in the presence of a new personality" (*CW* 336). The youth later heard a strange voice that tried to shame Mason as "crazy" (357). And as this alien hissing in his head turned into a tempting friend, Tarwater continued to fall under the stranger's invidious influence while trying to avoid being disgraced by Rayber. The rape in the woods consummates the way that Tarwater has been steadily submitting himself to the spirit of malign kinship. He has entrapped himself in the shame that leads to violence and in the violence that leads to shame.

O'Connor makes the violence sexual because the naked body is the premier site for shame in a postlapsarian world. In the past Tarwater eschewed such carnality, not so much out of chastity as out of a greater permissiveness toward sins of the head and heart. Although the pubescent Tarwater was proud that he knew the meaning of "whore," he "was intolerant of unspiritual evils and with those of the flesh he had never truckled" (*CW* 355, 468). Yet when the mighty angel of a woman at the crossroads store indicted Tarwater for not burying Mason, "It shames the dead" (467), the youth uttered an obscenity as if trying to shame his accuser in return. She did not flinch, and Tarwater only shamed himself. The foul-mouthed teen is then shamed in the woods, for his violent word assumes violent flesh when the stranger abuses him. Tarwater feels in the private depths of his own wracked body precisely how he has sinned against Mason's and Bishop's bodies. Born in a car wreck, he is left, bare and bound, a wreck by this violent anti-father who picks him up in a car and makes him suffer what can hardly be borne. Tarwater is so outraged that he sets fire to the spot in the woods where he was exposed and molested as if the sheer violence of the flames could bear his shame away.

"FROM THE BLOOD OF ABEL"

Tarwater's rape could easily inspire him to perpetuate the cycle of shame and violence. Gilligan explains that child abuse may kill the self by depriving it of much-needed love and thus turn the shamed victim into the ruthless victimizer (47). However, after being violated, Tarwater is not just offended; he senses how he has offended against others and against God. His shame gets transfigured into guilt for dishonoring the fatherly Mason and for killing the brotherly Bishop. Tarwater's remorse is not the self-referenced kind that destroyed his birth father after the car wreck; rather, it motivates the sinner to assume responsibility in a fallen world. Rejecting the violence of shame, Tarwater chooses what O'Connor calls the "violence of love" (*HB* 382). Such a compelling passion is, according to Susan Srigley, "an inward orientation of discipline and restraint done for the love of God and the Kingdom" (100). This violence bears away shame, for the self no longer lives for its own esteem as reflected in the eyes of another but for a community that transcends the striving and strife of Tarwater's family.

O'Connor offers the child of shame and violence the possibility of a different family with a different kind of father. She virtually bears Tarwater's old family life away so that she can imagine such relationships anew. Having suffered abasement at its most penetrating, Tarwater seeks a kinship not based on literal bloodlines and leading to bloodshed. O'Connor never shows how such bonds might actually be lived out on an ordinary Wednesday afternoon; instead, she gestures toward a transfigured understanding of domestic relations. When Tarwater returns to Powderhead, his embrace widens as he encounters Buford Munson, the African American neighbor who actually buried Mason while the teen lay drunk. In the first chapter Tarwater had denigrated Munson as a "nigger" when his great-uncle's old friend stopped to buy some home-brewed liquor. But now the youth no longer wants to shame the visitor who performed his own duty as Mason's kin; instead, Tarwater seeks to share a meal with his benefactor. That everyday table fellowship is reinterpreted in eschatological terms when Tarwater witnesses Jesus' feeding of the multitude. Eagerly waiting to be nourished among the crowd is Mason. The daily bread sought in the "Our Father" is given at this messianic banquet. Tarwater's final vision hallows Mason's fatherly providence and makes peace with his great-uncle's fury by including him in the family to come.

Although Mason may not have completely understood the mutual significance of his vocations as prophet and parent, he intuited the source of a new community that extends beyond blood connections. Whereas Rayber's cynical and materialistic father did not care if his son ever returned from a stay at Powderhead, Mason taught his nephew that "his true father was the Lord and not the simpleton in town." The prophet took pleasure that ever afterward Rayber "never could forget that there was a chance that that simpleton was not his only father" (CW 371, 372–73). In fact, Rayber once acted like the lost son when he tried to return to the backwoods farm "to hear more about God his Father" (371). Mason's contrast between biological and divine parenthood parallels the way Jesus undermines the patriarchal family of his time by identifying mother, sister, and brother with those who do the will of God (Mark 3:33–34). As Robert Hamerton-Kelly explains, "Jesus called people away from the bondage of kinship, the ties of fate, to relationships based on freedom and joined in love" (70). Paul's letters

to the Romans (8:12–17) and the Galatians (4:1–7) as well as his attrib-
uted letter to the Ephesians (1:5) continue this renovation of the family
by their unique reliance on adoption imagery. Paul claims that Christians have not received the spirit of slavery but the "spirit of adoption"
that enables them to call God their "Father" (Romans 8:15).

Mason felt the servitude that Paul regards as contrary to member-
ship in the divine household when the old man was placed in a strait
jacket and confined to the mental hospital for four years; Tarwater felt
it when he was bound by his rapist. "You were born into bondage,"
Mason preached as if echoing Paul, and then he proclaimed how the
enslaved can be "baptized into freedom, into the death of the Lord"
(*CW* 342). Pauline adoption is the opposite of the thralldom, enclo-
sure, and captivity that beset the uncles and nephews in O'Connor's
novel. Its holy spirit was so imaginatively and theologically powerful in
the ancient Church that such Fathers as Origen, Athanasius, Augustine, and Irenaeus explored the metaphor to understand how Jesus'
followers became children of God. The legal, biblical, and spiritual
meaning of such family life was later pondered by Thomas Aquinas,
O'Connor's own favorite.[12]

At the end of *The Violent Bear It Away* Tarwater is adopted into a
family history that goes beyond the deaths of his birth parents and the
debacles of his would-be parents. In its final images of generation, the
novel seems to unwrite Tarwater's violently penned "NOT HIS SON" and
rewrite it as an extended text on affiliation. Tarwater senses his participation in this transcendent family when he feels how the swell and
surge of his spiritual hunger "rose in a line of men whose lives were
chosen to sustain it . . . . He felt it building from the blood of Abel to
his own, rising and engulfing him" (*CW* 478). This momentum spins
Tarwater around, where his vision of a flaming tree links him to such
biblical ancestors as Moses, Elijah, and Daniel. And when the offspring
of this prophetic breed hears God's command, "GO WARN THE CHIL-
DREN OF GOD OF THE TERRIBLE SPEED OF MERCY," "[t]he words were as
silent as seeds opening one at a time in his blood" (478). As a descen-
dant of Abel, Tarwater stands in the line of the first victim, who was
murdered because Cain felt his offering was not respected by God. And
just as Abel was killed out of shame, such prophets as Moses, Elijah,
and Daniel were all reviled and persecuted because their tidings dis-

comfited their audience. Tarwater faces a kindred fate when he heads "toward the dark city, where the children of God lay sleeping" (479). To be adopted into the line from Abel through the prophets and unto Jesus is not to do violence but to risk becoming a victim, not to assert superiority but to accept shame.[13] If Tarwater can bear such a vocation, he will find his identity neither as the baby born in the wreck nor as the conflicted child of adoptive fathers who let violence bear themselves away. Rather, the orphan will be reborn into a new form of sonship. Like his listeners in the sleeping city, Tarwater will live as one of the children of God.

NOTES

1. In 1938, the year O'Connor's family left Savannah, the orphanage was moved to a new site on Victory Drive. In 2000 it provided a home for twenty-five to thirty boys and girls (*One Faith* 277–78).

2. O'Connor might have recalled such donations to St. Mary's when in "The Lame Shall Enter First" Sheppard asks what his son Norton would do if the boy won a thousand dollars: "Wouldn't you like to give some swings and trapezes to the orphanage?" (*CW* 598).

3. O'Connor was clearly familiar with the comic strip's heroine, for in a 1956 letter she wrote, "All my books are spotted with Ovaltine which has put me and Little Orphan Annie to sleep these many years" (*HB* 151). Ovaltine sponsored the Little Orphan Annie radio serial in the 1930s.

4. Butterfield traces how the southern legacy of honor, as reinterpreted by long-victimized African Americans, has influenced over a hundred years in the history of the Bosket family. As Pud Bosket (1889–1924) warned, "Don't step on my reputation" (63).

5. *Being Adopted: The Lifelong Search for Self* by Brodzinsky, Schechter, and Henig applies Erikson's stages of identity to adoptees.

6. Mason also views Tarwater as thrice-born: once, at the accident; again, through baptism; and a third time when he was rescued and raised by the old man himself (*CW* 356). Stevenson-Moessner writes of how adoptees experience three births—by nature, nurture, and the Spirit.

7. Lifton (*Journey* 28–35) likewise discusses the trauma of separation from the birth mother. Although Verrier and Lifton tend to view all adoptees as hurt by this separation and the subsequent secrecy of the closed adoption system, Brodzinsky, Schechter, and Henig recognize that the ways and extent of grieving vary widely among adoptees (73–74).

8. Other references in the novel to "blood connection" can be found on pages 339, 347, and 364 in the *Collected Works*.

9. Although O'Connor once altered "NOT HIS SON" to "BELONGS TO HIS SELF," Sally Fitzgerald suggested to her that the revision was "too self-conscious for Tarwater" (*HB* 345). O'Connor let her editor Robert Giroux decide about the phrase, and he recognized that her earlier version was the better choice. The bold negation expresses how Tarwater disowns his pseudo-father.

10. Oedipus has become a compelling figure in adoption studies. Lifton writes of "Oedipus, My Brother" (*Lost and Found* 147–48); Novy (chap. 2) discusses the role of adoption in *Oedipus*. However, O'Connor wondered, "But do we have to see Oedipus in every man who doesn't like his father?" (*HB* 375).

11. Novy focuses on the role of adoption in Albee's drama (160–66, 179–81).

12. Widdicombe provides a thorough review of adoption in the work of Origen and Athanasius. Aquinas considers adoption in such sections of the *Summa Theologica* as III, q. 23, and supp. q. 57.

13. Burke discusses how Pauline adoption imitates Roman law in conferring honor on all members of the new household (159–72). Indeed, Paul claims that the honor of being God's children implies identification with the inglorious suffering of Jesus (Romans 8:17).

WORKS CITED

Albee, Edward. *The American Dream*. New York: Coward-McCann, 1961.

Anderson, Maxwell. *Bad Seed*. New York: Dodd, Mead and Co., 1955.

Berrick, Jill Duerr. "When Children Cannot Remain Home: Foster Family Care and Kinship Care." *Families by Law: An Adoption Reader*. Ed. Naomi R. Cahn and Joan Heifetz Hollinger. New York: New York University Press, 2004. 111–14.

Brinkmeyer, Robert H., Jr. *The Art and Vision of Flannery O'Connor*. Baton Rouge: Louisiana State University Press, 1989.

Brodzinsky, David M., Marshall D. Schechter, and Robin Marantz Henig. *Being Adopted: The Lifelong Search for Self*. New York: Doubleday, 1992.

Burke, Trevor J. *Adopted into God's Family: Exploring a Pauline Metaphor*. Downers Grove, IL: InterVarsity Press, 2006.

Butler, Judith. *Antigone's Claim: Kinship between Life and Death*. New York: Columbia University Press, 2000.

Butterfield, Fox. *All God's Children: The Bosket Family and the American Tradition of Violence*. New York: Knopf, 1995.

Carp, E. Wayne, ed. *Adoption in America: Historical Perspectives*. Ann Arbor: University of Michigan Press, 2002.

Carp, E. Wayne. "Introduction: A Historical Overview of American Adoption." Carp, ed., 1–26.

Cash, Jean W. *Flannery O'Connor: A Life.* Knoxville: University of Tennessee Press, 2002.

Derrida, Jacques. *Dissemination.* Trans. Barbara Johnson. Chicago: University of Chicago Press, 1981.

Desmond, John F. "Violence and the Christian Mystery: A Way to Read Flannery O'Connor." *Literature and Belief* 17 (1997): 129–47.

Erikson, Erik. *Identity and the Life Cycle.* 1959. New York: Norton, 1980.

Garbarino, James. *Lost Boys: Why Our Sons Turn Violent and How We Can Save Them.* New York: Free Press, 1999.

Giannone, Richard. *Flannery O'Connor, Hermit Novelist.* Urbana: University of Illinois Press, 2000.

Gill, Brian Paul. "Adoption Agencies and the Search for the Ideal Family, 1918–1965." Carp, ed., 160–80.

Gilligan, James. *Violence: Reflections on a National Epidemic.* New York: Random House, 1997.

Gooch, Brad. *Flannery: A Life of Flannery O'Connor.* New York: Little, Brown, 2009.

Gordon, Sarah. *Flannery O'Connor: The Obedient Imagination.* Athens: University of Georgia Press, 2000.

Hamerton-Kelly, Robert. *God the Father: Theology and Patriarchy in the Teaching of Jesus.* Philadelphia: Fortress Press, 1979.

Hartman, Ann, and Joan Laird. "Family Treatment after Adoption: Common Themes." *The Psychology of Adoption.* Ed. David M. Brodzinsky and Marshall D. Schechter. New York: Oxford University Press, 1990. 221–39.

Hutchinson, Dorothy. *In Quest of Foster Parents: A Point of View on Homefinding.* New York: Columbia University Press, 1943.

Lane, Roger. *Murder in America: A History.* Columbus: Ohio State University Press, 1997.

Lifton, Betty Jean. *Journey of the Adopted Self: A Quest for Wholeness.* New York: Basic Books, 1994.

———. *Lost and Found: The Adoption Experience.* Updated edition. New York: Harper and Row, 1988.

———. *Twice Born.* New York: McGraw-Hill, 1975.

March, William. *The Bad Seed.* 1954. New York: Dell, 1972.

Melina, Lois Ruskai. *Raising Adopted Children: A Manual for Adoptive Parents.* New York: Harper Perennial, 1986.

Melosh, Barbara. "Adoption Stories: Autobiographical Narratives and the Politics of Identity." Carp, ed., 218–45.

Nelson, Claudia. *Little Strangers: Portrayals of Adoption and Foster Care in America, 1850–1929.* Bloomington: Indiana University Press, 2003.

Nisbett, Richard E., and Dov Cohen. *Culture of Honor: The Psychology of Violence in the South.* Boulder, CO: Westview Press, 1996.

Novy, Marianne. *Reading Adoption: Family and Difference in Fiction and Drama*. Ann Arbor: University of Michigan Press, 2005.

O'Connor, Flannery. *Collected Works*. Ed. Sally Fitzgerald. New York: Library of America, 1988.

———. *The Habit of Being: Letters of Flannery O'Connor*. Ed. Sally Fitzgerald. New York: Farrar, Straus and Giroux, 1979.

———. *Mystery and Manners: Occasional Prose*. Ed. Sally Fitzgerald and Robert Fitzgerald. New York: Farrar, Straus and Giroux, 1969.

One Faith, One Family: The Diocese of Savannah, 1850–2000. Syracuse, NY: Signature Publications, 2000.

Paton, Jean. *Orphan Voyage*. New York: Vantage Press, 1968.

Pertman, Adam. *Adoption Nation: How the Adoption Revolution Is Transforming America*. New York: Basic Books, 2000.

Prown, Katherine Hemple. *Revising Flannery O'Connor: Southern Literary Culture and the Problem of Female Authorship*. Charlottesville: University Press of Virginia, 2001.

Ragen, Brian Abel. *A Wreck on the Road to Damascus: Innocence, Guilt, and Conversion in Flannery O'Connor*. Chicago: Loyola University Press, 1989.

Ricoeur, Paul. "Fatherhood: From Phantasm to Symbol." Trans. Robert Sweeney. *The Conflict of Interpretations: Essays in Hermeneutics*. Ed. Don Ihde. Evanston: Northwestern University Press, 1974. 468–97.

Schulz, Joan. "Orphaning as Resistance." *The Female Tradition in Southern Literature*. Ed. Carol S. Manning. Urbana: University of Illinois Press, 1993. 89–109.

Shengold, Leonard. *Soul Murder: The Effects of Childhood Deprivation and Abuse*. New Haven: Yale University Press, 1989.

Singley, Carol J. "Building a Nation, Building a Family: Adoption in Nineteenth-Century American Children's Literature." Carp, ed., 51–81.

Spellman, Francis. *The Foundling*. New York: Scribner's, 1951.

Srigley, Susan. *Flannery O'Connor's Sacramental Art*. Notre Dame, IN: University of Notre Dame Press, 2004.

Stevenson-Moessner, Jeanne. *The Spirit of Adoption: At Home in God's Family*. Louisville, KY: Westminster John Knox Press, 2003.

Stolley, Kathy S. "Statistics on Adoption in the United States." *The Future of Children* 3.1 (1993): 26–42.

Verrier, Nancy Newton. *The Primal Wound: Understanding the Adopted Child*. Baltimore: Gateway Press, 1999.

Wasson, Valentina P. *The Chosen Baby*. New York: Lippincott, 1939.

Widdicombe, Peter. *The Fatherhood of God from Origen to Athanasius*. Oxford: Clarendon Press, 1994.

Wyatt-Brown, Bertram. *Southern Honor: Ethics and Behavior in the Old South*. New York: Oxford University Press, 1982.

CHAPTER 4

Abstraction and Intimacy in Flannery O'Connor's
The Violent Bear It Away

JASON PETERS

Abstraction is the death of religion no less than the death of
anything else.
                    —Allen Tate, "Remarks on the Southern Religion"

Flannery O'Connor's humor is sometimes so effective that its purpose
seems almost to divert us from our own. I have in mind for example, in
"Good Country People" Manley Pointer's telling Mrs. Hopewell that he
is "not even from a place, just from near a place" (*CS* 279) or, in "Parker's Back," Sarah Ruth's impressive outrage at Parker's tattoo of the Byz-
antine Christ, an outrage so complete and convincing that her accusing
Parker of idolatry is the least of it: she also beats him with a broom
until large welts form on the face of Jesus, then stomps on the broom,
and at last shakes it out the window "to get the taint of him off it" (*CS*
530). The humor is high, and we understand why O'Connor had to
prepare for public readings of her work by rehearsing it aloud straight-
faced in private.

But both of these jokes speak to conditions conducive to a kind of moral failure about which O'Connor felt strongly, especially by the time she resumed work on *The Violent Bear It Away*. Manichean is the word she often used for such conditions, eager as she was to point out that in the modern habit of mind an ancient and pernicious dualism obtains. But she especially wanted to scrub clean that old residual suspicion of the flesh and of the material order of creation—even as she herself was occasionally obliged to admit astonishment at the emphasis the Church places on the body (*HB* 100). One of her principal tutors on Catholic theology was Fr. William Lynch, who taught her that the infinite is achieved by the "penetration" of, not contempt for, the finite.[1] She was of course amicably predisposed to this hard affirmative doctrine, but Lynch's articulation of it was clearly signal in the development of her thought. Thus by the 1950s placelessness—which is not limited to "Good Country People" and certainly impinges upon *The Violent Bear It Away*—was not only an artistic concern of hers but a theological one as well. The condition of placelessnesss tells us something about the sort of scoundrel who believes in nothing and runs off with other people's wooden legs or glass eyeballs. Placelessness is not a morally neutral condition for the writer who said that "somewhere is better than anywhere" (*MM* 200).

And the taint that Sarah Ruth tries to shake off the broom is Parker's only in a reading as analogically obtuse as she is. It is clear that she is trying to shake off the taint of Jesus, and we realize a half-sentence too late that we have been laughing at a grimly comedic reenactment of the *via dolorosa*. Like Manley's placelessness, Sarah Ruth's outrage tells us something about the failed vision of those whose lives are essentially variations on George Rayber's: they are ghostly denizens of a world that is dense and heavy and palpable—that is, intolerable, for in it God has taken on human flesh and ratified its primal goodness.[2] Sarah Ruth is the consummate idolater of a world in which God is dead: she cannot countenance an image because she cannot see what stands on the other side of it. Indeed, for her there can be no such thing as an image. There are only idols in the literal and therefore limited world of her conjuring. So another joke—and Sarah Ruth's greatest offense—is what amounts to a flat denial of God: God "don't *look*. . . . He's a spirit. No man shall see his face." That she seems quite capable of beating that face with a broom only confirms what she unwittingly admits: that the God tattooed on Parker's back—the incarnate God—"ain't anybody I know" (*CS* 529). The welts she causes are the stripes with which she might be healed, but like Lucette Carmody, the child-preacher in *The Violent Bear It Away,* who has plenty to say about the Word but precious little about the Word-made-flesh, she serves the God of the Gnostic, who holds, as one eminent literary critic unapologetically holds, that Creation and the Fall were one and the same event (Bloom 261). And, once again, O'Connor tells us something about the conditions conducive to abuse given what *The Violent Bear It Away* calls the "threatened intimacy of creation" (*VBA* 22). Posit an incarnation, and you cannot live in contempt of the flesh; live in contempt of the flesh, and you deny the incarnation. Lacking a Word-made-flesh, we are at liberty to be as placeless as Manley Pointer and as literal as Sarah Ruth. We prepare an airy world inhabited by such displaced persons as they— a world in which it is impossible for the prophet Francis Marion Tarwater to trudge "off into the distance in the bleeding stinking mad shadow of Jesus" (221), for in such a world Jesus can neither bleed nor stink.

I give these examples from the short fiction for two reasons. One is that they remind us of how thoroughly suspicious O'Connor was of abstraction, which is Rayber's besetting malady in *The Violent Bear It Away*.[3] That so many early readers should have identified with him only speaks to the pervasiveness, and perhaps the insidiousness, of the malady.[4] It is nothing less than the default mode of the machine age; Rayber is the emblem of that age no less than its dependent.

The second reason is that these examples testify to the compact consistency of O'Connor's way of seeing: when O'Connor says "somewhere is better than anywhere" she is speaking about writing fiction, not about a central Christian mystery; when she allows Sarah Ruth to declare her utter ignorance of the second person of the Trinity, she is speaking about a central Christian mystery, not about fiction. And yet both instances suggest that the making of good fiction, like the making of a moral life, is grounded not in the general but in the particular, not in the abstract but in the concrete, not in placelessness but in place, not in the idea of God but in the person of Jesus, born of Mary.[5] Manley's placelessness and Sarah Ruth's inability to see the face of God are theological offenses for which there are artistic corollaries. Like Mrs. Hopewell, Sarah Ruth is "good Chrustian folk," but whatever she believes in is not an improvement upon the nothing in which Manley believes. She may as well join Onnie Jay Holy's Church of Christ Without Christ.

Belief is certainly one of Rayber's problems in *The Violent Bear It Away*. But O'Connor suggests that such a problem is not an island entire of itself. It bears with it a host of other problems and is marked by conditions and symptoms that—given the modern tendencies to idolatry that ensnare Sarah Ruth—only the vision of a prophet and his hunger for the bread of life can reveal. These symptoms and conditions I call abstraction—as will O'Connor in an important scene preceding the murder/baptism of Rayber's son Bishop. The etymology of the word *abstract*—to pull or draw away from[6]—is instructive: it implies a measurable physical distance despite implying a *departure* from all that is physical. That is, the word signifies in two important ways: in thought and in actuality. You may be abstracted, drawn up into thought or into a flight of fancy, too lost in theory to grow a rutabaga, just as you may also be abstracted—that is, physically distant—from the sources that give you your rutabagas. A philosopher theorizing in his ivory tower is no less abstracted than a sexton eating at a downtown diner, far removed from the fields that yielded his food. The one has forgotten his body, the other his bodily dependencies. One of the grimmest lessons of history is that abstraction of the first kind inevitably leads to abstraction of the second kind, and that abstraction of both kinds leads to abuse. We have been told this time and time again—from Jonathan Swift, who railed against the absentee English landlords prospering at the expense of an Irish peasantry they never set eyes on, to Wendell Berry, who has railed against the absentee corporations that control and profit from industrial farming. And yet no one seems to notice what happens to bodily health when people give themselves only to mental work, or what happens to topsoil and aquifers when too many people who like to eat and drink live too far from the sources that sustain them. From the so-called R&D sector to absentee landlords to absentee colonial powers, whether national or industrial, abstraction—distance *from*—permits ruin and encourages abuse as certainly as intimacy or proximity does not.

This may seem tangential to *The Violent Bear It Away,* but it most certainly is not. Every bit of it applies to Rayber exactly. He is abstracted—drawn up into thought—as much as he is disengaged from the life of the flesh. He wishes to live in the realm of pure thought, which is to say the world of the machine, the difference between the two being negligible. That he carries a machine with him at all times is the salient indicator of this: the man who forgets the body and its life in the created order to live only in ideas will necessarily need machines to do what his body does not or cannot do—as surely as the Manicheans against whom St. Augustine raged, distrustful as they were of the material world, nevertheless needed food, which they enlisted others to pick for them.[7] Rayber may intuit the power of proximity to disrupt his abstraction; he may have a dim knowledge of an intolerable intimacy that threatens it. But he is a modern Manichean. The food "system" feeds him and a machine hears for him. It is the burden of this essay to build a case against Rayber by implicating him in the theological offense—call it Manichean or Gnostic or technological—of abstraction and the violence that necessarily attends it.

WE KNOW THAT MASON AND RAYBER PROVIDE THE GOVerning tension in *The Violent Bear It Away,* that they contend in spiritual, physical, and imaginative warfare for Tarwater's soul.[8] But two scenes involving minor characters may also serve as the conceptual markers between which the novel's thought and action take place, and I point to them in an attempt to enlarge our thinking about the novel. One, involving Buford, was already part of O'Connor's previously published story "You Can't Be Any Poorer Than Dead" out of which the novel grew; the other, involving Lucette Carmody, the child-preacher, grew out of a failed story O'Connor had "laid by" and then pulled out to help solve the "difficulty" of Rayber, a problem frequently mentioned in her letters in the spring and early summer of 1959.[9] In the first of these scenes Buford says that Mason "deserves to lie in a grave that fits him" because "he was deep in this life, he was deep in Jesus' misery" (*VBA* 48). That he says this to a boy poised to follow in the "bleeding stinking mad shadow of Jesus" (221) only adds to the novel's emphasis on the body: any talk of mind or spirit that holds the flesh at a discount will not be permitted, and O'Connor makes Mason amply corpulent lest we forget.

In the second of these scenes the child-preacher says,

> Listen, world . . . Jesus is coming again! . . . The mountains will know Him and bound forward, the stars will light on His head, the sun will drop down at His feet, but will you know the Lord Jesus then? . . . If you don't know Him now, you won't know him then. Listen to me, world, listen to this warning. The Holy Word is in my mouth. (133)

That she says this to Rayber—she "turned her eyes again on his face in the window" (133)—only adds to the novel's countervailing attention to mind, to *gnosis:* Rayber too believes that salvation comes by knowledge. He is the modern Gnostic who harbors the comfortable but fragile Manichean heresy about which O'Connor so often remarked in her letters and essays. (In fact we learn later that Rayber's eyes are "shadowed," not illumined, "with knowledge" [*VBA* 56]). In "Everything That Rises Must Converge," Julian Chestny, to whom "true culture is in the mind, the *mind*" (*CS* 409), speaks in his story the only language Rayber can understand in his. Both are spiritually akin to Thomas Paine, whom O'Connor might have invented for fiction had not history already invented him for itself—Paine, who famously proclaimed that his mind was his church. Such Gnostics as Julian and Rayber and others like them populate O'Connor's fiction because they populate the concrete world she set out to render justly. She believed fully that her readers would identify with them. And, as it happens, they did.[10]

These two scenes—the one with Buford and the other with Lucette Carmody—illustrate the fundamental difference O'Connor is at pains to paint between Mason and Rayber: one is, and one is *not,* deep in this life. Even a dead Mason seems deeper in this life than a living Rayber: Rayber cannot hear much of anything; he denies "his senses unnecessary satisfaction" and pays "scarce attention" to food, whereas Tarwater even in death sits with "his stomach caught just under the edge of the table" and his eyes "focussed on the boy across from him" (*VBA* 11). In life Mason always insisted on being put in the ground; Rayber attempts to float above it in the airy realm of thought. That is to say, he is abstracted from the life of the body, a condition that turns out to be a great convenience to him and a grave danger to others.

The evidence for this abstraction is everywhere, of course, and it ranges from the obvious to the subtle. One of the first things we learn about Rayber—in the novel's second paragraph—is that he wants to raise Tarwater according to his "ideas" (4), which is a remark sensible and common enough until in short order Rayber emerges as a man of ideas only, a man unlike Tarwater, who is made of "dust" and "blood and nerve and mind," made "to bleed and weep and think" (91). O'Connor's descriptions of the two principal domiciles underscore Rayber's abstraction. Whereas the house at Powderhead is cluttered with sacks of feed and scrap metal and wood shavings, and the downstairs is "all kitchen" (10), Rayber's house has "little in it but books and papers" (19), and Rayber himself keeps a "rigid ascetic discipline" by sleeping in a "narrow iron bed," sitting "in a straight-backed chair," and eating "frugally" (114).[11] It is only because he once spent four days at Powderhead that he has ever "seen woods before or been in a boat or caught a fish or walked on roads that were not paved" or plowed a field (64). In short, Rayber's is a life abstracted from the created order; to him the body is an impediment to the life of the mind. One of his senses is deficient, and there is little doubt that he would gladly suffer the other four to fail as well. One critic has well said that Rayber is "trying to turn flesh into word" (Lake 51).

Rayber's abstraction from dust and blood and nerve accounts for his enthusiasm for technology and all the man-made emblems of what he is pleased to think of as progress. He takes Tarwater on escalators. He takes him to railroad yards. He tells Tarwater that he can have his own car when he is sixteen. Rayber even says there is something wrong with Tarwater if the thought of flying does not stir his imagination. But Tarwater, like his great-uncle, prefers doing to thinking, and he seems to intuit what the schoolteacher is too sophisticated to see: that the machine represents an assault on the body. Own a car? Tarwater "could walk on his two feet for nothing without being beholden" (*VBA* 108). Ride in an airplane? He has already been in one, he says, and the "houses weren't nothing but matchboxes and the people were invisible—like germs. I wouldn't give you nothing for no airplane" (173).

There is a grave seriousness to this, which I will discuss presently. But not surprisingly there is also a good joke at work. Tarwater's deft dismissal of what Rayber predictably calls "the greatest engineering achievement of man" prompts Rayber to say to him that Mason has "warped your whole life. . . . You're going to grow up to be a freak if you don't let yourself be helped" (173)—this from a man strapped for life with a hearing aid inside a clumsy metal box, a comic prop that O'Connor serves up to Tarwater, who dutifully executes the joke by wondering whether Rayber's head lights up and by suspecting that Rayber thinks with the box rather than with his head. O'Connor apparently believed that a man who lives in contempt of the body and yet needs a machine to help the body perform a necessary function is laughable. He is ridiculous and therefore deserves ridicule. So ignorant is he of his condition as a physical as well as an intellectual creature that he has to be told by an uncle whom he takes to be a lunatic that "you can't change a child's pants in your head" (75).

The desire to live by thought only, the desire to abstract oneself from the conditions of an earthly life that even God during the reign of Caesar Augustus did not spurn, has consequences that can be rightly named only by red-eyed prophets sensible enough to make cracks about changing a child's pants. *Nothing* necessary for the body can be done in the head. You cannot grow food in your head. You cannot keep dry or warm in your head. Literary criticism feeds and shelters no one. Trees and sweet basil do not take root in the pages of *PMLA,* nor do streams flow therefrom. Tarwater's remark about the airplane is important because it directs Rayber's attention—and also ours—to the earth, to the conditions of life, which are not theoretical but material. They are conditions in which even God says, "I thirst."

Rayber is not prepared to admit that the reduction of houses to matchboxes, and of people to germs, is a great convenience to those who, like him, live only by thought. He cannot see that such a reduction is a fundamental necessity to his way of thinking. If you are going to live in contempt of the flesh and turn everything into a piece of information that fits into your head, you will need to abstract yourself from the flesh; you will need the distance that the view from high above affords. Proximity will destroy that comfortable contempt; only abstraction can preserve it.

The novel bears this out, and the implications of it are not exactly trivial. That Rayber sees his uncle as a "type" (*VBA* 15) is obvious enough from Mason's outrage at being the object of a study. But even Rayber's "normal way of looking on Bishop was as an *x* signifying the general hideousness of fate" (113), and Tarwater knows that under Rayber's care he would be "in school, one among many, indistinguishable from the herd" (18). Unable or unwilling as he is to distinguish an individual from his class or type, Rayber could conceivably be anything from a sexual researcher to a sexual predator, and so here we must introduce a third meaning of *abstract:* when you see others as mere undifferentiated members of a group, you have turned them into abstractions; you have prepared for them an atrocity, indulged a sentimentality that can lead as quickly to the gas chamber as to rape or pillage. The mind given to abstractions necessarily generalizes, and when it sees the general rather than the particular it has already predisposed itself to abuse.

If Rayber knows this, he knows it only intuitively. It has not risen to the light of conscious day. Not so O'Connor, however, which is why she sometimes permits Rayber to look long and carefully enough to see a person rather than a type, whereupon something quite unexpected— and for Rayber unbearable—happens. In the case of Bishop he experiences "a love for the child so outrageous" that he is left "shocked and depressed for days, and trembling for his sanity" (113).[12] Is it any wonder Rayber prefers abstraction? It is indeed a very great convenience— as much to him as to colonizing kings and researchers and predators and captains of industry—especially if it fends off shock and depression.

What could so affect a man whose habit is to grind things up in his head until he can spit out a number—what but the very proximity that made God weep for Jerusalem? For the likes of Rayber nothing so threatens the cherished heresy as the heft of a child on his lap: "When he finished tying the shoes, he [Rayber] continued to hold the child, sprawling and grinning, in his lap. The little boy's white head fitted under his chin. . . . Without warning his hated love gripped him and held him in a vise. He should have known better than to let the child onto his lap" (141).

Which is to say that there's a threatened intimacy of creation, to be sure, but there is also a created intimacy that threatens. A man whose guts are in his head could not be thus moved. That Rayber feels a similar tenderness toward the child-preacher means only that his guts are in the same place as everyone else's. At such moments he might be capable of extricating himself from the ancient grip of the Manicheans, save that he has neither eyes to see nor ears to hear. It is true that when he hears the drowning Bishop bellow he will grab the metal box "as if it were clawing his heart" (202)—which at that moment he certainly will *not* believe is in his head—but by then he will have successfully converted all flesh into a piece of information ready to be spat out like a number. As critics have rightly noted, we are not left wondering whether Rayber is complicit in the murder of Bishop. By now it is clear that abstraction is a kind of violence—a violence perpetrated against a created unity, a sundering of what God has joined together and built into the moral structure of the universe, a violence that, like all violence, generates more, which generates more, which generates more.

I have said Rayber's abstraction is a great convenience to him. He could test this by thinking a little about the greatest achievement of the technological age: high above the earth, floating in the blue serene, a fighter pilot might find easy permission to push a button and annihilate a village from which he is comfortably abstracted. But, standing before a child from that same village, that same pilot will wait a long time— forever, let us hope—before he strangles her while she looks into his eyes. Again: there is a threatened but also a threatening intimacy of creation.

And then there is the airplane itself to think about, and the button and the bomb—that is, the machines. Tarwater's distrust of machines that do the body's work makes perfect sense to anyone who takes seriously the doctrine of the incarnation. The flesh matters; that which replaces it, and in so doing sets it at a discount, must give us pause.

RAYBER COMMITS ONE MORE EGREGIOUS ACT OF ABSTRACTION that cannot go unremarked simply because O'Connor does not apparently subject it to the usual ridicule. It is significant as a measure of the kind of judgment about which I will have more to say at the end.

Bishop and Rayber have left Tarwater in the Cherokee Lodge and gone for a drive: "The car apparently of its own volition had turned onto a dirt road which without warning pierced . . . [Rayber's] abstraction with its familiarity." Without meaning to, Rayber has come to the road that leads to Powderhead. Suddenly he realizes that, Mason's being dead, Powderhead is now his:

> The trees stood rising above him, majestic and aloof, as if they belonged to an order that had never budged from its first allegiance in the days of creation. His heart began to beat frenetically. Quickly he reduced the whole wood in probable board feet into a college education for the boy. His spirits lifted. (*VBA* 185)

We already know that familiarity has a way of piercing Rayber's abstraction and leaving him shocked and depressed; the effect is always salutary, and this scene is no exception. He will presently do Bishop a kindness (pick him a berry) even as he apparently begins to consider a benefit to Tarwater. But Rayber lives by thinking, by abstraction, by drawing away, and even here his selflessness involves the quick reduction of the majestic trees into something else: a college education ultimately, but obviously into board length—that is, cash—first. To do this he must disrupt "an order" that has "never budged from its first allegiance in the days of creation."

"Reduced" is precisely the right word: in an economy based on abstract as opposed to real wealth, simplification—reduction—is always the requisite first move; nature must be reduced to the price it can fetch in the here and now. The health of a place, its reproductive capacity, the real costs of converting productivity to money—especially those costs that are obviously charged to the future—all these bookable charges must be kept off the books if the likes of Rayber are to have their way.

And they have their way precisely because, having inevitably defended such acts of abstraction in the name of charity, they succeed in reducing a mystery to the limiting terms of their own limited understanding. I pause to point out what I hope is obvious: in this scene the name for that mystery is *fertility;* it is something about which Tarwater knows a thing or two, else why would he think to bury his great-uncle under the fig tree where his rotting corpse can do the tree some good? Fertility is not anything upon which O'Connor ever expostulated, but she certainly would have noted, had she cared to, that a kind of death and resurrection presents itself both actually and analogically in the processes of fertility.

But Rayber can no more see analogically than Manley Pointer or Sarah Ruth can, so down with the trees.

To object at this point on grounds that O'Connor never proffered anything like a criticism of the extractive economy would, I think, be a serious mistake.[13] It would blind the critics already prone to myopia to that compact consistency of which I spoke at the beginning. That she is not explicitly critical of Rayber's economy only means that she is not explicitly critical of Rayber's economy. But reducing the complexity of the forest to "board length" is an act of economic simplification that accords with all of Rayber's other acts of simplification—and it confirms something Allen Tate understood thirty years earlier: "economy is the secular image of religious conviction" ("Remarks" 168). Rayber's economy could be none other than what it is. But whatever frustration Rayber caused O'Connor in the spring of 1959, he is certainly no longer a "difficulty." He never once steps out of character.

And so after reducing the forest to board length what does he do? Explanations do not deepen mysteries for him. He limits a mystery—an order that has never budged in its faithfulness to the creation that God pronounced good and then died for—to the limiting terms of his own limited understanding:

> He decided that he would put the whole thing verbally before the boy. He would not argue with him but only tell him, tell him in so many plain words that he had a compulsion and what it was. Whether he answered, whether he cooperated, he would have to

listen. He could not escape knowing that there was someone who knew exactly what went on inside him and who understood it for the good reason that it was understandable. (*VBA* 187)

This is the language of idolatry. This is the language of someone who says that a sound does not exist because he cannot hear it—even though all the dogs around him are howling. It is the language of those for whom, as we know, O'Connor consciously wrote.

The intimacy of creation is plenty frightening, for it always presents itself as the kind of mystery that explanation only deepens. Bishop presents himself to Rayber in just this way. But the majestic trees, mysterious in their way, do not elicit the hated love that Bishop does. Rayber is armed against them in the manner of a confirmed city-dweller and absentee owner: he cannot love them because he has spent his life abstracted from them; he does not know them because he is distanced from them. All that he does and thinks and schemes in this scene overlooking Powderhead accords perfectly with his intellectual habits and commitments. He may as well be in an airplane—as poised there to push a button as he was elsewhere to hold a boy's head under water. But note which of these two conditions is inimical to violence: when the victim is intimate, proximate, the murder fails. When Bishop does finally die, Rayber will be at a comfortable distance—a distance that the flick of a switch will easily increase. That is, he will be abstracted. And, as usual, violence will ensue.

For Rayber cannot see the whole Bishop any more than Sarah Ruth can see the whole Parker, certainly not that part of him that bears the *imago dei*—cannot see what Tate says religion always insists upon, which is *everything*: the whole horse. Rayber's is the modern mind, the mind, Tate says, that

> sees only half of the horse—that half which may become a dynamo, or an automobile, or any other horsepowered machine. If this mind had much respect for the full-dimensioned, grass-eating horse, it would never have invented the engine which represents only half of him. The religious mind, on the other hand, has this respect; it wants the whole horse, and it will be satisfied with nothing less. ("Remarks" 157)

But Rayber is always satisfied with less—believing, always, that the less he has is more. He is, as Tate says, "trying to discover the place that religion holds with logical, abstract instruments, which of course tend to put religion in some logical system or series, where it vanishes" (163).

I SUGGESTED THAT WE THINK OF THE SCENES WITH BUFORD and Lucette Carmody as conceptual markers. I did so not because O'Connor makes much of them but because, inasmuch as they involve minor characters, they show the extent to which a mind-body opposition pervades the novel, an opposition dramatized principally in Rayber and the dead old man, who engage in a battle over Tarwater's soul. But more is at stake than the boy's soul; a doctrine of God and therefore a doctrine of man are also at stake: a theology, an anthropology, a cosmology, and issuing from them an economy, an ecology, and a mode of consciousness—that is, a habit of being. When abstraction does violence to any one of these, it perpetrates a disruption in all of them. A first allegiance to creation has been broken, and with it the moral and physical orders—which are not really two orders but one—also snap.

If we see the child-preacher as a version of Rayber—they are both in their ways Gnostics, not to mention physically deformed—we should be able to complete the case against him. That she happens to believe in God and Rayber does not, hardly matters: all that either of them demands is knowledge. Even the girl speaks only of the word, not the word made flesh. Like Manley Pointer she is placeless and rootless, poised like her parents (who come from Texas and Tennessee and who travel the world but belong nowhere) to become an itinerant charlatan. The bleeding stinking Jesus whom Tarwater follows is no one any of them know; they would be as likely as Sarah Ruth to thrash the nearest Parker. Some critics have argued—properly, I think—the importance of Lucette's sermon. I do not dispute that she is the vehicle of a partial truth. I wish to point out only that her message, like her body and her mode of living, is defective. Ultimately hers is a theology impermissible to someone who said, "better somewhere than anywhere." Place matters. That is a fact that must occur to anyone who has read the Old Testament.[14] If Lucette is not careful, she could become an "innerleckchul," which as we know is an incorrigibly gnostic champion of unconscionable hypermobility.

MY AIM HERE HAS BEEN TWOFOLD: TO GO TO WORK ON THE novel and to ask the novel to go to work on us—in the manner of those, descended from Dr. Johnson but now long since dead, in whom the old tradition of ethical criticism still had some purchase: scholars who were capable of learning not only about but also from their books. For there is really no use reading O'Connor if all we bring to the task is a strained nervousness and sterile "objectivity." Certainly we do no violence to O'Connor's vocation as a writer—and none to Tarwater's as a prophet—if we allow that those who judge books are also judged by them, that the use of a book extends beyond its covers and even perhaps, like an operation of grace, outside of time. The children of God may make short work of Tarwater, and even of O'Connor, but only because the children of God, like Rayber, are in the thrall of an ancient heresy. They have preferred horsepower to horses; they have preferred *un*carnation to incarnation. A neglected flesh and a despoiled creation are none other than the physical manifestations of such theological confusion as bedevils Rayber and the moral offenses he necessarily perpetuates, for (again) the physical and moral orders are not two orders but one.

NOTES

1. Lynch 61; O'Connor, *MM* 163. I have elsewhere suggested the influence of Lynch on O'Connor; see "The Source" 48–53.

2. Christina Bieber Lake reminds us that "[i]n the view of Pierre Teilhard de Chardin and Claude Tresmontant, writers O'Connor read and respected, Christ's incarnation validated the created world and encouraged people to be a part of its ongoing creation, growth, and evolution" (52). I have discussed this validation at some length; see "Flannery" 31–40.

3. As Richard Giannone, among others, has noted. See, for example, Giannone 122, 128.

4. See, for example, O'Connor's letter to Janet McKane, 27 August 1963 (*HB* 536).

5. And the novel's "truths are more particular than general" (*HB* 438).

6. *Abstract: abs* off, away + *tractus,* pa. ppl. of *trahĕre* to draw (*OED*).

7. "As for your not plucking fruits or piling up vegetables for yourselves, while you get your followers to pluck and pull and bring them to you, that you may confer benefits not only on those who bring the food but on the

food which is brought, what thoughtful person can bear to hear this?" (Augustine 84).

8. O'Connor tells us this (*HB* 350); Lake offers a useful warning (45).

9. "You Can't Be Any Poorer Than Dead" was published in *New World Writing* 8 (October 1955). O'Connor writes, "Lucette was part of a story I started a long time ago and saw it wasn't going to come off and put it up. I am glad I had it laid by" (*HB* 342). On the "difficulty" of Rayber, see *HB* 327, 329, and 332.

10. "The modern reader will identify himself with the schoolteacher," she said of Rayber, "but it is the old man who speaks for me" (*HB* 350).

11. It must be noted that Rayber does not understand the spiritual and intellectual effects of physical askesis. His "rigid ascetic discipline" is not a spiritual discipline; it is an example of his according the body little attention and in doing so setting it at a discount.

12. We do well to remember that O'Connor said that this "is the purest love I have ever dealt with" (*HB* 379).

13. And at any rate, the extent to which economic relations had become abstract did not escape her notice: "everybody wants the good things of life, like supermarkets," O'Connor said in an interview with Robert Penn Warren. "Everyone wants the privilege of being as abstract as the next man" (O'Connor, *Conversations* 30).

14. Philip J. Lee has a fine discussion of this in *Against the Protestant Gnostics* (30ff, 214). On the importance of place to O'Connor see, for example, her letter to Cecil Dawkins from July 1957: "I stayed away from the time I was 20 until I was 25 with the notion that the life of my writing depended on my staying away. I would certainly have persisted in that delusion had I not got very ill and had to come home. The best of my writing has been done here" (*HB* 230).

WORKS CITED

Augustine. *On the Morals of the Manichæans.* Trans. Richard Stothert. *Nicene and Post Nicene-Fathers.* Ed. Philip Schaff. Vol. 4. Peabody, MA: Hendrickson, 1994. 69–89.

Bloom, Harold. *Where Shall Wisdom Be Found?* New York: Riverhead, 2004.

Giannone, Richard. *Flannery O'Connor and the Mystery of Love.* Urbana: University of Illinois Press, 1989.

Lake, Christine Bieber. "Called to the Beautiful: The Incarnational Art of Flannery O'Connor's *The Violent Bear it Away.*" *Xavier Review* 18.1 (1998): 44–68.

Lee, Philip J. *Against the Protestant Gnostics*. New York: Oxford University Press, 1987.

Lynch, William. "Theology and the Imagination." *Thought* 29 (1954): 61–86.

O'Connor, Flannery. *The Complete Stories*. New York: Farrar, Straus and Giroux, 1971.

———. *Conversations with Flannery O'Connor*. Ed. Rosemary M. Magee. Jackson: University Press of Mississippi, 1987.

———. *The Habit of Being: Letters of Flannery O'Connor*. Ed. Sally Fitzgerald. New York: Farrar, Straus and Giroux, 1979.

———. *Mystery and Manners: Occasional Prose*. Ed. Sally Fitzgerald and Robert Fitzgerald. New York: Farrar, Straus and Giroux, 1969.

———. *The Violent Bear It Away*. New York: Farrar, Straus and Giroux, 1960.

Peters, Jason. "Flannery O'Connor on Fiction and a Mood for 'Christian' Intellectual Labor." *Intégrité* 4.2 (Fall 2005): 31–40.

———. "The Source of Flannery O'Connor's 'Flung' Fish in *The Violent Bear It Away*." *American Notes and Queries* 18.4 (Fall 2005): 48–53.

Tate, Allen. "Remarks on the Southern Religion." *I'll Take My Stand: The South and the Agrarian Tradition*. By Twelve Southerners. 1930. Baton Rouge: Louisiana State University Press, 1977. 155–75.

CHAPTER 5

Transfiguring Affliction

Simone Weil and Flannery O'Connor

RUTHANN KNECHEL JOHANSEN

The growth of the seed within us is painful.

—Simone Weil

Whoever does not bear his own cross and come after me, cannot be my disciple.

—Luke 14:27

During the last two decades, attentive scholars have noted Flannery O'Connor's interest in two European Jews, Simone Weil and Edith Stein. Of these two philosophers, Simone Weil receives greater attention both in O'Connor's letters and in recent O'Connor scholarship. Although the draw O'Connor had toward Weil seems initially surprising because, unlike Stein who converted to Catholicism, Weil remained outside the Church, this chapter posits an intellectual-spiritual kinship between O'Connor and Weil that will be examined through the philosopher's essays and the fiction writer's second novel, *The Violent Bear It Away.*

In his 1987 study *Simone Weil: A Modern Pilgrimage,* Robert Coles described Weil as "not only a brilliant and original social observer, political theorist, and moral philosopher, but an extraordinary pilgrim of the twentieth century" (xix). In the same year, Sarah Gordon described O'Connor's attraction to Weil in her essay "Flannery O'Connor, the Left-Wing Mystic, and the German Jew." Highlighting biographical details and philosophical ideas of the French philosopher, political activist, and mystic, Gordon traces O'Connor's fascination with Weil through O'Connor's letters, particularly her correspondence with Elizabeth Hester, and interprets suggestive hints of Weil in O'Connor's well-known stories such as "The Displaced Person" and "Good Country People."

Subsequent essays on the provocative, if sometimes confounding, fascination of O'Connor for Weil's thought by Lee Sturma, Jane Detweiler, and John Desmond have enriched O'Connor scholarship during the last decade.[1] The present analysis of *The Violent Bear It Away,* particularly the enigmatic part three of the novel, is indebted to such scholarship but goes further by arguing that O'Connor does not merely study nor characterize, or worse, caricature, selected ideas of Weil, as Sturma, Detweiler, and Desmond imply. By reading *The Violent Bear It Away* in light of three essays by Weil—"A War of Religions," "The Love of God and Affliction," and "Forms of the Implicit Love of God"—I suggest that O'Connor as fiction writer presses the philosopher beyond philosophical abstraction by embodying through her characters the monstrous struggle precipitated by affliction to turn toward God rather than to become an accomplice in one's own affliction.

During her second year at Georgia State College for Women (1943–44), Flannery O'Connor published in the campus literary journal *Colannade* "Home of the Brave," a short story satirizing the "home-front hypocrisy displayed by a group of small-town women who have gathered to wrap bandages for the war effort" (Cash 63). In the same year, Simone Weil, preoccupied throughout her life with injustice, war, and religious questions, addressed the perennial dream of abolishing the religious problem in her essay "A War of Religions." There she argues that human beings are not able to "evade the religious problem . . . because when offered the choice by the devil to follow God and thus be "unfree because you can do only good" or to follow the devil and have "the power to do good or evil as you choose," human beings continually opt to follow the devil. Once having made that choice and finding it like a red-hot coal, however, it is difficult to escape from the choice.

Weil proposes three paths of response to the religious problem. The first is the irreligious way, which "consists in denying the reality of the opposition between good and evil." The second is idolatry, by which Weil means "the adoration of the social under various divine names"; this way is most frequently employed by scientists and artists who "often make science and art a closed area within which there is no place for virtue or vice, whence they conclude that in their capacity as scientist or artist they are absolved from all moral responsibility." The third path is the mystical way through which human beings pass "beyond the sphere where good and evil are in opposition," making possible the "union of the soul with the absolute good" ("War on Religions" 211–14). Of these three ways, the first two are impossible, asserts Weil. And the third, "supernatural one (the mystical way) is only difficult, [for] the sole access to it is through spiritual poverty." For Weil, affliction offers "almost the only opportunity" of learning spiritual poverty necessary for the mystical way (216, 218).

In *The Violent Bear It Away*, Flannery O'Connor, likewise concerned with the religious problem in a secular age drawn by both the irreligious and idolatry as modes of escape from the problem of good and evil, depicts the protracted spiritual contest of the Tarwater family between idolatry and mystery. In this novel the eighty-four-year-old backwoods prophet Mason Tarwater, who believes himself obedient to God and "is too orthodox to grant evil any sort of dualistic equality with good" (Wood 228), has his great-nephew under his tutelage, wishing to commission the fourteen-year-old Francis Marion Tarwater to succeed him as a prophet.

Although young Tarwater dreams of glamorous and thrilling prophetic acts, Mason promises not glory but pain and ignominy. The boy's vocation as prophet will begin when the old man dies and the boy performs his first act of burying him deep enough in the ground to prevent the dogs from unearthing him and placing a cross at the head of his grave. His second prophetic task will be to baptize Bishop, the "idiot son" of his uncle George Rayber, a school psychologist and Nietzschean nihilist who has opted for the freedom to choose his response to the problem of good and evil. Rayber believes that Mason invented his prophetic calling, treats him like a deluded specimen for psychological study, and considers his own son Bishop a worthless creature who should have been aborted. The novel opens with Mason's death, and with his first prophetic task at hand, young Tarwater labors for half a day to dig the grave only to abandon his spade work in disobedience, heading off to his great-uncle's whiskey still to numb his conscience and satisfy his thirst. Depicting the struggle between good and evil that extends across generations, O'Connor presents Tarwater's spiritual re-bellion through an inner voice that takes paradoxical forms as both stranger and friend throughout the novel. Sometimes the voice arises from within the boy's own rebellious will and sometimes appears as a demonic force beyond his control. As Tarwater succumbs to the effects of the whiskey, the voice encourages Tarwater to exercise his independence from his great-uncle's commands, and Tarwater performs the one act prohibited by Mason: rather than bury his body in the ground, he sets fire to the house containing his great-uncle's corpse. In part two of the novel, Tarwater heads to the city to the home of his uncle Rayber, who undertakes to reform the boy of Mason's influence. Here Rayber contends mightily with Tarwater against his second prophetic task, to baptize Bishop.

O'Connor labored over this enigmatic novel for eight years (1952–60). During this time we know from O'Connor's letters and from critics such as Detweiler, Gordon, and Desmond that O'Connor read the work of Simone Weil, or work about her, at least as early as 1952. One of the earliest pieces O'Connor may have read was an essay in *Third Hour*, a journal edited by Helene Iswolsky, a professor at Fordham University who was a great-aunt of Erik Langskjaer.[2] The essay, written by Gerda Blumenthal and entitled "Simone Weil and the Cross of Dividedness," describes Weil's preoccupation with the infinite separation between the natural plane, subject to the laws of time and weight, and the super-natural plane of absolute truth or the absolute good, the plane of grace in which human beings are suspended (19). Like Weil, O'Connor wrestled with the mystery of this infinite distance but rendered her wrestling in parabolic fiction, not philosophical abstractions. Weil argues in "The Love of God and Affliction" that the only way this infinite separation becomes infinite unity is through the power of love that brings one to the foot of the cross, and she explicates this movement toward the cross through affliction and love. It is in part three of *The Violent Bear It Away,* laid next to "The Love of God and Affliction," that the third path, the mystical way, becomes shockingly visible.

In her essay Weil describes the characteristics of affliction, which include social, psychological, and physical degradation. She distinguishes it from suffering because affliction "takes possession of the soul" and makes the soul affliction's slave ("Love" 117). In affliction there is an uprooting of life that is the equivalent of death, making God appear absent for a time, an experience, Weil contends, known to Christ when he cried from the cross, "My God, why hast Thou forsaken me." If the soul stops loving in this state of extremity, God's absence becomes final, and little by little the soul becomes affliction's accomplice. The misery of affliction gets our attention and gives us a choice: on the one hand, "the infinite precious privilege of sharing in this distance between the Son and the Father" *or,* on the other, the turning away from God where everything simply becomes obedient to the mechanism of necessity. "If, however," Weil suggests, "we transport our hearts beyond ourselves, beyond the universe, beyond space and time to where the Father dwells . . . what seemed to be necessity becomes obedience" ("Love" 128). No one can escape obedience to God; the only choice is to desire obedience or not to desire it. Choosing obedience moves us *through* affliction toward a demanding apprenticeship in love.

In placing O'Connor's second novel next to Weil's briefly sketched ideas on affliction, no one can miss the social, psychological, and physical degradation that all three Tarwater males endure. The affliction is lodged in the family, as Rayber senses,

> It lay hidden in the line of blood that touched them, flowing from some ancient source, some desert prophet or pole-sitter . . . . Those it touched were condemned to fight it constantly or be ruled by it. The old man had been ruled by it. He at the cost of a full life, staved it off. What the boy would do hung in the balance. (*CW* 402)

It is the fourth Tarwater male, the so-called idiot child Bishop, who is not afflicted, as Detweiler reminds us, because he cannot choose to desire or not to desire obedience to God. As "a part of creation, and never apart from God, he is a figure for the presence of affliction" (Detweiler 5), or what I might call an enfleshed icon on which Rayber's and Tarwater's eyes are riveted and their responses to affliction depend. Bishop becomes the novel's fulcrum on which refusal of obedience or the desire to obey hinge.

In their wrestling with the affliction passed to them through blood, both Rayber and Tarwater exist at the foot of the cross, the farthest distance from God. O'Connor exposes Rayber's direction when he tells Tarwater, "I may not have the guts to drown him [Bishop], but I have the guts to maintain my self-respect and not to perform futile rites over him. I have the guts not to become prey of superstitions. . . . My guts are in my head" (*CW* 437). Despite his conviction of his freedom, Rayber's struggle between compulsion and denied affliction rages in his head where "he had known . . . that his own stability depended on the little boy's presence. He could control his terrifying love as long as it had its focus in Bishop, but if anything happened to the child, he would have to face it in itself. Then the whole world would become his idiot child" (442). Continuing his effort to save Tarwater from being driven by his obsessions and himself from terrifying love, Rayber explains that "baptism is only an empty act. If there's any way to be born again, it's a way that you accomplish yourself, an understanding about yourself" (450–51). At the Cherokee Lodge, Rayber offers Tarwater a glass of water and gives him permission to baptize Bishop as a way of weeding out his compulsion. Refusing the challenge, Tarwater retorts, "I can pull it up by the roots, once and for all. I can do something. I ain't like you. All you can do is think what you would have done if you had done it. Not me. I can do it. I can act" (451). Which indeed he does when he drowns Bishop with the words of baptism.

As we follow Tarwater's journey home following the baptismal murder, O'Connor's own artistic ability to be a prophet imaginatively expands what is required to move *through* affliction toward attention and obedience. Although both Weil and O'Connor suggest that affliction provides the occasion, the opportunity for the soul to turn toward God, through young Tarwater's journey back to Powderhead, O'Connor presses Weil by fleshing out what choosing obedience demands. She incarnates four obstacles that confound yet make known the path toward obedience. In depicting these obstacles, O'Connor simultaneously makes visible, through her metaphoric language, the analogy between the vocations of prophecy and art for bridging the infinite distance between the natural and the supernatural.

The first obstacle that affliction makes clear and that gives occasion for and even hinders obedience is egoism. While Rayber constructs his defense of egoism through his nihilistic intellectualism, Tarwater's struggles with egoism are complexly depicted through the ambiguous voices that accompany Tarwater from the beginning of the novel. As both stranger and friend, the voices continue to attend him through the baptismal event, which Tarwater rationalizes as "an accident and nothing more" (*CW* 465), and are with him on his way to Powderhead. Edward Kessler asserts that the metaphor of voices, which O'Connor considers Tarwater's wrestling with the devil, displaces Tarwater from the social community and "connects him with his true history and community" (156), a community that, according to Weil, he will find through affliction.

Taking different disguises and poses throughout the novel, even at times going into Rayber, the egocentric voices taunt Tarwater to pride for saving himself until he sees himself as "a gaunt stranger, the ghost who had been born in the wreck" (*CW* 465) and encounters the stranger in the man wearing lavender attire who precipitates in rape Tarwater's final confrontation with evil, his own rebellion and self-division that are both interior and external. The stranger prepares Tarwater for his violation by offering him powerful liquor that obliterates his senses. Whereas at the beginning of the novel whiskey from his great uncle's still emboldens young Tarwater toward rebellion and self-sufficiency, at the end the fiery liquor ushers him back to creation and his true vocation. Ironically, O'Connor has given Mason and young Tarwater the name of a drink with healing properties (tar-water) made from the pine or fir tree. The drink and its medicinal qualities were described in George Berkeley's *Siris: Philosophical Reflections and Inquiries Concerning the Virtues of Tar-Water* (1744) as having power to restore well-being in the afflicted.[3]

O'Connor not merely understands "the difficulty of penetrating disguises . . . that good and evil can take," concluding that "the 'real look' of good or evil remains invisible, mysterious" (Kessler 95); she makes that difficulty visible as a shocking means of grace for the ego. Through his violation, a metaphor for the world's rape, argues Kessler, Tarwater moves in nakedness from the foot of the cross—the greatest possible distance from divine Presence—to be nailed, as it were, to it. Although not chosen, Tarwater's violation reflects a central theme of Weil's thought: "To consent to being anonymous, to being human material (Eucharist), to renounce prestige, public esteem—that is to bear witness to truth: namely, that one is composed of human material, that one has no rights. It is to cast aside all ornament, to put up with one's nakedness" (*Notebooks* 217).

A second obstacle faced by Tarwater on his path toward obedience is to get the devil behind him. This he does after waking from his violation and setting fire to every part of the evil ground that the stranger touched. O'Connor returns Tarwater to the natural world of Powderhead, moving him closer to home through the recalled sound of one thrush "hidden some distance ahead of him, [calling] the same four notes again and again, stopping each time after them to make a silence" that he had heard shortly after Mason's death (*CW* 357). Now upon return his senses are stunned and his thoughts too seem suspended: "Somewhere deep in the wood a woodthrush called and as if the sound were a key turned in the boy's heart, his throat began to tighten . . . the woodthrush called again. With the same four formal notes it trilled its grief against the silence" (474). Tarwater endeavors to avoid the threatened intimacy of creation. Anticipating a blow he instead "felt a breeze on his neck as light as breath . . . and a presence as pervasive as an odor . . . a violet shadow hanging around his shoulders." And the voice of his friend whispers one last time, "Go down and take it. . . . It's ours. We've won it" (475). The world before him could be his own, but at this temptation, Tarwater "shuddered convulsively. . . . tore off another pine bough," and set it afire, watching as the grinning presence of "his adversary would soon be consumed in a roaring blaze" (475).

As Tarwater continues moving through each obstacle, I have already alluded to the third: the alteration of his senses. With unveiled vision, his familiar country "look[s] like strange and alien country" (473). Although nothing has changed in the external world, O'Connor shrinks the infinite distance between the natural and the supernatural planes through the metaphor of "a transformed world and renovated vision" (Kessler 139). In Weil's argument,

> he whose soul remains . . . turned toward God though the nail pierces it[,] finds himself nailed to the very center of the universe . . . without leaving the place and the instant where the body to which it is united is situated, can cross the totality of space and time and come into the very presence of God. ("Love" 135–36)

Tarwater's death to the world ushers him to silence and attentiveness, necessary for the apprehension of mystery, which gives birth to obedience. Following his vision of "dim figures seated on the slope" (*CW* 477) being fed from a single basket and after the divine injunction to prophesy fades, "[t]he words [of God's mercy] were as silent as seeds opening one at a time in his blood" (478). Or, in Weil's terms, "as soon as we have a point of eternity in the soul, we have nothing to do but to take care of it, for it will grow of itself like a seed" (*Gravity and Grace* 172–73).

Although at the end of the novel it is unclear what shape Tarwater's obedience to his vocation will take, two conditions prevail: first, Tarwater seems to grasp Weil's insight that "love is a direction, not a state of the soul . . ." ("Love" 135). Second, through his vision of the multitude eating the loaves and fishes, he discovers a superhistorical, supernatural community—Kessler calls it a mythic community—that will influence his relationship to the human community. Is it possible that through affliction Tarwater confronts a fourth obstacle, the invitation to hear, which O'Connor places both in the call of the wood thrush and puzzlingly in the middle of the novel in the voice of a young girl?

In contrast to Rayber, Tarwater listens toward the vision annunciated by Lucette Carmody, the physically crippled and psychologically exploited child preacher who, Ralph Wood suggests, "instinctively understands the whole creation as a trope of God. Not to discern analogies between the book of nature and the book of salvation is to be unfaithful to both" (174). Or in Weil's terms, the beauty of the world provides implicit evidence of God's love ("Forms" 137–214). Lucette's preaching infuriates and terrifies the eavesdropping Rayber who refuses to hear by turning off his hearing aid as she says:

> 'I want to tell you people the story of the world, . . . I want to tell
> you why Jesus came and what happened to him. . . . Do you know
> who Jesus is? . . . Jesus is the Word of God and Jesus is love. The
> Word of God is love and do you know what love is, you people?
> Listen you people! . . . the world knew in its heart, the same as you
> know in your hearts and I know in my heart . . . Jesus grew up and
> raised the dead . . . and the world shouted, 'Leave the dead lie. The
> dead are dead and can stay that way. . . . Listen world, Jesus is com
> ing again! The mountains are going to perch on His shoulder and
> when He calls it, the sun will drop down at His feet, but will you
> know the Lord Jesus then?' (*CW* 412–14)

Twelve-year-old Lucette recalls the image of another child preaching to temple elders and the deaf and the words of another prophet (Isaiah) who foretold that "the wolf shall dwell with the lamb . . . and a little child shall lead them" (Isaiah 11:6). In response to the young girl's message, the deaf Rayber "had the wooden look it wore when his hearing aid was off," but, in grabbing Tarwater, he could see that "for the first time the boy's eyes were submissive" (*CW* 415).

Having confronted these obstacles, Tarwater comes to silence, to an attentiveness that makes him conscious of a community he desires and to which he belongs:

> He felt his hunger no longer as a pain but as a tide. He felt it rising
> in himself through time and darkness, rising through the centu
> ries, and he knew that it rose in a line of men whose lives were cho
> sen to sustain it, who would wander in the world, strangers from
> that violent country where the silence is never broken except to
> shout the truth. (*CW* 478)

Through the words of a child preaching about the Word that became flesh, Tarwater recognizes in his body his hunger for bread. Through this realization of hunger, which turns into a vision of the dim figures being fed from a single basket when he returns to Powderhead, O'Connor shortens the distance between the natural and supernatural planes. The mystical power of words that evoke the Eucharist drop seeds in the blood that feed Tarwater's hunger and change his direction.

At the end of "The Love of God and Affliction," Simone Weil describes the person whose soul is turned toward God as being nailed at the cross pieces to the center of the universe. "It is the true center," she says, "not in the middle; it is beyond space and time; it is God" ("Love" 135). O'Connor as visionary artist, one who described "the prophet as a realist of distances" (*MM* 44), takes readers to this true center through the language of metaphor that releases the mind from the confines of both time and space. The visionary poet-novelist and the philosopher-mystic wrestle on the plane of language with words that have allowed us to denature nature, that are drained of flesh and blood through abstraction, that continually throw us into entrapping webs of words and yet that may, however wobbly, bridge the infinite distance between the natural and the supernatural. In moments of grace—defined by Marion Montgomery as "God's gesture of love"—there is no separation of the natural and the supernatural, of grace from nature or imagination from reason (274). "One may sense the separation of grace from nature, accomplished by man's willful intellect (i.e., Rayber), without understanding that the problem's only solution must be found in superhistorical and supernatural drawings of the spirit" (102).

O'Connor, like Weil, did understand the problem and attempted to startle her audience into awareness by using metaphor as her instrument for accommodating transcendent vision. Using the common materials of prose fiction and human affliction, O'Connor draws attentive readers to hear the wood thrush's song that beckons them, deep in their own forests, to silence in the infinite distance crossed by divine Love. In her essay "Morality and Literature" Weil describes what I think O'Connor attempted:

> There is something . . . which has the power to awaken us to the truth. It is the works of writers of genius, or at least of those with genius of the very first order when it has reached its full maturity. They are outside the realm of fiction and they release us from it. They give us, in the guise of fiction, something equivalent to the

actual density of the real [what I might call the unity of the natural and the supernatural], that density which life offers us every day but which we are unable to grasp because we are amusing ourselves with lies. ("Morality" 292)

In O'Connor's reference to Simone Weil as the perfect blending of the Comic and the Terrible and a woman about whom she would like to write a comic novel, responsible readers and critics must include O'Connor's personal association with this perfect blending. Acknowledging that the Comic and the Terrible "may be opposites sides of the same coin," O'Connor continues in her letter to Elizabeth Hester: "In my own experience, everything funny I have written is more terrible than it is funny, or only terrible because it is funny" (*CW* 478). What the Georgia writer could not dominate, as in a single character, she embodied in her own life work, presenting us visions from the artist as prophet whose vocation it is to "Go warn the [afflicted] children of God of the terrible speed of mercy" (478).

In bringing young Tarwater from obsessive rebellion through affliction to attentive acceptance, O'Connor in microcosm points toward the reunion of the natural and supernatural planes made possible through spiritual poverty. Weil, of course, was concerned about the affliction of conquered peoples and how to escape from nationalistic idolatries. She argued the need for an *elite* "to inspire the virtue of spiritual poverty among the ill-used masses," an *elite* that "would be part of the masses and in direct contact with them" ("War" 216). Tarwater's journey makes visible the terrible demands—indeed the violence—involved in refusing idolatry's obsessions and accepting the mystical path by which the infinite separation of the natural and the supernatural becomes infinite unity through the power of love.

The obligation of love that can bridge the infinite separation of the natural and the supernatural is expressed in the commandment "Thou shalt love the Lord thy God." Until God awakens that love in a person, Weil argues, love must have another object. This she calls "the indirect or implicit love of God." There are "only three things on earth in which God is really though secretly present. These are religious ceremonies, the beauty of the world, and our neighbor. . . . The combination of these loves constitutes the love of God in the form best suited to the preparatory period, that is to say the veiled form" ("Forms" 138). In *The Violent Bear It Away* O'Connor depicts how these three implicit forms of the love of God—the religious ceremony of baptism, the beauty of the world, and the love of neighbor—can be perverted through rebellion, denial, and violation. In so doing, she exposes the intense struggle necessary to avoid becoming an accomplice in one's own affliction and to realize spiritual poverty in which the transfiguring seed of love can grow.

NOTES

1. See Lee Sturma's "Flannery O'Connor, Simone Weil, and the Virtue of Necessity; Jane Detweiler's "Flannery O'Connor's Conversation with Simone Weil: *The Violent Bear It Away* as a Study in Affliction"; and John Desmond's "Flannery O'Connor and Simone Weil: A Question of Sympathy."

2. Erik Langskjaer was a textbook salesman for Harcourt Brace who visited Andalusia on several occasions in 1953 and with whom O'Connor fell in love.

3. I am grateful to E. Jane Doering for alerting me to Arthur L. Herman's "The Philosophy of Tar-Water: Bishop Berkeley and Medico-pyro-pantheism I," *Aryan Path* 37.6 (June–July 1966): 271–75.

WORKS CITED

Blumenthal, Gerda. "The Cross of Dividedness." *Third Hour* 5 (1951): 17–24.

Cash, Jean W. *Flannery O'Connor: A Life.* Knoxville: University of Tennessee Press, 2002.

Coles, Robert. *Simone Weil: A Modern Pilgrimage.* Reading, MA: Addison-Welsey, 1987.

Desmond, John F. "Flannery O'Connor and Simone Weil: A Question of Sympathy." *Logos: A Journal of Catholic Thought and Culture* 8.1 (2005): 102–16.

Detweiler, Jane. "Flannery O'Connor's Conversation with Simone Weil: *The Violent Bear It Away* as a Study in Affliction." *Kentucky Philological Review* 6 (1991): 4–8.

Gordon, Sarah. "Flannery O'Connor, the Left-Wing Mystic, and the German Jew." *Flannery O'Connor Bulletin* 16 (1987): 43–51.

Kessler, Edward. *Flannery O'Connor and the Language of Apocalypse,* Princeton, NJ: Princeton University Press, 1986.

Montgomery, Marion. *Why Flannery O'Connor Stayed Home*. La Salle, IL: Sherwood Sugden and Co., 1981.

O'Connor, Flannery. *Collected Works*. Ed. Sally Fitzgerald. New York: Library of America, 1988.

———. *Mystery and Manners: Occasional Prose*. Ed. Sally Fitzgerald and Robert Fitzgerald. New York: Farrar, Straus and Giroux, 1969.

Sturma, Lee. "Flannery O'Connor, Simone Weil, and the Virtue of Necessity." *Studies in the Literary Imagination* 20.2 (1987): 109–21.

Weil, Simone. "Forms of the Implicit Love of God." *Waiting for God*. New York: Harper and Row, 1951. 137–214.

———. *Gravity and Grace*. Trans. Arthur Wills. Lincoln: University of Nebraska Press, 1997.

———. "The Love of God and Affliction." *Waiting for God*. New York: Harper and Row, 1951. 117–36.

———. "Morality and Literature." *Simone Weil Reader*. Ed. George A. Panichas, Wakefield, RI: Moyer Bell, 1999. 290–95.

———. *Notebooks*. Trans. Arthur Wills. London: Routledge, 1956.

———. "A War of Religions." *Selected Essays, 1934–1943*. Trans. Richard Rees. London: Oxford University Press, 1962. 211–18.

Wood, Ralph C. *Flannery O'Connor and the Christ-Haunted South*. Grand Rapids, MI: Eerdmans, 2004.

CHAPTER 6

Only Love Overcomes Violence

The Violent Bear It Away as Case Studies
in Theological Ethics

SCOTT HUELIN

As far as I can tell, Flannery O'Connor never wasted a line of prose. So when we run across a line in her fiction that bears the weight of a long tradition of philosophical and theological argumentation, we should pause and take note. Here is one such line from the *Violent Bear It Away*: Rayber "did not believe that he himself was formed in the image and likeness of God but that Bishop was he had no doubt" (*VBA* 113). On the face of it, this line is darkly comic, and doubly so, for it is at once a stinging indictment of Christian notions of God and an ironic deployment of the popular yet loathsome genre of "retard" jokes. However, the allusion to Genesis 1:26 suggests that much more may be at stake here than just a few misplaced laughs. In fact, this allusion firmly places the novel's drama within a long and ongoing conversation about the nature of human beings (that is, in the tradition of theological anthropology) and their proper flourishing (that is, in the tradition of theological ethics). This is so because any Christian ethics must answer the following question: What exactly does it mean to say that human beings are made "in the image and likeness of God"? Three answers have dominated Western theological ethics—*imago Dei* as reason, as will, and as love—and Flannery O'Connor's second novel explores each of these from the inside, as it were, through its portrayal of the distinctive lifeworlds inhabited by three of the novel's major characters: George Rayber, Francis Marion Tarwater, and the boy Bishop.

REASON

The most ancient and most common account of the *imago Dei* identifies reason as the hallmark of humanity. Though reason carries significantly different connotations for several proponents of this position, all associate it with some form of cognitive function. Plato, Aristotle, and the Stoics held such a view, and some early church fathers baptized it quite eagerly. St. Thomas Aquinas further developed this tradition, and it continued to influence philosophical anthropology throughout modernity (esp. Kant and Hegel). Even our species name, *homo sapiens,* would seem to imply such a view.

In *The Violent Bear It Away,* this rationalist model is embodied in the person of Rayber, the number-crunching technocrat and aspiring sociologist[1] who sports an electronic hearing aid instead of a heart; whose house is full of books and papers instead of food and moonshine; who treats his mentally handicapped son as a problem to be solved as efficiently as possible. Bishop is, of course, subhuman in his father's eyes, precisely because he does not have the capacity for reason. Tarwater, reflecting his uncle's tutelage, makes this point with excruciating clarity: "The only difference between me and you and a hog is that me and you can calculate, but there ain't any difference between [Bishop] and one" (*VBA* 116–17). If the ability to calculate is what separates humans from animals, Bishop certainly cannot be counted among the members of the human species.

Modern versions of this rationalist anthropology generally have trouble dealing with three other features of human existence: passions, bodies, and other human beings. Recall what we know of Rayber's relation to his own emotional life: "He had kept it [his hated love] from gaining control over him by a rigid ascetic discipline. . . . He was not deceived that this was a whole or full life, he only knew that it was the way his life had to be lived if it were going to have any dignity" (114). To be dignified, therefore, is to be passionless, that is, to be fully in control of one's emotions at all times.[2] Since emotions respond to events and objects in the world outside of the self, they are dangerously volatile and unreliable because they undermine the project of rational self-sufficiency.[3] Thus a perverse asceticism—perverse because it constricts rather than enlarges the heart—comprises Rayber's way of life both in his own practice and in what he hands down to his protégé Tarwater (Browning 77–78). "For Rayber, freedom means control," that is, keeping things external to the soul under control for the sake of freeing the soul from their attachments (Brinkmeyer 120). The schoolteacher's highest wish for himself is to "conquer this pain [his love for Bishop], face it and with a supreme effort of his will, refuse to feel it," thus becoming "a free man" (*VBA* 141). His highest wish for Tarwater is that the boy learn to make reasonable choices that are "not driven by a compulsion [he doesn't] understand. What we understand we can control" (194). His highest wish for Bishop is that he would just go away. He is, after all, only an idiot, and one who can be difficult to control.

Despite his best efforts to achieve this passionless ideal, Rayber frequently finds himself overtaken by anger, joy, or compassion. Think of Rayber's confrontation with Mason after Tarwater's baptism. In that moment Rayber feebly tries to conceal his rage: "That can't even irritate me. That only makes me laugh" (72). After blaming Mason for ruining his life, Rayber loses control, screaming, "I'm not always myself, I'm not al . . ." (73). Even though Rayber clearly thinks he has managed to get beyond the influence of Mason, his behavior suggests otherwise. Even in his efforts to reject everything he associates with Mason, he is still orienting his life around Mason, though negatively now rather than positively. Thus Rayber eventually observes that his very self is divided into two: a rational self and a violent self (139). The violent self is precisely that portion of himself that feels, the part that was nurtured at Powderhead and that opens himself to the world and to suffering; the rational self is that which seeks to extinguish all feeling, the part that was nurtured in and through his schooling and that seeks self-sufficiency. For Rayber, indifference is power (200–201), the power to remain aloof from attachment to the mundane things of this world, thus saving himself from suffering, even as he hopes to save the suffering children (133).

Because he is so committed to a narrowly rational life, Rayber also has difficulty acknowledging the bodily dimension of being human. When Tarwater asks why Rayber never returned to Powderhead to reclaim him, Mason quips, "It was because he found you a heap of trouble. He wanted it all in his head. You can't change a child's pants in your head" (75). Unlike the farmhouse at Powderhead, which is stocked with food (nourishment for the body), Rayber's home is wall-to-wall books (nourishment, or distraction, for the mind). And whenever Bishop touches Rayber, his "hated love" for the boy grips him. At the fountain in the park, Rayber muses that "[h]e should have known better than to let the child onto his lap" (141). Bodies, for Rayber, pose an even greater threat to the project of rational self-sufficiency than emotions do. Like emotions, bodies are essentially dependent upon external goods—food, clothing, shelter—but unlike emotions, bodies are utterly essential to the life of rational self-sufficiency, even if reason despises its necessary dependence upon the body. Moreover, the body is the site of the soul's engagement with the external world and the objects of emotional attachment, as Rayber's mechanical ear reminds us. "Tuning out" is thus more than a mere defensive strategy when confronted with an offensive spectacle like Lucette Carmody's sermon; it also emblematizes Rayber's entire way of being-in-the-world as detachment from all things physical.

This inability to deal with passions and bodies makes it impossible for Rayber to have any meaningful sort of relationship with either his natural or his adopted son. It is with a good measure of irony that we must call Rayber a schoolteacher, for his profession seems much more like that of the school counselor, an activist bureaucrat wielding social-scientific methods of testing. If so, his choice to work with figures rather than flesh-and-blood students is telling, for it reveals his preference for reducing other human beings to nothing more than data to be plugged into complex statistical analyses, for tying them up inside his head. This hunch is confirmed by Rayber's resolute avoidance of look-ing at Bishop, always looking away from or beyond him, so as not to arouse feeling. In refusing to see Bishop, Rayber turns his son into an abstraction, yet another number like the students at his school: "His normal way of looking on Bishop was as an *x* signifying the general hideousness of fate" (113). While his failure to see Bishop stems from his hyperrationality, Rayber sometimes fails to see when his violent side, his emotions, gets the best of him: "He did not see [Tarwater's] ex-pression at all. His rage obliterated all but the general lines of his figure" (135). When he is not consumed by his passions, he tends to see in Tar-water not the real human being in all his embodied particularity, but rather an ideal child who can be molded into his own image. After Tar-water boasts of having burned Mason, Rayber "gazed through the ac-tual insignificant boy before him to an image of him that he held fully developed in his mind" (90). As far as I know, it is impossible to have a genuine relationship with an imaginary friend, much less an imagi-nary son.

This same pattern obtains with respect to Rayber's relation to the natural world. When he sees the forest surrounding Powderhead for the first time in several years, Rayber quickly *calculates* how much money he could get for the lumber (185). This utilitarian relation to nature stands in stark contrast to what happens if he looks at anything too long:

> It could be a stick or a stone, the line of a shadow, the absurd old man's walk of a starling crossing the sidewalk. If, without thinking, he lent himself to it, he would suddenly feel a morbid surge of the love that terrified him—powerful enough to throw him to the ground in an act of idiot praise. It was completely irrational and abnormal. (113)

So a rational and autonomous life requires an inhuman, machinelike indifference to the things of this world, an indifference nicely figured in Rayber's hearing aid. At the same time, the world's enduring ability to summon love from someone like Rayber seems to suggest that Rayber's rationalism, rather than the temptation to "idiot praise," should be re-garded as abnormal.

WILL

Another way of grounding a theological anthropology is to focus on the phenomenon of human willing. In the late medieval period, theologians began to think of God's being as centering on his will rather than his intellect, thus inevitably transforming the *imago Dei* from a rationalist to a voluntarist model. Such a view necessarily locates God's image in the human will, that is, in our capacity for responsible choice and, therefore, moral agency. William of Ockham, seeking out an alternative metaphysics after the collapse of high medieval scholasticism, first systematized this view, and it was the anthropological inheritance of both Renaissance humanism[4] and Reformation theology,[5] as well as of modern secular parodies such as Nietzsche's will to power and existential authenticity. *The Violent Bear It Away* explores this way of being human through the person of young Tarwater.

Tarwater shares with his uncle the desire to be autonomous, but he seeks this end through the exercise of a different human faculty, the will.[6] Whereas Rayber wants to be free of the physical world, including the emotions that accompany our bodies, Tarwater wants to be free of limits and obligations. Nearly his first thought after the death of Mason reveals this desire: "I'm going to move that fence," Tarwater said. "I ain't going to have any fence I own in the middle of a patch" (*VBA* 12). Shortly thereafter, as Tarwater digs Mason's grave, he thinks to himself in the voice of the stranger, "Nobody to bother me, he thought. Ever. No hand uplifted to hinder me from anything; except the Lord's, and he ain't said anything. He ain't even noticed me yet" (24).

Tarwater's rejection of limits includes the rejection of paternal authority and filial obligation. In response to his uncle's overtures, he lashes out, "I ain't ast for no father" (106), and even more poignantly, he prints on the back of the card at the Cherokee Lodge: "Francis Marion Tarwater. Powderhead, Tennessee. NOT HIS SON" (157). Witness also Tarwater's determination to repay the cost of all of Rayber's provisions so as not "to be beholden" (116). This desire for freedom from relational obligations seems to be the point of Tarwater's refusal to bury Mason in a Christian manner: "'You don't owe the dead anything,'

Tarwater said in a loud voice. . . . 'Nor they you,' said the stranger. 'And that's the way it ought to be in this world—nobody owing nobody nothing'" (51). Tarwater's ideal, as articulated by the stranger, is of a world of isolated individuals for whom interpersonal contact always amounts to interpersonal conflict. Hell, it seems, is other people, especially in the cramped quarters of mutual obligation.

The point of the removal of limits seems to be freedom of action, and through action, of self-definition. Tarwater prides himself on his ability to act, in contrast to the paralysis generated by Rayber's intellect: "I can do something. I ain't like you. All you can do is think what you would have done if you had done it. Not me. I can do it. I can act" (196; cf. 76). Moreover, Tarwater's insistence upon wearing clothes that Rayber finds as bizarre as some ethnic costume helps the uncle to realize the boy's fiercely independent streak (100). This pride of Tarwater in setting himself apart drives the events of the end of part two to their terrible conclusion, as his motivation in murdering Bishop has everything to do with resisting obligation, namely his calling to baptize and prophesy, which is simultaneously an obligation to Bishop (the baptizand), Mason (the ordaining authority), and God (the one who, strictly speaking, calls). To free himself from this web of obligation would be a step in the right direction, as far as Tarwater is concerned.

Freedom is a value also shared by Mason. However, Tarwater does not share his great-uncle's understanding of freedom. This distinction becomes readily apparent in Tarwater's habitual response to Mason's oft-repeated story of rejecting Rayber's social-scientific study of his own uncle:

> Something of his great-uncle's glee would take hold of Tarwater at that point, and he would feel that he had escaped some mysterious prison. He even felt he could smell his freedom, pine-scented, coming out of the woods, until the old man would continue, "You were born into bondage and baptized into freedom, into the death of the Lord, into the death of the Lord Jesus Christ." Then the child would feel a sullenness creeping over him, a slow warm rising resentment that this freedom had to be connected with Jesus and that Jesus had to be Lord. (20–21)

While Mason holds to a positive conception of freedom, that is, freedom to be renewed in Jesus Christ, Tarwater thinks of freedom entirely in negative terms: free from outside interference in his choices, free from obligations, and thus free to be no one's son.

Despite his protests, Tarwater is, in many ways, rather like his bookish uncle. Both are deeply alienated from the human and natural worlds around them. Tarwater scornfully deflects all of Bishop's attempts to be playful or show affection, and he avoids Bishop's eyes just as studiously as Rayber does. Even more striking, however, is the way that Tarwater also avoids looking too carefully at the created world:

> He tried when possible . . . to see no more than what was in front of his face and to let his eyes stop at the surface of that. It was as if he were afraid that if he let his eye rest for an instant longer than was needed to place something—a spade, a hoe, the mule's hind quarters before his plow, the red furrow under him—that the thing would suddenly stand before him, strange and terrifying, demanding that he name it and name it justly and be judged for the name he gave it. He did all he could to avoid this threatened intimacy of creation. (22)

Unlike Rayber, Tarwater is not so much worried about emotions running amok as he is afraid of an obligation both to creation and to its creator. Anyone can name things however they want for their own manipulative purposes (e.g., calling civilian deaths "collateral damage"). Who, besides Adam, can name them justly (i.e., according to their nature) and then stand before the Creator to have our naming judged? No wonder, then, that Tarwater avoids looking through or beyond or behind created things, because they would point him once again to the highest source of obligation, the One whose invocation makes the boy's resentment rise.

LOVE

A third anthropological option explored in this novel locates the *imago Dei* in love or *caritas,* that is, in the capacity for self-giving and other-receiving that characterizes interpersonal relationality. Rooted in the

New Testament claim that God is love (1 John 4:19), this view was elaborated by both St. Augustine[7] and St. Thomas Aquinas[8] and has enjoyed a renaissance of late thanks to new developments in Trinitarian theology[9] and to Pope Benedict XVI's encyclical *Deus caritas est*. Its secular parodies include Romanticism's revaluation of the emotions as well as contemporary therapeutic discourse. In O'Connor's novel, this way of orienting human life is preached by Lucette Carmody and embodied in the person of Bishop.

Unlike either Rayber or Tarwater, Bishop has no illusions of independence. He knows that he requires the assistance of others, and this despite Rayber's calloused habit of treating him as a bachelor housemate (*VBA* 112). Bishop's neediness makes him open to the kind of giving and receiving in relationship that offends to Rayber's and Tarwater's quests for autonomy. Bishop's constant longing for and offering of physical touch, which both Rayber and Tarwater studiously avoid, suggests precisely this combination of dependence and openness. It also manifests itself in Bishop's gaze, his tendency to look long and lovingly on things and people. Whereas Tarwater cannot look at anything too long for fear of sensing his obligation to it, and Rayber cannot gaze upon his son lest he be overwhelmed by his hated love, Bishop lives a wide-eyed existence, one of wonder and fascination. As Rayber pejoratively says of him, "All he can do is stare at you and he's very friendly. He stares at everything that way" (92). Bishop gazes with wonder not only at people but at things: Rayber had to drag him along those four days of city-touring because he kept stopping to examine some bit of detritus on the sidewalk. Whereas his father and cousin resist opening themselves to the world for fear of feeling obligated to it or feeling love for it, Bishop puts up no such resistance. He instinctively understands himself to be vitally connected to the world and to other people.

Bishop's wonder-filled gaze is often accompanied by a gaping mouth, and this serves to reinforce the notion of gaze as openness to others. Take, for example, his visit to Powderhead. En route, Bishop "was hanging his head out the window, his mouth open, letting the air dry his tongue" (180). Once there, "Bishop could barely walk for gaping. He lifted his face to stare open-mouthed above him as if he were in some vast overwhelming edifice" (184). Such an expression might be mistaken for slack-jawed stupidity, but here it clearly suggests that

Bishop sees more precisely because he is open to doing so. He understands that the forest of Powderhead is not a commodity to be sold; rather it is a temple, a vast edifice, for the worship of its Creator. Bishop's open mouth also recalls the typical posture of Catholic communicants in the 1950s, who would receive the host (the bread of life) directly into their open mouths and upon their outstretched tongues. Because Bishop is more open to everyone and everything around him, he is therefore also more open to God. He receives the world sacramentally, as "an allegory of love to be interpreted by love" (Ward 189).

Precisely because he is open to and therefore connected with the world in lifegiving ways, Bishop is the most emotional of the three characters we are discussing. He delights in the dancers at the Cherokee Lodge, entranced by them while his cousin "stared through them" (*VBA* 190), and therefore audibly registers his displeasure when the dancing ends. His enjoyment of the fountain turns into howls of frustration when he is removed (165), and he bellows when his overtures of love are rejected (93). Bishop's openness leads directly to emotional attachments. For to be open to the goodness of the world is to identify particular goods (dancing, playing in water, touching), and particular goods so identified necessarily cause grief when they are lost. Tarwater's struggles against his desire for the bread of life epitomizes his struggle against recognizing his own need for any external goods, while Rayber's efforts to keep his love for Bishop in check demonstrates his commitment to rational *apatheia* as a way of life. Bishop's outbursts may produce frustration for his stoic caregivers, but his emotions make him seem far more alive than they do.[10]

Bishop's wondering gaze and receptive mouth might remind us of what Simone Weil has called creative attention, the ability to see things not only as they are but as they might be: this, Weil argues, is the beating heart of neighbor love (*Waiting for God* 92). Such vision has the power not only to transform the mundane into the sublime in the beholder's eye but also to transform the objects of vision themselves. When others return Bishop's gaze, they also are drawn into the giving and receiving that is love: both Rayber and Tarwater, despite their best efforts to the contrary, save the idiot child they are trying to drown, though they do so in dramatically different ways.

ONLY LOVE OVERCOMES VIOLENCE

Many critics have made much of the violence in *The Violent Bear It Away,* but few have traced the violence to its source. Susan Srigley, however, has rightly named it: the original act of violence is to separate oneself from others through an illusion of and desire for autonomy or independence, "to resist submission to the fact of one's limitation and need," and thereby to "resist being completed by God" (94). One of the most famous definitions of sin ever produced in the Christian tradition speaks of sin as curving in of the self upon itself (*incurvatus in se*).[11] It is a striking metaphor: sin is like an extremely advanced case of osteoporosis. If human beings were created to love, to look others deeply in the eye and see them for who they are (and for who they might be), then it will be difficult to fulfill our created purpose while narcissistically hunched over upon ourselves.

Tarwater's first glimpse of this understanding comes during his first visit to the city with Mason, when Tarwater is stunned to find that passersby would just ignore other human beings on the sidewalk, averting their eyes and avoiding any kind of emotional connection with strangers even when they have had the physical contact of a collision. In a flash of insight, Tarwater diagnoses the spiritual malady of the city: "Then he had realized, almost without warning, that this place was evil—the ducked heads, the muttered words, the hastening away. He saw in a burst of light that these people were hastening away from the Lord God Almighty" (*VBA* 27). To shut oneself off from other human beings (or from the natural world, as we have seen) is also to shut oneself off from God. Closing in upon oneself may seem safe, but it is lonely and deadly because it necessarily alienates oneself from precisely the means by which one might unbend the self.

As dependent erotic animals, human beings become progressively less human when we pursue lives like those of Rayber and Tarwater. Sin is its own punishment, as St. Augustine teaches, and their rejection of the proper nature of human beings as dependent erotic animals has left them abnormal, misshapen, crippled. If sin is to be curved in on oneself, to be grotesquely deformed, then who are the freaks in this novel? Not Bishop, but rather Rayber and Tarwater. While Bishop certainly lacks some of the abilities of a fully functioning human being, he is not lacking in that which is most essential to his humanity—his capacity for love. He remains open to the world and to others through his wide gaze, his gaping mouth, and his persistent touching. Moreover through this openness he remains open to that which lies behind and beyond perception, that which is truly Other. Rayber and Tarwater, on the other hand, who possess all of the common human faculties, nonetheless have truncated themselves by resisting limits and attachments, that is, by failing to embrace their creaturely neediness. No wonder they see little more in nature than commodities or occasions for self-assertion. No wonder they see other human beings as opportunities for self-replication or provocations to self-assertion. The violence of rending their selves from the nexus of heaven, earth, and human community now perpetuates itself *ad nauseum*. The contrast between the ways of being-in-the-world embodied by Bishop and his kin could not be more starkly opposed: "Whereas the other members of his family tend to confront everyone and everything as an obstacle to be opposed, Bishop views all before him without antagonism. He lives by the Johannine Logos of love rather than the logos of violence" (Ciuba 148).

This originary violence—the violence of rending oneself from what is—finds its great opposite in the grace of God, in that sun that by turns seems ominous and life-giving, threatening and healing, depending on the spiritual state of the one who gazes upon it. If the aim of divine grace is to restore in sinful human beings the lost image of God, their capacity to love, such grace will necessarily seem violent because it will seek to undo what both legacy and habit have cemented. The restoration of the lost image of God, the first and most proper human nature, will require an act of violence against this second nature, and the violence of the means will be proportionate to the severity of the deformation (Lake 35). In the words of Lucette Carmody, the exploited girl preacher, "The Word of God is a burning Word to burn you clean, burns man and child, man and child the same, you people!" (*VBA* 135). Christ, the physician of souls, inflicts the salutary wounds that sin has made necessary. This kind of salutary violence is not so much the will of the physician as the requirement of the condition. There are, after all, two kinds of fire: the Lord's, which cleanses and heals, and the world's, which destroys, "Be saved in the Lord's fire or perish in your own!" (135). The self-truncating asceticisms of Rayber and Tarwater embody the latter and produce only death; the Christian asceticism of Mason aspires to the instinctive charity of Bishop, and such charity is the outward and visible sign of the motions of divine and salutary grace.

Suffering is the lot of dependent erotic animals like ourselves. Because we are dependent, we can be crippled by unmet needs. Because we are erotic, we can be crippled by unfulfilled or misdirected desires. Because we are animals, our bodies can fail us, suffer disease or injury, and will surely die. So the only reasonable question to ask about suffering is not how to avoid it but what to do with it: "The extreme greatness of Christianity lies in the fact that it does not seek a supernatural cure for suffering, but a supernatural use of it" (Weil, *Gravity and Grace* 132). To rightly use our suffering would be to allow it to unbend us so that we might be restored to life-giving relationships with the natural world, other human beings, and our Creator. This, it seems, is the reason why Tarwater's rape can, despite the perpetrator's intentions, become a moment of grace: this horrific crime shatters this proud young man's illusions of autonomy and self-sufficiency and has *opened* him, both physically and spiritually. (Moreover, it explains the symbolic significance of the corkscrew/bottle-opener.) For O'Connor, humanity is constituted by its capacity to enter into meaningful, responsible, and responsive relationships with others, and the unbending of the self, its opening to the other, precisely is the restoration of the image of God, for "God, we might say, is relationship without remainder" (Hart 170).

Christians worship the Father, Son, and Holy Spirit, three divine persons whose unified "being is . . . an act of communion" that comprises the single Godhead (Zizioulas 44). Whereas the god of theism *is* by virtue of its metaphysical isolation from all other being, the Triune God "*is* as the differing modalities of replete love . . . whose relatedness is his substance" (Hart 172). Though Christians confess that the Son is begotten of the Father and the Spirit proceeds from the Father,[12] this does not mean that the Father was once the lone monad of philosophical theism, waiting for someone to join him in the ranks of the immortals. Rather, the Son was, as the Nicene Creed puts it, *eternally* begotten of the Father. Therefore, there never was a time when the Son was not, and there never was a time when the Father was alone. Thus "begotten" here designates a mode of relationship rather than a punc-tiliar beginning to existence, an essential difference that is never eclipsed but made productive through love. In *begetting* the Son, the Father opens himself, makes a space for another; in begetting a *son,* the Father's love is always already reaching out in love and receiving love in return. The eternal begetting of the Son is the eternal begetting of dif-ference, and this difference opens the Godhead to a non-narcissistic self-love.

"God is love. Whoever lives in love lives in God, and God in him" (1 John 4:16). The eternal begetting of the Son thus establishes the Godhead as "an 'economy' of the gift" (Hart 268), where "Christ's dif-ference begets the creative circulation of kenotic giving."[13] The Father's *kenosis* makes room for the Son, while the Son's *kenosis* surrenders himself to his Father as Father.[14] This eternal exchange of love eternally brings forth a third Person, the Spirit, for he "interprets" the Son to the Father, and vice versa;[15] that is, the Spirit traverses the distance of dif-ference, freely crossing the boundaries of sameness and otherness in the service of love.[16] Though the Spirit is closely associated with the love shared by Father and Son, he cannot be reduced to that love for he is no impersonal force. The Holy Spirit proceeds from love because the nature of love is excessive; it naturally seeks to exceed boundaries, to overflow with abundance, to share the goodness of love with an other. Thus the Spirit "is not only the bond of love [between the Father and the Son], but also the one who always breaks the bonds of self-love. . . . The Spirit is that other in whom Father and Son meet 'again,' in the commonality of their love *for another*" (Hart 176). The mutual love of the three Persons for one another is thus neither narcissistic nor exclusive. It is essentially ecstatic: the divine Persons find their "selves" outside themselves in the giving and receiving of their mutual rela-tions, that is, in their unified Godhead.

If relation is the very being of God, how much more so must it be for dependent erotic animals like ourselves? To live, then, is to be in relation. Only inanimate objects, things with no life, dead things can be regarded as completely solitary, independent, and self-sufficient. Ironi-cally, this is exactly how the theology of modernity has envisioned God: the isolated, needless, self-contained monad, utterly unlike any-thing else and therefore utterly unrelatable.[17] The roots of such a notion stretch far back into Western intellectual history, all the way to Plato and Aristotle.[18] Early modernity revived this kind of philosophical theology (calling it "theism") as a way of talking about god without resort to the conflicting confessions of particular churches, a theology purportedly without dogma. This conceptual strategy, however, can never escape Feuerbach's trenchant critique: theism merely fashions an idealized image of humanity, projects it upon the heavens, and bows down to worship it.[19] Theism is modernity's golden calf, a projection of our own desire to be done with others. Theism imagines a paradise of unity without plurality; in other words theism and Sartre (both sons of modernity) would agree that hell is being with others. When the radical theologians of the 1960s announced that "God is dead," they were not so much radical as brutally honest, for the god of modernity, as utterly solitary, independent, and self-sufficient, cannot be otherwise. Insofar as Rayber and Tarwater manifest the image of God, they image theism's lifeless idol.

Rayber was therefore right to proclaim that, unlike him, Bishop is in the image of God, for Bishop images the living God, the God of Abraham, Isaac, Jacob, and Jesus, not the dead god of wannabe rationalists and hillbilly Nietzsches.[20] Human beings, like the God who is Three-in-One, exist only in relation to others. To live fully in these relations is to retrieve and reanimate the image of God lost through sinful self-absorption. To live apart from these relations is to do violence to the human, thus descending to the animal and mechanical. If all such relations are fully and finally severed, as they are for Rayber at the drowning of Bishop, what is left but death, the image and likeness of modernity's god? Only Love can overcome such sacralized violence.

NOTES

1. David Eggenschwiler rightly calls him "a false prophet of sociology" (137).

2. Passionlessness, or *apatheia,* is an ancient ethical ideal; its roots lie in ancient Stoicism, but some early church figures embraced it as well (e.g., St. Antony as depicted in St. Athanasius's biography of the desert monk), despite St. Augustine's admonition that it was an impossible and inhuman ideal (*City of God* 14.9).

3. For a critique of rational self-sufficiency as ethical ideal, see Nussbaum.

4. As Pico della Mirandola once opined, "To [humanity alone] it is granted to have whatever he chooses, to be whatever he wills" (225).

5. Luther and Calvin regard the *imago Dei* as the original righteousness of Adam and Eve, understood as their ongoing and unquestioned obedience to God in both desire and act.

6. "For what is centrally involved in this struggle [between Tarwater and Rayber] are two radically divergent concepts of freedom" (Browning 81).

7. "When you see charity, you have seen the Trinity" (*The Trinity* 8.8.12).

8. "Now the intellectual nature imitates God chiefly in this, that God understands and loves Himself" (Aquinas, *Summa Theologica* I, q. 93, art. 4).

9. For a good summary of recent developments, see Shults.

10. "Bishop's powerful affection—compared with Rayber's monotonous logic—makes him appear full of life, despite his intellectual deficiency" (Srigley 120).

11. The metaphor has its origin in Augustine but was significantly advanced by Martin Luther. See Jenson.

12. Western Christians affirm that the Spirit proceeds from the Father *and the Son,* while Eastern Christians regard the latter addition (the notorious *filioque*) as unwarranted and illegitimate. I do not wish to enjoin this debate now, so I merely state that which Eastern and Western Christians agree upon, the Father's spiration of the third Person.

13. Ward 145. Note that Ward distinguishes *kenosis* from self-annihilation: "The nature of love is not just to give, it is to create a space for reception. It is not simply a pouring out, an emptying of oneself on behalf of the other, it is the creation, by that kenosis, of a place for the entry of the other, for participation" (149–50).

14. Here I am referring to the eternal *kenosis* of the Son that responds to the eternal *kenosis* of the Father and that must be distinguished from the temporal *kenosis* of incarnation and passion that is hymned in Philippians 2. See Moltmann 140.

15. St. Symeon the New Theologian qtd. in Hart 185.

16. Cf. Gunton 182.

17. For an extended argument on this point, see Gunton.

18. Platonic and Aristotelian philosophy derived the concept of monotheism by means of privation and amplification, that is, by removing from its concept of god all unworthy features of created being (god is *im*mortal, *immu*table, *in*visible, *in*finite, etc.) and intensifying those remaining features (god is *omni*scient, *omni*potent, *omni*present, etc.).

19. See, for example, Feuerbach, though he would not have approved of this use of the term *theism.*

20. Cf. Pascal, *Pensées* frag. 690.

WORKS CITED

Aquinas, Saint Thomas. *Summa Theologica*. 3 vols. Trans. Fathers of the English Dominican Province. New York: Benziger, 1947–48.

Augustine of Hippo, Saint. *The City of God against the Pagans*. Ed. and trans. R. W. Dyson. Cambridge: Cambridge University Press, 1998.

———. *The Trinity (De trinitate)*. Trans. John Rotelle. Hyde Park, NY: New City Press, 1991.

Brinkmeyer, Robert H., Jr. *The Art and Vision of Flannery O'Connor*. Baton Rouge: Louisiana State University Press, 1989.

Browning, Preston M., Jr. *Flannery O'Connor*. Carbondale: Southern Illinois University Press, 1974.

Ciuba, Gary M. *Desire, Violence, and Divinity in Modern Southern Fiction*. Baton Rouge: Louisiana State University Press, 2007.

Eggenschwiler, David. *The Christian Humanism of Flannery O'Connor*. Detroit: Wayne State University Press, 1972.

Feuerbach, Ludwig. *The Essence of Christianity*. Trans. George Eliot. Buffalo: Prometheus, 1989.

Gunton, Colin E. *The One, the Three, and the Many: God, Creation, and the Culture of Modernity*. New York: Cambridge University Press, 1993.

Hart, David Bentley. *The Beauty of the Infinite: The Aesthetics of Christian Truth*. Grand Rapids, MI: Eerdmans, 2003.

Jenson, Matt. *The Gravity of Sin: Augustine, Luther and Barth on 'Homo Incurvatus in Se.'* New York: Continuum, 2007.

Lake, Christina Bieber. *The Incarnational Art of Flannery O'Connor*. Macon, GA: Mercer University Press, 2005.

Moltmann, Jürgen. "God's Kenosis in the Creation and Consummation of the World." *The Work of Love: Creation as Kenosis*. Ed. John Polkinghorne. Grand Rapids, MI: Eerdmans, 2001. 137–51.

Nussbaum, Martha. *The Fragility of Goodness: Luck and Ethics in Greek Tragedy and Philosophy*. Cambridge: Cambridge University Press, 1986.

O'Connor, Flannery. *The Violent Bear It Away*. New York: Farrar, Straus and Giroux, 1960.

Pascal, Blaise. *Pensées*. Ed. and Trans. Roger Ariew. Indianapolis: Hackett, 2005.

Pico della Mirandola. *Oration on the Dignity of Man*. *The Renaissance Philosophy of Man*. Ed. Ernst Cassirer, Paul Oskar Kristellar, and John Herman Randall, Jr. Chicago: University of Chicago Press, 1956. 223–54.

Shults, F. LeRon. *Reforming the Doctrine of God*. Grand Rapids, MI: Eerdmans, 2006.

Srigley, Susan. *Flannery O'Connor's Sacramental Art.* Notre Dame, IN: University of Notre Dame Press, 2004.

Ward, Graham. *Christ and Culture.* Challenges in Contemporary Theology. New York: Blackwell, 2005.

Weil, Simone. *Gravity and Grace.* Trans. Arthur Wills. Lincoln: University of Nebraska Press, 1997.

———. *Waiting for God.* Trans. Emma Craufurd. 1951. San Francisco: Harper Perennial, 2001.

Zizioulas, John. *Being as Communion: Studies in Personhood and the Church.* Crestwood, NY: St. Vladimir's Seminary Press, 2002.

CHAPTER 7

"Jesus Is the Bread of Life"

Johannine Sign and Deed in *The Violent Bear It Away*

P. TRAVIS KROEKER

Flannery O'Connor's *The Violent Bear It Away* concerns the nature and meaning of the prophetic vocation, a vocation to which old Mason Tarwater is called in the apocalyptic biblical tradition epitomized in the New Testament gospels by John the Baptizer. The central action of the novel, as O'Connor herself suggested, is a baptism (*MM* 162). The title and epigraph of O'Connor's novel are taken from Matthew 11:12— "From the days of John the Baptist until now, the kingdom of heaven suffereth violence, and the violent bear it away"—one of the great conundrums of the New Testament.[1] Yet the novel's central sacramental tropes of baptism, water, prophetic signs, and the bread of life come from the fourth gospel, the Gospel according to John.[2] The hidden yet obvious connections between the title and the tropes can only be discerned through the apocalyptic vision of faith. Matthew 11:12 is situated within Jesus' extended reflection on the wilderness prophet, John, with whom his own public life dramatically intersects at decisive points. This coinherence between Jesus and John exists because their scandalous authority (*exousia*) derives from the same source (Matthew 21:23–27)—not the visible authority of dominant central religious, political, and educational institutions, but the invisible wisdom of the kingdom of heaven that comes into view only from the margins and yet is publicly though ambiguously evident in visible deeds of divine power. For those whose vision is focused upon the human power game of the dominant centers, this authority (and in Greek *exousia* is closely related to freedom and power to act, "from being") can only create scandal—as it does dramatically and repeatedly in the words and deeds of Jesus in John's gospel. I wish to show how this apocalyptic prophetic pattern is echoed and displayed in *The Violent Bear It Away*, particularly in the central tropes of baptism and Jesus as the bread of life (the scandal scene in John 6), which are no less scandalous in O'Connor's art, especially as concerns the question of violence. This sacramental vision mediates the freedom to act, but only for those who do not judge merely by appearances.

In Matthew 3 the message of John the Baptist is summed up pithily: "Repent, for the kingdom of heaven is at hand" (3:2). His voice cries out in the wilderness preparing the people for the messianic apocalypse through a baptism of repentance: "I baptize you with water for repentance, but he who is coming after me is mightier than I, whose sandals I am not worthy to carry; he will baptize you with the Holy Spirit and with fire" (Matthew 3:11). Like the biblical Baptist, Mason Tarwater is a wilderness prophet who proclaims a message of judgment and repentance, a baptism not only with water but also with the Spirit and with fire. Indeed Mason himself has experienced a "baptism by fire" that transforms his own message of judgment from one of divine destruction of the *massa damnata,* the sinful world, to one of divine salvation from destruction—but which of the two visions is "more violent" is a misplaced question. In fact the transformation of his prophetic vision is represented in Mason's own consciousness by his kidnapping of his great-nephew Francis Tarwater from his nephew Rayber the schoolteacher: "That time his rage of vision had been clear. He had known what he was saving the boy from and it was saving and not destruction he was seeking. He had learned enough to hate the destruction that had to come and not all that was going to be destroyed" (*VBA* 6). This "saving deed," however, is not without violence. It offends conventional moral understandings not only in terms of the means employed by Mason to "liberate" young Tarwater—he kidnaps the child from his rightful guardian and shoots a wedge out of Rayber's right ear when Rayber comes to Powderhead to reclaim the child—but also in terms of the form of life for which he saves him, to all appearances a rather uncivilized one, of backwoods imbecility.

That is, Mason "saves" young Tarwater from the deterministic, corrupting influences of modern education—in particular the secular scientistic rationalism represented by the educator Rayber and his "welfare-woman" wife, Bernice Bishop—in order to raise him for a prophetic vocation (15), a calling that Mason identifies with freedom: "I saved you to be free, your own self!" (16). It is a freedom taught in a dramatic alternative form of education: "he was left free for the pursuit of wisdom, the companions of his spirit Abel and Enoch and Noah and Job, Abraham and Moses, King David and Solomon, and all the prophets, from Elijah who escaped death, to John whose severed head struck terror from a dish" (17). It is an education that frees the self to act in a cosmic, historical divine-human drama (76–77), in contrast to the herd conformity and stultifying abstraction of "factual information" represented in the numbers and charts of modern schoolrooms. Tarwater is easily transported by his great-uncle's perorations on freedom. But much to young Tarwater's displeasure, this freedom is closely tied by Mason to baptism "into the death of the Lord Jesus Christ" (20)— a Jesus who is "the bread of life": "In the darkest, most private part of his soul, hanging upsidedown like a sleeping bat, was the certain, undeniable knowledge that he was not hungry for the bread of life" (21). The paradoxical ways in which freedom to act is linked to the prophetic vocation and the messianic meaning of the claim that "Jesus is the bread of life" constitute the spiritual trial and existential crisis Tarwater undergoes in the novel.

O'Connor as a novelist is attuned to the spiritual and artistic implications of apocalyptic messianism, particularly in the "Christ-haunted" South.[3] The Southern writer, she says, must "make his gaze extend beyond the surface, beyond mere problems, until it touches that realm which is the concern of prophets and poets" (*MM* 45).[4] That realm is the realm of mystery—*mysterion* in Greek, which in Latin is translated *sacramentum*. This means that surface visibility always points beyond itself to what remains hidden and yet real, becoming visible (or "unveiled," "apocalypsed") only in signs that are traces of both inner and outer movement. For those not freely attuned to the movement above and below the surface of things, these signs remain impenetrable, meaningless, foolish. Not only for the writer of fiction, therefore, but also for the reader of fiction, "everything has its testing point in the eye, and the eye is the organ that eventually involves the whole personality, and as much of the world as can be got into it. It involves judgment" (91).

One of the areas for which the current age lacks a sharp eye, in O'Connor's view, is "the almost imperceptible intrusions of grace" that are generally preceded and followed by violence, lines of spiritual motion that often remain undiscerned: "The devil's greatest wile, Baudelaire has said, is to convince us that he does not exist" (112).[5] And so the inner voice of "the stranger," who quickly becomes Tarwater's friend and mentor, tells Tarwater when the boy suggests his choice is "Jesus or the devil": "No, no no, . . . there ain't no such thing as a devil. I can tell you that from my own self-experience. I know that for a fact. It ain't Jesus or the devil. It's Jesus or *you*" (*VBA* 39). Of course, based on the self-experience of the once-born in which Jesus can only be a fully human historical influence on the surface level of things, facts are facts and one had best judge them astutely if one is to save oneself and not be duped. If there is no Christ sent from heaven, it would be foolish to believe in the devil "as a real spirit who must be made to name himself . . . with his specific personality for every occasion" (*MM* 117). And yet, just this is O'Connor's claim, rooted in apocalyptic vision in which the spiritual pulls of good and evil, truth and lie, are fully incarnate in the cosmic drama in which the human self is always in critical condition, confronted with the choice of how to interpret and respond to these pulls, to decide which self to become.

In John's gospel, the hidden Word that underlies and illumines, literally "enlivens" all created reality, becomes incarnate in the human being, Jesus, whose deeds bear witness as signs to divine truth. However, according to John, to see this requires a rebirth in which one is given the power oneself to become a child of the divine (1:12–13). As Jesus tells Nicodemus in his nocturnal visit: "Truly, truly, I say to you, unless one is born anew [*anothen,* which can also be translated "from above"], one cannot see the kingdom of God" (John 3:3). This is a rebirth that Nicodemus finds difficult to understand—is it physical, is it spiritual, is it some strange mix of the two? Jesus responds that "unless one is born of water and the Spirit, one does not have the power to enter the kingdom of God" (John 3:5). The water here seems to refer to John the Baptist's water baptism—and it is itself a sign of Jesus' strange divine power when, rather than requiring John to stoop before him to carry his sandals, he stoops and invites John to baptize him with the baptism of repentance. The Spirit, who descends "like a dove" from heaven (John 1:32–33) and "blows where it wills, and you hear the sound of it, but you do not know whence it comes or whither it goes" (John 3:8), is the power that enables the mysterious movement between earthly things and heavenly things, human things and divine things.

John's entire gospel displays the struggle to discern the significance of Jesus' mysterious words and deeds that manifest the archetypal light, life, and truth of divine glory in ways that shatter conventional human wisdom and authority. In so doing they provoke a crisis of belief, or of discernment and the question of which authority speaks and acts from insight into the true character and power of reality, its divine origin and end. This is not only an intellectual or doctrinal question but above all an existential question concerning what it means to become a human being who is raised up to eternal life. That is, discernment is not a matter of direct speech and direct intellectual understanding, but a matter of the existential relationship between faith and enactment (word and deed) that brings together the spiritual and material, invisible and visible truth of a wisdom that is ultimately possessed by God alone.

THE PROPHETIC VOCATION: JOHN THE BAPTIZER

Matthew 11:12 is one of the great scriptural paradoxes that has given rise to many different interpretations in the Christian tradition. The desert fathers, as O'Connor herself points out in one of her letters concerning her title, interpret it in terms of "the violence of love, of giving more than the law demands, of an asceticism like John the Baptist's, but in the face of which even John is less than the least in the kingdom"

(*HB* 382). Perhaps the best concise text displaying this view is in John Cassian's "Twenty-fourth Conference of Abbot Abraham: On Mortification":

> For not the slothful, or the careless, or the delicate, or the tender take the kingdom of heaven by force, but the violent. Who then are the violent? Surely they are those who show a splendid violence not to others, but to their own soul and who, by a laudable force, deprive it of all delights in things present, and are declared by the Lord's mouth to be splendid plunderers, and by rapine of this kind, violently seize upon the kingdom of heaven. For, as the Lord says, "The kingdom of heaven suffereth violence and the violent bear it away." Those are certainly worthy of praise as violent, who do violence to their own destruction . . . . For our destruction is delight in this present life, and to speak more definitely, the performance of our own likes and desires, as, if a person withdraws these from his soul and mortifies them, he straightaway does glorious and valuable violence to his own destruction . . . .[6]

Such asceticism, associated externally in John the Baptist with his clothing of camel hair, his diet of locusts and wild honey (as Jesus says, "John came neither eating nor drinking," Matthew 11:18), is also closely related to the eschatological prophetic mission of Elijah, proclaiming the apocalyptic "great and terrible day of the Lord" (Malachai 4:5; cf. Matthew 11:14, 17:9–13). Redemption of the people is preceded by a cosmic battle, an ultimate conflict that Jesus suggests has already been joined from the days of John the Baptist and marked by the crisis of repentance from deeds of destruction. Particular ascetic deeds in themselves, however, are not a reliable marker—as Jesus himself is distinguished from John the Baptist as a glutton and a drunkard because he eats and drinks with sinners. "Yet," says Jesus, "wisdom is justified by her deeds" (Matthew 11:19). The context of Jesus' reflections in Matthew 11 is that disciples of the now imprisoned John have been sent by John to find out more about Jesus' messianic identity, and Jesus answers with reference to his deeds of saving power, concluding with the words "blessed are they who take no offense at me" (11:6).

Clearly there is a paradoxical and ambiguous relation between inner and outer, thought and deed, in the violent asceticism of love that calls out for wise discernment. The problem with the present generation, according to Jesus, is that they lack wisdom—like fickle children they are complacent spectators with a variety of contradictory interests and desires who want above all to be entertained by spectacles upon which they make pronouncements without discernment. And so they judge John and Jesus harshly for different reasons, but equally without understanding. They look for hopeful "signs" that confirm their desires but are unable to interpret the signs of the times with reference to the agency of the divine word, and this is related by both John and Jesus to an unwillingness to bear fruitful deeds of repentance rooted in the mortification of their own disordered desires. Such spectators remain offended at the prophetic proclamation of repentance, both in word and in deed.

So too is Tarwater offended at the prophetic vocation in and for which his great-uncle has sought to raise him. While he welcomes his freedom from the conformism of conventional education in order to act out of "his own self," he experiences "a sullenness . . . a slow warm rising resentment that this freedom had to be connected with Jesus and that Jesus had to be the Lord" (*VBA* 20–21). The boy is afraid of his great-uncle's mad hunger for the bread of life, his desire to "hasten to the banks of the Lake of Galilee to eat the loaves and fishes that the Lord had multiplied. 'Forever?' the horrified boy asked. 'Forever,' the old man said" (21). Afraid of being torn open by such a hunger, Tarwater keeps his vision focused on the surface level of things, avoiding the "threatened intimacy of creation" of old Mason's prophetic vision, hoping that the Lord's prophetic call to him will come "from out of a clear and empty sky, . . . untouched by any fleshly hand or breath" (22). He shares this fear of threatened intimacy with his uncle Rayber who both longs for and is offended by the old man's mad eyes that communicate irrational love—"insane, fish-coloured, violent with their impossible vision of a world transfigured" (114). Rayber controls his own experience of this madness—mediated above all in his outrageous love for his dim-witted child Bishop but which then "like an avalanche covered everything his reason hated"—through a rigid ascetic discipline that "denied his senses unnecessary satisfactions," a program of rational self-salvation to a dignity free from the extremes of spiritual vision (114).

Upon the death of his great-uncle, the boy who has hitherto "always followed his uncle's customs" (13) experiences a challenging change, represented by the internal dialogue involving the voice of a stranger who calls old Mason's teachings into question. Tarwater is now freed from the direct authority of his living guardian and mentor in prophecy in order to decide for himself how to respond to what he has been taught and "how much of it is true" (79). This he will do in the company of his urban uncle Rayber, whose own rationalist asceticism stands against the prophetic. The immediate challenge for Tarwater, however, is how to respond to Mason's insistent and repeated request that Tarwater bury him in Christian fashion, thus confronting the boy with the question concerning the status of the dead. The old man has taught him: "The world was made for the dead. Think of all the dead there are" (16). Christian burial names the dead as living. Tarwater, prompted by the internal stranger, states by contrast that "you can't be any poorer than dead" (24, 35) and that in effect nothing is owed the dead (51). Rayber concurs: "A dead man is not going to do you any good" (104). The heart of the difference in status concerns the question of resurrection. For old Mason, the dead will be raised in the flesh at the resurrection where they will eat the loaves and fishes at the heavenly banquet, whereas Rayber asserts dogmatically that the dead will not rise again (110).

This contrast has everything to do with the second challenge Tarwater faces, the prophetic vocation to baptize Bishop, a mission the elder Mason Tarwater has laid upon the younger that offends Rayber's rationalist vision and young Tarwater's self-aggrandizing images of prophetic greatness. It bespeaks a very different conception of human dignity—"Precious in the sight of the Lord even an idiot!" proclaims Mason—from the one Rayber propounds: "You could slosh water on him for the rest of his life and he'd still be an idiot. Five years old for all eternity, useless forever. Listen . . . he'll never be baptized—just as a matter of principle, nothing else. As a gesture of human dignity, he'll never be baptized" (33–34). For Rayber, the great dignity of man is the capacity for rational humanist self-assessment, the ability to say "I am born once and no more. What I can see and do for myself and my fellowman in this life is all of my portion and I'm content with it. It's enough to be a man" (172).[7] On such a measure Bishop is not fully human, of course; hence the indignity of the outrageous love for him that Rayber feels at times—"powerful enough to throw him to the ground in an act of idiot praise" (113), a love without reason that threatens to cause him foolishly to lose control of his life. It is precisely such a morbid love rooted in "the bleeding stinking mad shadow of Jesus" (91, 221) that Rayber fears and resists. By contrast Rayber's normal view of Bishop is "as an *x* signifying the general hideousness of fate," (113), a "mistake of nature" (117, a view also shared in the novel by certain offended adolescents, 190).

Hence when Tarwater experiences the prophetic call to baptize, not from his great-uncle, but precisely in the fleshly hand (93) and heavy breathing (82–83, 90) of the child Bishop, he is faced with the stunning and yet unremarkable implication of the revelation:

> his own stricken image of himself, trudging into the distance in the bleeding stinking mad shadow of Jesus, until at last he received his reward, a broken fish, a multiplied loaf. The Lord out of dust had created him, had made him blood and nerve and mind, had made him to bleed and weep and think, and set him in a world of loss and fire all to baptize one idiot child that He need not have created in the first place and to cry out a gospel just as foolish. (91–92)

The prophetic act of baptism is one that proclaims Bishop is capable of rebirth into the mysterious heart of a love that cannot be reduced to or measured by a merely human rationality. A prophetic rationality, connected incarnationally to blood and nerve, relinquishes its own hold on naming reality. If the first test, that of burial, raises the question about the meaning of the body, the second test, that of baptism into the death of Jesus and thus another kind of burial, raises the question about the human spirit and its named dignity.

While Tarwater, like Rayber, rebels against the messianic prophetic calling, he is determined not to rebel merely intellectually in the manner of the abstract rationalist. Unlike Rayber, whose guts are in his head (172), and like the prophetic great-uncle in this respect, he will prove capable of dramatic action that names the world in freely chosen, self-called agency. He will give vulgar, concrete expression to Rayber's theoretical anthropology with regard to Bishop's life both in word—"He's like a hog . . . . He eats like a hog and he don't think no more than a hog and when he dies, he'll rot like a hog. Me and you too . . . will rot like hogs. The only difference between me and you and a hog is me and you can calculate, but there ain't any difference between him and one" (116–17)—and in deed, by successfully drowning (an act Rayber initiated but could not complete) the hideous mistake of nature that Bishop represents. In this regard the drowning is a classic anti-prophetic act that enacts in starkly symbolic but utterly incarnational terms the naming of its vision. In this murderous act of anti-sacramental burial/baptism Tarwater will decisively define himself over against both the great-uncle and the uncle, thus liberating himself to be his own self. As Miles Orwell puts it, Tarwater's act of drowning is intended to achieve a double renunciation, of old Mason's mad prophetic mission and of Rayber's impotent scientism (97). By not only saying no to the prophetic vocation but by enacting that negation, Tarwater will return to the wilderness to take full charge of his life.

It does not turn out that way. His act of drowning Bishop, he explains cryptically to the trucker who picks him up afterward, was accompanied by the accidental, involuntary utterance of the words of baptism: "I didn't mean to . . . I only meant to drown him. . . . You're only born once. They were just some words that run out of my mouth and spilled in the water" (*VBA* 209). Tarwater's deed is rooted in self-division, the destructive separation of word and deed, which plagues the boy. He is hungry but unable to eat, has a thirst he cannot quench, and he is unable to shut down the inner eye of his spiritual consciousness. Indeed, as he relives the murderous baptism in his dream in the truck cab, he feels himself being engulfed, like the runaway prophet Jonah, in a monstrous darkness: "He grappled with the air as if he had been flung like a fish on the shores of the dead without lungs to breathe there. . . . Suddenly in a high raw voice the defeated boy cried out the words of baptism, shuddered, and opened his eyes" (216).[8]

While it might be said that the enclosing darkness is his empathic reliving of Bishop's drowning that his conscience will not allow him to forget, it is also quite clearly an experience of his spiritual condition with regard to both the dead whose bodies he has tried to desecrate in word and in deed. It is worth recalling here that in the baptism chapter (3) of the Gospel of John, "water and spirit" (3:5) form an important hendiadys in Jesus' response to Nicodemus's incredulous reaction to Jesus' claim that to see the kingdom of God requires a rebirth "from above" (3:3). Only a rebirth from above by the spirit beyond human knowing and control (3:8) enables one to "breathe" in the interpenetrating domain (the earthly and the heavenly, 3:12) that constitutes the mysterious realm of divine sovereignty, a sacramental realm in which the meaning of life and death, of visible matter and invisible spirit, of truth and lie, are quite otherwise than in the merely once-born realm of the ruler of darkness (3:19) where evil deeds shun the judgment of heavenly light.

Tarwater's violent act is rooted in a horrifying lie, a destructive self-delusion, a theory and practice from which Tarwater must be violently extricated. He must indeed be saved from his own self-destructive desire for freedom on his own terms, his taking offence at the prophetic teaching that Jesus is the bread of life whose undignified, intimate sovereignty in creation undermines the autonomy of his own divided self. In the shriving light of his conscience young Tarwater's destructive deeds are defeated by the words of baptism, as he shudders into wakefulness, opens his eyes, and hears "the sibilant oaths of his friend [the hidden spiritual mentor] fading away on the darkness" (*VBA* 216). And yet he deliberately and forcefully closes the inner eye of possible rebirth, determined to go back to take charge of that other site of desecration, "to live his life as he had elected it, and where, for the rest of his days, he would make good his refusal" (218).

Tarwater continues to believe he can save himself through negation, that "in the order of things, a drowning was a more important act than a few words spilled in the water" (221). And of course according to the structure of values in this once-born cosmology he is joined by many a reader of O'Connor's scandalizing story, who focus in horror only upon the drowning. But O'Connor continues, lovingly and violently, to force open the inner eye of her character by means of the colloquy of spiritual voices that continue to speak. In the face of the all-knowing woman (from whom he wishes to buy a "purple drink") who stands in judgment "fixed from the foundations of time" upon his attempted desecration of Mason's dead body, Tarwater is conscious "that he was called upon by some force outside them both to answer for his freedom and make bold his acts" (225). Plumbing the depths of his soul for the bold answering voice of his "mentor" he involuntarily voices an obscenity. Again the division within himself makes it shockingly evident that he is not "in charge" of himself or anything else. It is a discomfiting truth that makes him begin to hunger for companionship as much as for food and drink, in order to explain himself "with the right words to wipe out the obscenity that had stained his thought" (226).

It is at this very point of Tarwater's greatest desire to prove his autonomous, self-liberating agency, where Tarwater notes, "nobody tells me what to do" (228), that he is violently mastered by a fleshly representative of his hitherto spiritual violet-eyed mentor (214–15, 227). He finds the fleshly companion, whom he ironically (but mercifully) seeks for spiritual self-confirmation, and, after consuming the anesthetizing anti-sacraments of weed and moonshine ("It's better than the Bread of Life!" [230]), is raped. This is a mercy that burns. I am not suggesting, of course, that the violent rape is a humanly mediated divine act, but here O'Connor herself provides us an interesting account: "In my stories a reader will find that the devil accomplishes a good deal of groundwork that seems to be necessary before grace is effective. Tarwater's final vision could not have been brought off if he hadn't met the man in the lavender and cream-colored car. This is another mystery" (*MM* 117). That is, as O'Connor puts it in another communication, "It is the violation in the woods that brings home to Tarwater the real nature of his rejection" (*HB* 368). He receives the judgment by which he has judged and wakes up to his true condition, mired in a self-destructive negation from which he cannot save himself. This time he does not resist the movement toward the apocalypse of rebirth for which he has been prepared by the inner eye "from above." In order to interpret this final revelation, however, we must pass through the scandalous apocalyptic symbolism of Jesus as the bread of life in John 6.

A MINOR HYMN TO THE EUCHARIST: JOHN 6
IN *THE VIOLENT BEAR IT AWAY*

There are two main symbols in [*The Violent Bear It Away*]—water and the bread that Christ is. The whole action of the novel is Tarwater's selfish will against all that the little lake (the baptismal font) and the bread stand for. This book is a very minor hymn to the Eucharist.

—Flannery O'Connor, *The Habit of Being*

According to John's gospel, the illumining light "from above" is neither simply celestial (the sun or the moon or "a brilliant marriage" between them [*VBA* 221]) nor the Platonic Good beyond being, the archetypical "light itself" that enlightens every earthly soul (*Republic* 506–17). John's scandalous testimony claims that the eternal light that shines in the darkness, through which all things were made, that joins the earthly and the heavenly in a recreating "new birth" from above in which sins are forgiven, has come into the world in a manner that reveals ("apocalypse" as verb, not noun) divine glory to those with eyes to see. This glory is no less than life eternal itself (*zoe aionios*) manifested through the movements (the "works," *erga*) of the "lamb of God" (an apocalyptic messianic title John uses for Jesus). This movement appears in particular human form, in Jesus who claims, scandalously, to be the "bread of life." In response to this apocalyptic movement, which provokes a "crisis" in the need to decide how to respond, human beings are "judged" according to their works—do they seek life or death? Do they seek the glory that comes from God alone and that may not be possessed, or do they seek their own glory, a reflected glory received from other human beings that turns out to be darkness? This is a difficult question, as it appears that the moving source of this glory is simply yet another particular human being who makes extravagant claims to know the truth about being.

In John's gospel it seems the only real decision is whether to force such a person to rule as universal king (6:15; 12:12–19) or to have him arrested for blasphemy. In either case, Jesus' movements provoke violence. But the violence does not end there. Jesus himself suggests (in

John's climactic twelfth chapter) that his cosmic glorification is tied not to life but to death—"the one who loves one's own *psyche* loses it, the one who hates one's own *psyche* in this world will keep it to life eternal" (12:25). By his death, lifted up on a criminal's cross, he will draw all things (12:32). That is, those desires (rooted in the possession of human glory) that evoke violent acts of coronation or crucifixion must themselves be violently mortified in the light of a messianic movement that draws the self, as Kierkegaard suggests, "through lowliness and abasement"—that is, through penitence.[9] The pathway of messianic drawing revealed through Jesus converges always only at one point, the consciousness of sin and the call to become a self by losing it.

It is precisely this prophetic messianic "being drawn" that Tarwater resists, for to trudge in the "bleeding stinking mad shadow of Jesus, lost forever to his own inclinations" (*VBA* 91, 221) is an offensive eucharistic calling. In John 6, the eucharistic chapter in which Jesus calls himself "the bread of life," the opening scene that "draws" the crowd is Jesus' miraculous feeding of five thousand with the five barley loaves and two fish. The breaking and distribution of bread by Jesus, after "giving thanks [*eucharista*]," evokes the admiration and astonishment of all who see it, and their desire, John tells us, is to "come and take him by force to make him king" (6:15). Jesus resists their coronating admiration—"Truly, truly, I say to you, you seek me, not because you saw signs, but because you ate your fill of the loaves" (John 6:26). In other words, they have not truly seen the significance of Jesus' works, the hidden movement of his words and deeds and their sovereign authority. Jesus resists the external glory-seeking orientation that motivates the crowd's movement. His miraculous deed is not primarily about "the food which perishes" (John 6:27).

When young Tarwater (like Nicodemus in John 3) goes for his surreptitious night walk, with Rayber secretly following him, the boy stops briefly in front of a shop window and Rayber observes that his face is "like the face of someone starving who sees a meal he can't reach laid out before him. At last, something he *wants,* he thought, and determined that tomorrow he would return and buy it." It turns out, however, that the place is only a bakery and what Tarwater has so hungrily observed is but an overlooked loaf of bread pushed off to the side of an otherwise empty display case. "Everything a false alarm, [Rayber] thought with disgust. If he had eaten his dinner, he wouldn't be hungry" (*VBA* 122). Rayber is unable to discern even the literal significance of the external loaves. If Tarwater has problems with food, it is not only because the city fare served up by his uncle is less appetizing than old Mason's country fare had been, but because he is wrestling with an inner hunger that has become an "insistent silent force" like that silent country into which he continues to refuse to enter. His inner mentor is adamant that he "refuse to entertain hunger as a sign" (160–62). And yet, as the inner mentor by his very presence continues to testify, Tarwater remains open in a way Rayber cannot because Tarwater is attuned to the spiritual significance of earthly food, an apocalyptic significance that can dispense neither with the spiritual nor with the fleshly, neither with the invisible nor with the visible. Tarwater now knows the apocalypse does not come from a "clear and empty sky" that is untouched by "fleshy hand or breath" but only through an inner rebirth from above to a restored intimacy with creation—through blood and nerve and mind in a world of loss in which he is called to bleed and weep and think in relation to an idiot gospel.

In this we are reminded of Jesus' wilderness temptations after his own baptism. In keeping with his response to the devil's suggestion that he miraculously turn stones into loaves—"Humans shall not live by bread alone, but by every word that proceeds from the mouth of God" (Matthew 4:4)—Jesus tells the people who have sought him out after his feeding of the five thousand, "Do not labor for the food which perishes, but for the food which endures to eternal life" (John 6:27). When he is asked what this labor is that brings eternal life, Jesus tells them to come to him, since "I am the bread of life" (6:35), and his food is to do not his own will but the will of the Father who has sent him from heaven. When this terse statement causes understandable murmuring ("Is not this Jesus, the son of Joseph, whose father and mother we know?"), Jesus elaborates by way of an even harder saying: "I am the living bread which came down from heaven; if any one eats of this bread, he will live forever; and the bread which I shall give for the life of the world is my flesh" (6:51). Jesus' "hard sayings" cause offense because of his complete fleshly identification with the will, word, and works of God, the Father who has sent him. It is a relation of "abiding" or dwelling that cannot be seen by those who focus only upon physical descent ("is not this the son of Joseph") or blood lineage, or the temporal, visible meaning of created reality.

To hear this word and not be offended requires faith in the eternal word that dwells within (cf. John 5:38), the spirit that gives life and draws from beyond the realm of the flesh, and yet fully abides within it. Jesus thus becomes in his movements the occasion of being confronted in the flesh by the apocalyptic movement of divine light and life itself—for those with eyes to see. Jesus is the bread and the giver of bread insofar as he gives himself, his flesh and his blood, completely for the life of the world. It is a giving that gives itself up completely for the divine movement, without holding anything back possessively, even unto death. It provokes a crisis in that it calls for a decision about the eternal meaning of life in relation to the unseen, to what remains unconsummated in the world. To decide to allow one's life to be drawn into an abiding in such a love—a prophetic new birth relation to what is hidden and unseen, yet claims in the flesh to be love itself—this is of all things most difficult. It requires the self to do what seems impossible—eat the flesh and drink the blood of the Son of man sent from the living Father (John 6:53–58), namely, to abide in the eternal life mediated in the bodily life of Jesus whose food is to enact the divine word.

Here is precisely the self-mortifyingly intimate drawing that both Rayber and Tarwater so desperately resist in O'Connor's novel. Rayber experiences it through his son, Bishop, horrifyingly (to him) formed in the image and likeness of God, who—in contrast to "love in general" (i.e., love as a policy, cf. *VBA* 50–51), which has its uses and therapeutic benefits—evokes in him in thoughtless or irrational moments "a morbid surge of love that terrified him" (113). This is a love without earthly uses, a love of a different order entirely: "It was not the kind that could be used for the child's improvement or his own. It was love without reason, love for something futureless, love that appeared to exist only to be itself, imperious and all demanding, the kind that would cause him to make a fool of himself in an instant" (113–14). It is, in effect, a love that violates all possessive desires, above all the desire to possess oneself, a love rooted in an impossible vision of a world transfigured. Rayber feels it as a drawing or a longing "like an undertow in his blood dragging him backwards to what he knew to be madness" (114). Tarwater also feels it as a madness, a hunger in his great-uncle Mason, and he fears it may be "hidden in the blood" and passed down to him, "the bottom split out of his stomach so that nothing would heal or fill it but the bread of life" (21). The eucharist, the blood and bread of life in O'Connor's novel, like baptism, is not an institutional act mediated by scripture or the Church. It is an enactment that requires a complete giving up of the self in obedience to the call of Christ, in which the only meaningful definition of dead and living resides in kinship relation, a complete consanguinity with the crucified yet lifted up Word that draws all in transfiguring relation to divine Life itself.

Without such eucharistic eyes to see, the final apocalypse in *The Violent Bear It Away* remains literally (which is to say, sacramentally) unbelievable, a stumbling block. The final scene is a movement at once penitential and liturgical—in the literal sense of the Greek word *lei-tourgia:* a work of public service to the world in the form of idiot praise and the enactment of an idiot gospel. It proclaims that the only true path to life is through the abasement of the cross. As Tarwater approaches Powderhead along the burning path following his rape, he sees what he expects to see, "an empty clearing" (*VBA* 237): "The clearing was burned free of all that had ever oppressed him. No cross was there to say that this was ground that the Lord still held. What he looked out upon was the sign of a broken covenant. The place was forsaken and his own" (237). His inner mentor, at once friend and adversary, admonishes him to go down and take the place that "they" have won for themselves together. Tarwater tries ineffectually to burn this tormenting presence from his consciousness and remains open to the mysterious quiet that pervades the clearing—which turns out not to be entirely forsaken. Buford Munson has remained faithful in his service there, tending the crop and completing the burial of Mason that Tarwater abandoned in drunken rebellion.

As Tarwater now sees that he has been saved from his own desecrating intentions by the faithful actions of Buford, his eyes are drawn downward to the cross on the grave "as if they followed below the surface of the earth to where its roots encircled all the dead" (240). The boy allows his vision to go below the surface and into the threatened intimacy of creation and he sees not only his old dead uncle, but he becomes "aware at last of the object of his hunger, aware that it was the same as the old man's and that nothing on earth would fill him. His hunger was so great that he could have eaten all the loaves and fishes after they were multiplied" (241). His hunger now binds him in diaspora kinship across time with all those lives prophetically called to sustain the world as strangers and victims in it, as citizens "from that violent country where the silence is never broken except to shout the truth" (242). His hunger now binds him in a lineage "from the blood of Abel to his own"; it immerses him penitentially in a tide that lifts and turns him from his own violent deeds to the commanding words that come "as silent as seeds opening one at a time in his blood," to "go warn the children of God of the terrible speed of mercy" (242). The old man's words that earlier dropped silently into his bloodstream (60–61) now open as a command heard from within. It turns out the words are not the possessions of Mason, nor rooted in a merely human madness, an inherited mental instability. They are rather the fleshly articulation of an inner word that Tarwater is now able to hear with "eyes to see"— much as in Job's final answer to the Lord who has allowed him to be afflicted with undeserved sufferings: "I had heard of thee by the hearing of the ear, but now my eye sees thee; therefore I despise myself, and repent in dust and ashes" (Job 42:5). And with that he is sent back into the dark city where the children of God lie sleeping.

This ending remains a scandal, "the futility, the ridiculous absurdity of performing the empty rite" as Rayber might put it (*VBA* 146). Whether that rite be baptism, penitence, or eucharist, it will not bring back the drowned Bishop, that innocent victim, nor will it "cure" Tarwater of his backwoods imbecility. What on earth could he possibly accomplish with the sleeping children of God in the city? I, like O'Connor, do not propose to answer that question—thus articulated it is posed by a once-born Rayberian humanism. A prophet is not a politician, nor indeed a schoolteacher or welfare worker. A prophet is called to become a witness to the mystery of spiritual motion in the everyday (*HB* 365) and such a witness is rooted in penitential self-denial, a kinship with the divine. It is a calling not accessible to purely external social or political conventions—in these respects to understand human agency and becoming a self in freedom sacramentally remains futile, since the whole point of such a calling is nonconformity to the fallen world.

The point of O'Connor's novel is not to display the moral transformation of her protagonist—he cannot undo or atone for his evil
murderous deeds rooted in rebellion, violent deeds provoked precisely
because of his spiritual attunement to what he is called to become by
the sovereignty of a crucified Messiah. Yet even he may be reborn, not
to a "better adjusted" human dignity or a more "normal" social psychology, but to a life of messianic responsibility before God in the only
life he has been given, his own. This requires penitence for his sinful
deeds—and whether the deed is rooted in saying no to the divine command to baptize a mentally defective child or in a "mercy killing" act
of euthanasia rooted in a tender compassion that cannot abide suffering makes no difference whatsoever—and an immediate disposition of
obedience to the divine will which is life itself. For O'Connor this will
must be seen eucharistically in relation to the apocalypse of Jesus as the
messianic "bread of life." This goes beyond a Mosaic prophetic escha-
tology (Moses who gave people water from the rock and bread from
heaven) to a revelation of eternal life related to the violent death of
Jesus who claims himself to be the food and drink of eternal life itself.
The path to life, then, for those with eucharistic vision, must pass
through a suffering and death in which Christ gives his flesh and sheds
his blood for all—a vision that remains as offensive today as it ever was,
world without end.

NOTES

1. See Davies and Allison 254f.

2. My reading of John's gospel is indebted especially to C. H. Dodd,
The Interpretation of the Fourth Gospel; see also Bultmann, *The Gospel
of John: A Commentary;* and Barrett, *The Gospel According to St. John.*

3. See the fine study by Ralph Wood.

4. O'Connor's comments on poetics and prophecy are well known:
"In the novelist's case, prophecy is a matter of seeing near things with
their extensions of meaning and thus of seeing far things close up. The
prophet is a realist of distances . . ." (*MM* 44). And again: "The prophet
is a realist of distances, and it is this kind of realism that goes into great
novels. It is the realism which does not hesitate to distort appearances

in order to show a hidden truth" (179). For an excellent discussion of O'Connor's prophetic art in relation to Thomas Aquinas's interpretation of prophetic vision, see Srigley (chap. 1).

5. O'Connor adds, "[I]n my own stories I have found that violence is strangely capable of returning my characters to reality and preparing them to accept their moment of grace. . . . This idea, that reality is something to which we must be returned at considerable cost, is one which is seldom understood by the casual reader, but it is one which is implicit in the Christian view of the world." Violence, then, "is the extreme situation that best reveals what we are essentially . . ." (*MM* 113). For an illuminating discussion of violence in *The Violent Bear It Away*, see John Desmond's "Violence and the Christian Mystery."

6. Cassian chap. 26. The definitive study of O'Connor's work in relation to the desert traditions is Richard Giannone's *Flannery O'Connor, Hermit Novelist*.

7. Compare the words of Dr. Rieux in Albert Camus, *The Plague:* "Heroism and sanctity don't really appeal to me, I imagine. What interests me is—being a man" (209).

8. See the fine discussion of this passage and its multiple "ichthyological" resonances in "The Source" by Jason Peters.

9. See no. III of Kierkegaard's *Practice in Christianity*.

WORKS CITED

Barrett, C. K. *The Gospel According to St. John*. 2nd edition. Philadelphia: Westminster Press, 1978.

Bultmann, Rudolph. *The Gospel of John: A Commentary*. Trans. G. R. Beasley-Murray Philadelphia: Westminster Press, 1971.

Camus, Albert. *The Plague*. Trans. Stuart Gilbert. London: Penguin Books, 1960.

Cassian, John. *The Conferences*. Trans. Boniface Ramsey. New York: Newman Press, 1997.

Davies, William David, and Dale. C. Allison. *A Critical and Exegetical Commentary on the Gospel According to Saint Matthew*. Vol. 2, *Matthew 8–18*. New York: T and T Clark, 1991.

Desmond, John F. "Violence and the Christian Mystery: A Way to Read Flannery O'Connor." *Literature and Belief* 17 (1997): 129–47.

Dodd, C. H. *The Interpretation of the Fourth Gospel.* Cambridge: Cambridge University Press, 1953.

Giannone, Richard. *Flannery O'Connor, Hermit Novelist.* Urbana: University of Illinois Press, 2000.

Kierkegaard, Søren. *Practice in Christianity.* Trans. Howard V. Hong and Edna H. Hong. Princeton, NJ: Princeton University Press, 1991.

O'Connor, Flannery. *The Habit of Being: Letters of Flannery O'Connor.* Ed. Sally Fitzgerald. New York: Farrar, Straus and Giroux, 1979.

———. *Mystery and Manners: Occasional Prose.* Ed. Sally Fitzgerald and Robert Fitzgerald. New York: Farrar, Straus and Giroux, 1969.

———. *The Violent Bear It Away.* New York: Farrar, Straus and Giroux, 1960.

Orwell, Miles. *The Invisible Parade: The Fiction of Flannery O'Connor.* Philadelphia: Temple University Press, 1972.

Peters, Jason. "The Source of Flannery O'Connor's 'Flung' Fish in *The Violent Bear It Away.*" *American Notes and Queries* 18.4 (Fall 2005): 48–53.

Srigley, Susan. *Flannery O'Connor's Sacramental Art.* Notre Dame, IN: University of Notre Dame Press, 2004.

Wood, Ralph C. *Flannery O'Connor and the Christ Haunted South.* Grand Rapids, MI: Eerdmans, 2004.

CHAPTER 8

Suffering Violence in the Kingdom of Heaven

The Violent Bear It Away

KARL E. MARTIN

Nearly everyone who has ever commented on Flannery O'Connor's *The Violent Bear It Away* has acknowledged the Gospel of Matthew as the source of its title and epigraph. But the novel borrows much more than its title and epigraph from Matthew. The immediate context for the novel's title are the words of Jesus as he announces the coming of the kingdom of heaven, contrasting his pronouncement to the understanding of the prior prophetic kingdom articulated by John the Baptist:[1] "From the days of John the Baptist until now, the kingdom of heaven suffereth violence, and the violent bear it away" (11:12). If we take the biblical relation of O'Connor's title and epigraph a step further and place the novel in the context of the gospel story, we see Francis Marion Tarwater being freed from the paradigm of the prophetic kingdom presented to him by his great-uncle Mason and being ushered into a vision of the kingdom of heaven exemplified by his cousin Bishop Rayber.

Early in the novel, Mason tells Tarwater that God is preparing a prophet whose message will be: "Go warn the children of God . . . of the terrible speed of justice" (*CW* 368). Mason proclaims, "The Lord is preparing a prophet with fire in his hand and eye and the prophet is moving toward the city with his warning" (368). In the novel's final scene, Tarwater feels the call of God on his life when he recognizes that the fire before him is "the fire that had encircled Daniel, that had raised Elijah from the earth, that had spoken to Moses and would in the instant speak to him" (478). Tarwater comes close to fulfilling the old man's prophecy—he sets fire to Powderhead with his own hands, and that fire is reflected in his eyes. However, the message he is given is subtlety but significantly different from the one prophesied for him by Mason. Tarwater hears the command to warn God's children—this time delivered with the emphasis of capital letters—"OF THE TERRIBLE SPEED OF MERCY" (478).

I contend that Tarwater's interactions with Bishop leads to this transformation of his prophetic calling. Such a reading of the novel suggests the young boy's influence on Tarwater surpasses that of Mason or even Tarwater's schoolteacher uncle, George Rayber. Rather than seeing Tarwater as pulled between the influences of Mason and Rayber, we should consider how Tarwater moves away from Mason and toward Bishop. Rightly considered, Bishop may be the novel's true protagonist, the character whose very presence determines many of the novel's most significant episodes.[2] If we read such episodes alongside the structure and imagery of the Gospel of Matthew, we see that it is Bishop who provides the means by which Tarwater is delivered into the kingdom of heaven.[3] Through the announcement of the messianic kingdom, a critique of the role of the prophet, and the experience of suffering, the gospel story informs the transformative action in O'Connor's novel.

This reading of *The Violent Bear It Away* follows the lead of previous critics who have placed the title and epigraph in its Matthean context. Shortly after the novel's publication in 1960, Summer J. Ferris noted the source and briefly provided alternative readings of the passage from *A Catholic Commentary of the Holy Scripture*.[4] Still, the verse O'Connor employs from Matthew is notoriously difficult to translate and interpret. What does it mean that the kingdom of heaven "suffereth violence" and who are the "violent" and just how do they "bear [the kingdom] away"? With the publication of O'Connor's letters in 1979, critics could add to their analysis O'Connor's insight into the verse. O'Connor wrote to her friend and frequent correspondent Elizabeth Hester in 1959, "St. Thomas's gloss on this verse is that the violent [ones that] Christ is here talking about represent those ascetics who strain against mere nature. St. Augustine concurs" (1101). Of this letter Susan Srigley writes, "According to O'Connor, the understanding of violence that is expressed by Christ in the Gospels suggests a pattern of self-sacrifice that the followers of Christ are called to imitate . . ." (100). Richard Giannone writes that although the passage seems to justify the use of violence in advancing the kingdom of heaven, "there is a counter meaning in the Matthean title that promises a dispensation after John the Baptist, namely, with Jesus, when humility takes the kingdom" (*Mystery* 116). Building on Giannone's reading, Gary M. Ciuba writes, "Especially when read out of context, the passage that provided O'Connor with her title and epigraph might seem to affirm a kingdom of sacred violence. However the gospel verse actually undermines such a bloody realm" (120). Given its complexity, establishing the context from Matthew seems crucial to understanding O'Connor's use of the passage.

THE MESSIANIC KINGDOM OF HEAVEN IN MATTHEW'S GOSPEL

As noted above, one difficulty of the epigraph from Matthew's gospel results from the phrase "suffereth violence." The notion of a suffering kingdom is an underlying theme in O'Connor's novel, as will be seen below. Another difficult element of the epigraph, however, is the use of the term "now"—"from the time of St. John the Baptist until now." For when Jesus makes this statement, John is imprisoned but still alive. In this sense, "the time of John the Baptist" is not yet over. "Now" would thus seem to relate to eschatological rather than chronological time. That is, the text relates to the announcement of the kingdom of heaven that plays such a crucial role in the relationship between John the Baptist and Jesus in Matthew's gospel. In chapter 3, for example, John is reported to be preaching in the wilderness of Judea. His message is,

"Repent, for the kingdom of heaven is at hand" (3:2).[5] Following his baptism and temptation in the wilderness, Jesus hears that John has been imprisoned. John's imprisonment may be seen as the symbolic end of the prophetic paradigm, for it is the event in Matthew immediately preceding the public ministry of Jesus. "From that time," that is, from the time of the imprisonment of John, "Jesus began to preach and say, 'Repent, for the kingdom of heaven is at hand'" (4:17). The message of Jesus is the same as John's, but John himself predicted that the times were changing (3:11). Even though Matthew relates the two pronouncements using the same words, Jesus, especially in his teachings in the Sermon on the Mount in chapters 5–7, begins to redefine the meaning of the kingdom of heaven and the means of participation within it. Chapter 5 of Matthew is notable for its repeated use of the trope, "You have heard that it was said" paired with, "But I say to you." The use of the trope also signals Jesus' new definition of the kingdom of heaven.

The concern of Jesus to redefine the meaning of the kingdom of heaven is made clear in Matthew's gospel through the series of parables and teachings recorded in chapters 11–13, and in the section of Matthew between the visit of John's disciples and in the account of John's beheading that leads directly to the story of the feeding of the five thousand in chapter 14. John has heard of the healing and teaching activities of Jesus and has sent his disciples to ask him, "Are you the Expected One, or shall we look for someone else?" (11:3b). To their question, Jesus responds, "Go and report to John what you hear and see: the blind receive sight and the lame walk, the lepers are cleansed and the deaf hear, the dead are raised up, and the poor have the gospel preached to them" (11:4–5). This litany is the familiar list of the works of the prophesied Messiah with two notable exceptions—liberty to the captives and freedom for the imprisoned are not listed as they are, for example, in Isaiah 61. The fact that Jesus does not promise John freedom may well be his way of informing John that the messianic kingdom of heaven will be marked by suffering—a crucial understanding for John and for readers of O'Connor's novel.

Another significant aspect of the new kingdom is reflected in Jesus' teaching about John's ministry and status. Jesus offers unparalleled praise for John when he proclaims, "Truly I say to you, among those born of women there has not arisen anyone greater than John the Baptist!" Nevertheless, in the very next breath, Jesus proclaims, "Yet the one who is least in the kingdom of heaven is greater than he" (Matthew 11:11). The verse employed by O'Connor for her epigraph and title appears after this contrast between the greatest man ever born of woman and the least in the kingdom of heaven—a fact that should alert us to attend to "the least" as they are present in O'Connor's narrative and encourage us to contemplate Tarwater's relationships with Mason and Bishop.

The central message of the section in Matthew in which O'Connor's epigraph appears concerns the values and structure of the messianic kingdom. So if we take O'Connor's choice of a text for her title and epigraph seriously and strive to place it in its original context, we are led to consider the parallels between the story of John the Baptist and Jesus (whom the Christian church, based on Luke 1:36, traditionally has considered to be related) and Tarwater and his ecclesiastically named cousin, Bishop. In addition, we are led to consider how the kingdom of heaven, a central image in Matthew, is characterized in the novel, a central element in the relationship between Jesus and John the Baptist as Matthew presents it. However, first we must explore the connections between Mason, John the Baptist, and the prophetic paradigm. For, despite their family connection, Mason and Bishop are emblematic of different paradigms.

THE PROPHETIC PARADIGM: JOHN THE BAPTIST AND MASON TARWATER

Drawing parallels between John the Baptist and Mason Tarwater is not difficult. Both are associated with the wilderness and a prophetic ministry focusing on judgment and calling for repentance. Like John, Mason is imprisoned for a time—Mason serves time in an asylum. Unlike John the Baptist, however, Mason has the ability to free himself from prison, to avoid the suffering and eventual death John the Baptist experiences. The condition required for Mason's freedom is a silencing, or at least a tempering, of his prophetic voice. Mason's decision to free himself from the prison of the asylum by moderating his speech signifies that, while he is indeed a prophet, he is not willing to fully endure the suffering required by his call. In addition to their shared imprisonment, both John the Baptist and Mason have as their primary prophetic activity the act of baptism. And both have a profound understanding that someone will follow them called to even greater work than they. Perhaps neither fully understands the form the ministry of the coming Messiah will take. Jesus indicates as much when he contrasts the relative greatness of John and "the least" in the kingdom. Perhaps Mason himself is confused, assuming Tarwater will take up the call and discounting Bishop's value and role.

Mason's vision of history is one of the strongest links between this backwoods preacher and the prophets of Israel, of whom John the Baptist is Matthew's example. O'Connor's narrative voice tells us of the history taught by Mason to his great-nephew. Mason teaches Tarwater "History beginning with Adam expelled from the Garden and going on down through the presidents to Herbert Hoover and on in speculation toward the Second Coming and the Day of the Judgment" (*CW* 331). The presentation is, of course, meant to be comic—but only partially so. Mason does not distinguish between the biblical account of history and the secular.

Consistent with a prophetic paradigm, the history of the world is seen by Mason fundamentally as the history of God's activity in history. So when the narrative voice declares that Mason has given the boy "a good education" (331), the judgment is not completely absurd. At the very least, Mason rejects the modern distinction between the sacred and the secular, incorporating all of history in his narrative of the history of the sacred, all of history as moving from the expulsion from the Garden to the Day of Judgment. The novel nowhere indicates that Tarwater renounces this vision of history taught to him as a boy. He certainly does not reject it in favor of any vision of history articulated by his uncle Rayber. In his study of O'Connor and the Desert Fathers, Giannone points out that Mason's solitary years—and the years he skips when he teaches Tarwater about the presidents but abruptly ends with Herbert Hoover—coincide with years of tremendous violence against the Jews. As Jews are being slaughtered, Mason is honoring their prophets in the wilderness of Tennessee (*Hermit* 48).

A crucial distinction between John the Baptist and Mason must also be noted—a distinction making Mason an essentially comic character and limiting the extent of his identification with the messianic kingdom of heaven. Whereas the ministry of John the Baptist occurs during the prophetic age, that is, before the advent of the kingdom of heaven ushered in by the Messiah, Mason is functioning in a prophetic mode *during* the messianic. Thus he gives readers a sense of being out of place, of being out of step not only with the modern, secular world (as any prophet should be) but also out of step with the kingdom of heaven as announced by and embodied in Jesus.

In her typically sly way, O'Connor may give us a hint of Mason's displacement, of his distance from the messianic kingdom. In Matthew, as Jesus is extolling the prophetic attributes of John the Baptist, he admonishes his listeners by saying, "He who has ears, let him hear" (11:15). If Rayber is one member of Mason's target audience, that is, if Rayber is one to whom Mason has been sent, then it is comically ironic that rather than helping Rayber hear God's message, Mason is responsible for Rayber's inability to hear and respond to that message. Mason causes Rayber's partial loss of hearing when he shoots off Rayber's ear with a shotgun blast when Rayber ventures out to Powderhead in an attempt to retrieve Tarwater. Later, when Rayber tells Tarwater about the first time he encountered Mason, O'Connor again indicates that, for Rayber, the old man's message is ineffective. Rayber tells his nephew, "I was six or seven, I was out in the yard playing and all of a sudden I felt something between me and the sun" (*CW* 436). If the sun represents the presence of God as it does elsewhere in the novel and elsewhere in O'Connor's prose, then—at least for Rayber—Mason is a hindrance rather than a help to God's work. Mason may be able to train a prophet, but he is presented as a poor evangelist of the messianic kingdom.

THE MESSIANIC KINGDOM

After associating Mason with the prophetic paradigm of the Old Testament carried into the New Testament in the person of John the Baptist, O'Connor employs Bishop as an emblem of the messianic kingdom inaugurated by Jesus. But aligning Bishop with the messianic kingdom is more problematic than aligning Mason with John the Baptist, for O'Connor has no intention of turning Bishop into a Christ figure or even a messianic figure. In a 1956 letter to Elizabeth Hester, O'Connor writes, "In my novel I have a child—the school teacher's boy—whom I aim to have a kind of Christ image, though a better way to think of it is probably just as a kind of redemptive figure" (*CW* 1015).[6] Regardless of its challenges, the association of Bishop with the messianic kingdom clarifies his role in the novel.

Bishop fits the description of Jesus' call in Matthew 11:11, as he is certainly deemed "the least" by those around him. In chapter one, we read of Tarwater's first visit to the city with Mason when together they visit Rayber's home and encounter Bishop. Mason tells Rayber that either he or Tarwater will someday baptize Bishop. Rayber responds by saying, "You could slosh water on him for the rest of his life and he'd still be an idiot. Five years old for all eternity, useless forever" (*CW* 351). When Tarwater returns to Rayber's home after the Mason's death, Rayber once again highlights Bishop's uselessness. He tells Tarwater of his plans for him while disparaging his own son when he says, "All the things that I would do for him—if it were any use—I'll do for you" (389). Rayber's final estimation is that Bishop's entire existence is a mistake. "His normal way of looking on Bishop was as an *x* signifying the general hideousness of fate" (401). For Rayber, Bishop is "just a mistake of nature" (403).

Even though Mason is committed to baptizing Bishop, he too seems to believe that Bishop is least among God's creation. On his visit to Rayber's home with Tarwater, Mason tells Rayber, "That boy cries out for his baptism" and proclaims, "Precious in the sight of the Lord even an idiot!" (350). When Mason suggests that if he does not succeed in baptizing Bishop, Tarwater will begin his ministry with this task, Tarwater resists the idea. "The boy doubted very much that his first mission would be to baptize a dim-witted child." Tarwater is partially motivated by his desire to break with his great-uncle, but he also seems to believe Bishop to be of little intrinsic worth. He believes God has greater things in mind for him. "And he thought of Moses who struck water from a rock, of Joshua who made the sun stand still, of Daniel who stared down lions in the pit" (335). Tarwater, in an especially harsh passage, associates Bishop with a hog. He tells Rayber that Bishop "eats like a hog and he don't think no more than a hog and when he dies, he'll rot like a hog." Tarwater insists he and Rayber will also rot like hogs; still, he maintains their superiority over Bishop when he says, "The only difference between me and you and a hog is me and you can calculate, but there ain't any difference between him and one" (403). Tarwater resists the idea that his primary prophetic task will be focused on someone as insignificant—as animal-like—as Bishop.

Although the other major characters in the novel downplay Bishop's importance, O'Connor's narrative voice places him in another light altogether and thus emphasizes his status in the kingdom of heaven as Jesus defines it. From the novel's first paragraphs, O'Connor associates the sun with the prophetic presence of God, and later in the novel she associates that divine presence with Bishop. In an episode reminiscent of the call of the prophet Isaiah, Mason is burned clean by God when "one morning he saw to his joy a finger of fire coming out of [the sun] and before he could turn, before he could shout, the finger had touched him and the destruction he had been waiting for had fallen in his own brain and his own body" (332). The connection to Isaiah's vision (Isaiah 6) is important, for Isaiah describes a vision of being in the very presence of God. O'Connor is suggesting the sun at Powderhead represents that divine presence.

O'Connor's intention to associate sunlight with the divine presence of God is also made later in the first chapter during Tarwater's early interaction with the voice of the stranger. When Tarwater resists digging the old man's grave as he had promised, "The sun was like a furious white blister in the sky" (345). In their visit to the city, a place seen by both Tarwater and Mason as a world inattentive to God, Tarwater sees the street below the lawyer's office as "a river of tin" and sees "glints on it from the sun which drifted pale in the sky, too far away to ignite anything" (347). The stranger tries to convince Tarwater that his redemption is meaningless, that the old man had led him astray: "You're left by yourself in this empty place. Forever by yourself in this empty place with just as much light as that dwarf sun wants to let in. You don't mean a thing to a soul as far as I can see" (352–53). Later, the stranger's voice more forcefully questions the presence of the Lord in Tarwater's life; he asks Tarwater directly, "[W]here is the voice of the Lord?"

When the question is posed, "[t]he sun was directly overhead, apparently dead still, holding its breath, waiting out the noontime" (356). As the stranger exhibits his influence on Tarwater, the images of the sun express the anger of God toward him. The sun is described as appearing "a furious white" and is described as "angry" (358).

Before Tarwater will fully experience God's calling in his life, Rayber will take him to the city park, which he considers the center of civilized, humane life, in an attempt to break Mason's control over him. There in the city is a piece of Powderhead: "the boy paled as if he were shocked to find a wood in the middle of the city." With the setting of the woods comes the reemergence of the sun as an image for God's presence. Tarwater sees the beauty of the natural world again, sees "the huge trees whose ancient rustling branches intermingled overhead" and "[p]atches of light sifting through them spattered the concrete walks with sunshine" (417). Here in the park a crucial interaction between Tarwater and Bishop takes place, also marked by the sun's presence, when Rayber observes Tarwater moving toward Bishop in the park fountain: "Rayber had the sense that [Tarwater] was moving blindly, that where Bishop was he saw only a spot of light." Fearing that Mason "*had* transferred his fixation to the boy, *had* left him with the notion that he must baptize Bishop," Rayber quickly removes Bishop from the fountain away from Tarwater (421). But O'Connor's narrative voice breaks in and challenges Rayber's interpretation of the incident. First, in chapter six, interrupting Rayber's consciousness, the narrator notes that Tarwater's "eyes were on the child in the pool but they burned as if he beheld some terrible compelling vision. The sun shone brightly on Bishop's white head" (421) and again, in chapter 8, when the same scene is told through Tarwater's consciousness, Tarwater senses the great significance of the sunlight falling on Bishop. When Bishop is in the pool,

> [t]he sun, which had been tacking from cloud to cloud, emerged above the fountain. A blinding brightness fell on the lion's tangled marble head and gilded the stream of water rushing from his mouth. Then the light, falling more gently, rested like a hand on the child's white head. His face might have been a mirror where the sun had stopped to watch its reflection. (432)

Tarwater sees not merely "a spot of light," as Rayber suggests, but the sun as a hand resting on Bishop's head. In one of her rare uses of a direct simile, O'Connor states that the sun "rested like a hand" on Bishop. Later in the novel she will also abandon her use of the less direct construction "as if" in relationship to Bishop as we shall see.

Here the connection between Bishop's stance in the fountain and the baptism of Jesus as recorded in Matthew is clear. In Matthew we read, "After being baptized, Jesus came up immediately from the water; and behold, the heavens were opened, and he saw the Spirit of God descending as a dove and lighting on Him" (3:16). The sun breaking through the clouds above the fountain resembles the scene of the opening heavens in Matthew. The dove in the gospel story has become a hand in O'Connor's narrative. The point here is not to establish Bishop as a Christ figure but rather to associate Bishop closely with the mysterious presence of God in the world and thus with the arrival of the messianic kingdom of heaven as defined by Jesus.

Along with the significance of the sun is the significance of water. In this first narration of the visit to the park, filtered through Rayber's consciousness, we also learn of the fountain's immediate draw for Bishop. When Bishop saw it, he "was flying toward it, his arms flailing like a windmill" (420), and, once in the pool, "the little boy stood there with a look of attention" (421). The characterization of Bishop standing at attention introduces us to the sense of anticipated action he exhibits when around water. Thus in the city park the sun reappears along with water as significant symbols associated with God's approving relationship with Bishop, with the one considered least. As Giannone writes, "The child lives alone and in the poverty of total dependence on God for his dignity." Giannone continues, "God never leaves the child; God is present at the sparkling fountain and God is with Bishop at the blackened lake" (*Hermit* 160).

In addition to being closely associated with the presence of God, Bishop, as an emblem of the least in the kingdom of heaven, also plays unsettling roles in the lives of both Rayber and Tarwater, eliciting from them emotional reactions and making them uncomfortable. Most of the time, Rayber is able to keep his love for Bishop contained, to define Bishop as unimportant and thus ignore his feelings for his son. However, on occasion his love for his son is overwhelming. "The little boy was part of a simple equation that required no further solution, except at the moments when with little or no warning he would feel himself overwhelmed by the horrifying love." The love is described as "powerful enough to throw him to the ground in an act of idiot praise"—a wonderful double entendre suggesting that Rayber would both be praising God the way an idiot might and praising his idiot son— another example of Bishop's mysterious association with the kingdom of heaven. Because Bishop lacks human potential in Rayber's eyes, because his love cannot improve the lot of the one he considers to be among the least of all humanity, Rayber considers his nonutilitarian love for his son as "completely irrational and abnormal" (*CW* 401). While Rayber's relationship with Bishop may trouble him deeply, it is Tarwater who has a complex yet sustained relationship with Bishop marked by physical contact until the moment of the child's death. This sustained contact marks the means by which Tarwater is drawn into the messianic kingdom.

Tarwater's first encounter with Bishop occurs early in the novel. After consulting with a lawyer in the city, Mason takes his great-nephew to Rayber's home. As they approach the house, Tarwater, "knew by some obscure instinct that the door was going to open and reveal his destiny. In his mind's eye, he saw the schoolteacher about to appear in it, lean and evil, waiting to engage whom the Lord would send to conquer him." However, when the door opens, it is not Rayber but Bishop who confronts them. "A small pink-faced boy stood in it with his mouth hung in a silly smile. He had white hair and a knobby forehead. He wore steel-rimmed spectacles and had pale silver eyes like the old man's except that they were clear and empty" (349). Mason looks at Bishop "as if he beheld an unspeakable mystery," but Tarwater perceives the boy as an immediate threat. In a voice "slow" and "emphatic," he tells the boy, "Before you was here, *I* was here" (350).

Tarwater next encounters Bishop following the death and burial of their great-uncle when he returns to the city and makes his way to his uncle's house. Bishop's presence is at first remote, through a telephone call made at the insistence of Meeks, the copper flue salesman with whom Tarwater has hitched a ride. Tarwater hears "what sounded like heavy breathing in his ear" (383). The breathing is heard again by Tarwater in his third encounter with Bishop upon reaching his uncle's house. After a brief conversation with Rayber, he senses his cousin's presence. "He heard a faint familiar sound of heavy breathing. It was closer to him than the beating of his own heart. His eyes widened and an inner door in them opened in preparation for some inevitable vision." A physical description allows the narrative voice to challenge Tarwater's claim that he preceded Bishop and thus takes precedent over him. For, we are told, Bishop "stood there, dim and ancient, like a child who had been a child for centuries" (388). Here O'Connor directly draws upon the relationship between John the Baptist and Jesus. Just as Tarwater precedes Bishop because he is older, so John the Baptist preceded Christ. But the temporal time is supplanted by the eternal nature of Christ. Again, the point is not to transform Bishop into a Christ figure but to associate him closely with the kingdom of heaven, older than the prophetic kingdom of John the Baptist because of its being rooted in the eternal Trinity.

The narrative voice is insistent. We read, "Then the revelation came, silent, implacable, direct as a bullet. Tarwater did not look into the eyes of any fiery beast or see a burning bush. He only knew, with a certainty sunk in despair, that he was expected to baptize the child he saw and begin the life for which his great-uncle had prepared him. He knew he was called to be a prophet and that the ways of his prophecy would not be remarkable" (388–89). Tarwater is both correct and mistaken in his understanding of this vision—correct that he is called to be a prophet—the novel's final scene connecting his call to the callings of Daniel, Elijah, and Moses makes this abundantly clear, mistaken in believing his great-uncle is the one who has prepared him for this life and mistaken in believing the baptism of Bishop will be the essential act of his prophecy. For Tarwater is called not to participate in the prophetic paradigm as exemplified by Mason but to be ushered into the messianic kingdom of Christ through his suffering. Only Bishop can lead him into this kingdom, and Bishop's leading marks the remainder of the relationship between Bishop and Tarwater and culminates in Bishop's death, Tarwater's experience of suffering, and his prophetic call.

That Bishop will take the lead in his relationship with Tarwater is made clear immediately after Tarwater's vision in the doorway of Rayber's house:

The boy heard nothing he said. The muscles in his neck stood out like cables. The dim-witted child was not five feet from him and was coming every instant closer with his lopsided smile. Suddenly he [Tarwater] knew that the child *recognized* him, that the old man himself had primed him from on high that here was the forced servant of God come to see that he was born again. The little boy was sticking out his hand to touch him. (389)

O'Connor's use of the male pronouns is confusing: Who has the old man "primed"? Which boy is "the forced servant of God"? Regardless, the final image is one of Bishop moving toward Tarwater.

The complex relationship between Bishop and Tarwater is made evident in chapter eight as Tarwater reflects on the events at the fountain in the city park, the same scene delivered through the consciousness of Rayber in chapter 6. This second telling of the scene not only calls into question Rayber's interpretation of the action at the fountain, as mentioned above, but also prepares readers for the competing versions of the climactic drowning/baptism scene later when Rayber, Bishop, and Tarwater take a trip to the lake. Unknown to Rayber, Tarwater enters the park with a sense of anticipation. "They had only but entered [the park] when [Tarwater] felt a hush in his blood and a stillness in the atmosphere as if the air were being purged for the approach of revelation." The wooded setting clearly reminds Tarwater of Powderhead. "The trees rustled thickly and the clearing rose to his mind's eye." As they moved closer to the fountain into which Bishop will rush, and, to Rayber, present himself for baptism, Tarwater "began to feel again the approach of mystery" (431). Here, in Tarwater's sense of approaching mystery, follows O'Connor's description of the sun resting like a hand on Bishop's head. Tarwater strongly feels Mason's presence: "The old man might have been lurking near, holding his breath, waiting for the baptism" (432).

Curiously, at this crucial moment, the voice of the stranger, the voice tempting Tarwater to disregard his redemption and resist the old man's influence, does not speak: "His friend was silent as if in the felt presence, he dared not raise his voice" (432). But why should this be so?

The stranger/friend is not silent earlier at Powderhead, and surely the old man's "felt presence" is stronger at Powderhead than now at the fountain in the city park. Perhaps it is not the "felt presence" of Mason that silences the stranger but God's approving hand on Bishop, or perhaps it is the combination of Bishop and the sense that Mason is present that function to silence the stranger. Either way, the stranger is silenced in a way he is not silenced at Powderhead, and the new element in the equation is Bishop with God's approving hand resting on his head.

Although, as Rayber suspects, Tarwater is tempted to move into the fountain and baptize the boy, he says, while "flinging the silent words" at his own face in the water, "I'd drown him first." "Drown him then, the face appeared to say" (432). But Tarwater does not attempt to either baptize or drown the boy at this point. As we recall, when the episode is told through Rayber's consciousness, Rayber places himself in the position of saving both Bishop and Tarwater from this moment of baptism: "Rayber sprang and snatched the child out of the water and set him down, howling, on the concrete" (421). When the episode is given through Tarwater's consciousness, Rayber's agency is removed; Tarwater moves away from the fountain as soon as he contemplates drowning Bishop:

> Tarwater stepped back, shocked. Scowling, he straightened himself and moved away. The sun had gone in and there were black caves in the tree branches. Bishop was lying on his back, roaring from a red distorted face, and the schoolteacher stood above him, staring at nothing in particular as if it were he who had received the revelation." (432–33)

By removing a description of Rayber's agency, the narrative suggests that Bishop's wailing is a direct reaction to Tarwater's refusal to act, Tarwater's refusal to baptize him. The sun's absence at this moment, the "black caves in the tree branches" that earlier had "[p]atches of light sifting through them" (417), may suggest that what God wishes for Bishop and Tarwater has not yet occurred, that some ritual has not yet been enacted. In Matthew, the baptism of Jesus by John the Baptist occurs uninterrupted; in *The Violent Bear It Away* it does not. As we turn to the day at the lake, the narrative of Bishop's last day of life, we see the young boy more aggressively leading his cousin to their final moment together.

SUFFERING VIOLENCE: TARWATER'S TRANSFORMATION

Twice Rayber proclaims of Bishop, "Nothing ever happens to him" (425). The first occasion is in response to the woman tending the reception desk at the Cherokee Lodge who asks whether Bishop can sit still in a boat; the second occurs when Rayber and Tarwater leave Bishop behind on the shore and set out together in the boat. Bishop, as in the scene at the park fountain, is again rushing toward water, this time toward Rayber and Tarwater's boat, but he is kept from falling off the dock by the woman who snatches him up at the last moment. Tarwater tells Rayber, "It wouldn't have been no great loss if he had drowned." And in response Rayber tells him, after a flashback of his attempt to drown Bishop one day at the ocean, "'Nothing ever happens to that kind of child' . . . . 'In a hundred years people may have learned enough to put them to sleep when they're born'" (435).

Rayber is both incorrect and correct about Bishop. He is incorrect because something momentous is about to happen to Bishop, and he is ironically correct in suggesting that nothing ever happens to a boy like Bishop because a boy like Bishop can act. Nothing may happen *to* him, but he may be able to *cause* things to happen, especially in Tarwater's life. This distinction becomes more evident during the scenes at the lake adjacent to the lodge. Behind all of the interchanges between Bishop and Tarwater lurks the relationship between John the Baptist and Jesus and their own scene of baptism, a scene marked by the confusion of just who should be baptizing whom. Jesus comes to be baptized, "But John tried to prevent Him, saying, 'I have need to be baptized by You, and do you come to me?'" (Matthew 3:14). The role reversal between Jesus and John should prepare readers for the ambiguous lake scene between Bishop and Tarwater.

On their way to the Cherokee Lodge and early in their stay, Bishop had continued his relentless pursuit of Tarwater. In the car, Rayber could see, "Bishop's face rise unorganized into the rearview mirror and then disappear as he attempted to crawl over the top of the front seat and climb into Tarwater's lap. The boy had turned and without looking at him had given the panting child a firm push onto the back seat again" (*CW* 423). Once at the lodge, "Tarwater came quickly around the side of the building with the distinct look to Rayber of being pursued" (424) by Bishop. As Tarwater filled out the registration card, he momentarily loses track of Bishop. "He was so taken up" with reviewing his registration, "that he did not see the little boy reaching out to touch him. The instant the child touched him, the country boy's shoulders leapt. He snatched his touched hand up and jammed it in his pocket. 'Leave off!' he said in a high voice. 'Git away and quit bothering me!'" (426).

Tarwater's violent reaction to Bishop's touch—reminiscent of the Misfit's reaction to the touch of the grandmother in "A Good Man Is Hard to Find"—makes the following episode between Tarwater and Bishop on the stairs even more startling. The episode makes sense—perhaps only makes sense—when read in the context of Matthew's narrative. When Tarwater tells Bishop to quit bothering him, the woman at the lodge hisses at him saying, "Mind how you talk to one of them there, you boy!" (*CW* 426). When Tarwater asks, "Them there what?" (426), the woman answers, "'That there kind,' . . . looking at him fiercely as if he had profaned the holy" (427). The woman's sense of Bishop as one of "the holy" suggests his place in the kingdom of heaven, again marking him as one of "the least" considered by Jesus as superior to John the Baptist. The woman's words bring a change to Tarwater who "seemed to see the little boy and nothing else, no air around him, no room, no nothing, as if his gaze had slipped and fallen into the center of the child's eyes and was still falling down and down and down." Bishop skips off with Tarwater, following "so directly that he might have been attached to him by a tow-line" (427). Bishop leads Tarwater up the stairs and "[t]hen suddenly he [Bishop] flipped himself around and sat down squarely in the country boy's way and stuck his feet out in front of him, apparently wanting his shoes tied." The woman who is watching feels certain that Tarwater will not tie Bishop's shoes. "He ain't going to tie them, she said, not him" (427). She has no reason to believe Tarwater will aid the boy, and readers have even less reason to expect Tarwater to tie Bishop's shoes. After all, Tarwater has reacted violently to Bishop's touch twice before on this same day. So why does Tarwater tie the boy's shoes? In Matthew, John the Baptist tells the Pharisees and Sadducees, "As for me, I baptize you with water for repentance, but He who is coming after me is mightier than I, and I am not fit to remove His sandals; He will baptize you with the Holy Spirit and fire" (3:11).

This is one of O'Connor's masterful strokes. Tarwater, raised by a wilderness prophet much like John the Baptist, is indeed not fit to untie Bishop's sandals, so he does the opposite and ties them, thereby signaling Bishop's preeminence. By so doing, he places himself in the position of a servant kneeling before the boy. The act also alludes to Jesus washing the feet of his disciples as recorded in the gospels. The act of foot washing, one of the great emblems of the messianic kingdom, is a clear sign that the kingdom of heaven is a kingdom marked by servanthood, a kingdom where the first are last and the last, first. Tarwater's actions perplex the woman watching who, "[c]onfused by this kindness," intends to ask him, "Whose boy are you?" (*CW* 427). The question remains unasked and, therefore, unanswered. But Tarwater, sensing the danger he is in because he senses himself being drawn ever closer to Bishop, tries to resist the draw by once again claiming his distinction based on his own ability to act.

As he consistently does during such moments in the novel, Tarwater claims protection in his ability to act, to negate Bishop's and Mason's influence by the force of his will. In response to the woman who warns him against doing devil's work at her lodge, Tarwater says, "You can't just say NO . . . . You got to do NO. You got to show it. You got to show you mean it by doing it, You got to show you're not going to do one thing by doing another. You got to make an end of it. One way or another" (427–28). Readers know this is a hollow boast based on a faulty assumption. Tarwater believes that he has burned his greatuncle's body when he has not. If he now acts to negate the influence of Mason and Bishop, it will be the first time he has accomplished such an action rather than an action informed and inspired by previous forceful action.

Although Tarwater senses that his uncle has a plan to try to trap him against his will, Tarwater's "mind was entirely occupied with saving himself from the larger, grander trap that he felt set all about him." The narrative voice provides a detailed description of this trap. "It was a strange waiting silence. It seemed to lie all around him like an invisible country whose borders he was always on the edge of, always in danger of crossing." Tarwater thinks back to walks in the city when his form appeared "transparent as a snakeskin"; the narrative voice tells us, "It moved beside him like some violent ghost who had already crossed over and was reproaching him from the other side." This silent country is closely associated with Bishop. "If he turned his head the opposite way," during these city walks,

> there would be the dim-witted boy, hanging onto the schoolteacher's coat, watching him. His mouth hung in a lopsided smile but there was a judging sternness about his forehead. The boy never looked lower than the top of his head except by accident for the silent country appeared to be reflected again in the center of his eyes. It stretched out there, limitless and clear. (429)

It is tempting here to associate Bishop's country with Mason's prophetic kingdom. But conflating Bishop into Mason and assuming that this "country" is the country they both occupy is far too easy. Doing so undervalues the differences between the old man and the "idiot" child. Mason is a man of violent action. The boy is one who suffers violence and experiences neglect, especially from his own father. Perhaps the country Tarwater sees reflected in Bishop's eyes is not the world of the prophetic paradigm, the world of his great-uncle, but instead the world of suffering and loss, the world where one absorbs affliction without retaliation and as a means of leading those who act in violence to a measure of redemption. In other words, perhaps the "country" is the messianic kingdom inaugurated by Jesus and represented in Tarwater's life by Bishop.

At the Cherokee Lodge, the stranger whose voice Tarwater has not heard since shortly after Mason's death intervenes again to aid Tarwater's resistance to the country he sees reflected in Bishop's eyes. His message to Tarwater confirms, by means of contrast, the nature of the kingdom of suffering love. When the stranger speaks, he is identified with leading Tarwater to action and is described as the one "who had kept [Tarwater] company while he dug his uncle's grave" (430). The stranger does not try to get Tarwater to discount his redemption as he did when Tarwater was digging the grave but rather tries to pull Tarwater back into a prophetic paradigm. "If you are a prophet," the stranger tells him, "it's only right you should be treated like one." The lure of the messianic kingdom exemplified by Bishop is not countered by secularism but by the supplanted prophetic kingdom associated with Mason. The equivalent in Matthew's gospel would be for John to reject Jesus and maintain that his understanding of the kingdom of heaven is sufficient and correct. Tarwater is tempted to associate himself not with Rayber but with Mason. The hunger he has been experiencing since leaving Powderhead is discounted by the stranger who "was adamant that he refuse to entertain hunger as a sign" (430), because for a prophet the sign is insufficient. However, hungering and thirsting for righteousness, for the values of the kingdom of heaven, is one of the beatitudes articulated by Jesus during the Sermon on the Mount (Matthew 5:6). Thus, such hunger is an appropriate symbol of the kingdom of heaven, represented in the novel by Bishop, not Mason.

When Rayber and Tarwater are alone on the lake, their conversation ends abruptly when Rayber tells the teenager he resembles Mason. "You're just like him. You have his future before you" (*CW* 439). In a scene reminiscent of Peter's actions recorded in John 21, Tarwater dives out of the fishing boat and swims to shore. In the gospel account, Peter swims toward the risen Christ. Tarwater's destination is Bishop, his motivation being Rayber's claim that his future is Mason's. The episode provides yet another example of the pull Tarwater feels, unacknowledged though it is, away from the prophetic kingdom of Mason and toward the messianic kingdom of Bishop. Indeed, when Rayber comes to shore, he is surprised at the evidence of a new relationship between Tarwater and Bishop. "When he came in, he was startled to see Tarwater lying on the far cot in his new clothes and to see Bishop sitting on the other end of it, watching him as if he were mesmerized by the steel-like glint that came from the boy's eyes and was directed into his own" (439–40). The narrative voice tells us Tarwater's body seems filled with excitement, "as if he had settled on an inevitable course of action." Now Tarwater is no longer ignoring Bishop. Now he looks "back at Bishop, triumphantly, boldly, into the very center of his eyes" (440).

Before the final interaction between Tarwater and Bishop, Rayber makes a final if half-hearted attempt to "save" his nephew, to convert him to the kind of rational self-control used by Rayber to contain the irrational love he feels for Bishop. Bishop's and Tarwater's interaction resumes after Rayber has taken his son to Powderhead, given Tarwater the gift of the corkscrew–bottle opener, and confronted Tarwater during a meal at the lodge. After receiving Rayber's gift in the room that they share, Tarwater, "returned his attention to Bishop as if this were its natural place" (447). He commands Bishop to follow him, and Bishop obeys, convincing Rayber that Tarwater's plan is to make a slave of the boy.

At the lodge restaurant, Rayber is confronted by the dancers who gaze at Bishop "as if they had been betrayed by a fault in creation, something that should have been corrected before they were allowed to see it." He is angered by their reaction to his son in part because it too closely resembles his own position. He is further angered because his reaction allows Tarwater to more fully recognize Rayber's disdain for Bishop. Tarwater "was looking directly at him with an omniscient smile, faint but decided. It was a smile that Rayber had seen on his face before. It seemed to mock him from an ever-deepening inner knowledge that grew in indifference as it came nearer and nearer to a secret truth about him" (448). Part of this truth is that Rayber disdains his son; however, a part also is that Tarwater seems to now understand how much Bishop moves Rayber, how much Rayber loves the boy. But Tarwater still believes that his decisive action, his killing of Bishop, will forever set him apart from Rayber and free him into a world of individual autonomy and self-determination. He does not recognize that Bishop plays a role in his life similar to the role he plays in Rayber's life, representing for them both an alternative way of being in the world.

At the lodge Tarwater's relationship with Bishop also takes a new turn. Tarwater

walked off, across the room to the screen door where he stood looking out. At once Bishop climbed down off his chair and started after him, putting on his hat as he went. Tarwater stiffened when the child approached but he did not move and Rayber watched as the two of them stood there side by side, looking out the door—the two figures, hatted and somehow ancient, bound together by some necessity of nerve that excluded him. He was startled to see the boy put his hand on Bishop's neck just under his hat, open the door and guide him out of it. (452)

Once again, Rayber misunderstands the interaction between Tarwater and Bishop, and perhaps too many readers have read the scene influenced by Rayber's perspective. Rayber is now quite certain that Tarwater plans to make a slave of Bishop and believes "Bishop would be at his command like a faithful dog" (452). And this should be the case, for Tarwater has never been more sure of himself than he is in this moment, never more sure he will be able to act, to drown Bishop and free himself from both Mason's and Bishop's control.

What is most interesting about this passage is the observation by Rayber that the two boys are "bound together by some necessity of nerve." Rayber does what he rarely does in relationship to Bishop—he assigns agency to the boy. The "necessity of nerve" is apparently something both boys share, something that binds them together but excludes Rayber. Both boys are now described as "somehow ancient," belonging to a world excluding Rayber. O'Connor uses Rayber's observation to prepare the reader for a portrayal of a much more assertive Bishop and to challenge Tarwater's misplaced confidence in his ability to act in defiance of Mason and Bishop. The difference between the two boys is that, now, Tarwater no longer resists Bishop's advances because he believes that he is in control of the situation. But his belief is built on the assumption that he can act, an assumption the reader knows is faulty.

Rayber, following Bishop and Tarwater out of the restaurant, notices a subtle but significant change between the two boys: "The two were in front of him half way down the dock, walking slowly, Tarwater's hand still resting just under Bishop's hat; but it seemed to Rayber that it was Bishop who was doing the leading, that the child had made the capture" (452). Once again, the agency denied to Bishop earlier in the novel is established as O'Connor prepares the reader for the novel's most significant scene—Bishop's baptism and drowning. And this time Tarwater and Bishop go out in the boat, and it is Rayber who is left behind. When the baptism and drowning scene is first introduced to the reader, it is presented in a most cryptic way. Rayber, awakening from a nap and realizing Tarwater and Bishop are still out on the lake, anticipates the death of Bishop, assumes Tarwater will drown his son even while saying words of baptism over him. Because we first experience Bishop's death as it affects Rayber, it is a challenge to read the later, more detailed, account of the events with an eye for the detail O'Connor provides. Such close attention, however, is essential if we are to understand the conclusion of O'Connor's novel.

A narrative jump occurs between the ending of chapter 9 and the beginning of chapter 10. Bishop is dead, and Tarwater has fled from Cherokee Lodge on his way to Powderhead. When a truck driver picks him up and insists that the hitchhiker talk to keep him awake, Tarwater attempts to speak. "There were queer ups and downs in his voice as if he were using it for the first time after some momentous failure" (457). What is initially unclear is the true nature of Tarwater's failure. To the truck driver, Tarwater says, "I drowned a boy" and "I baptized him." As if to once again underscore Bishop's status in his culture as a being of little value, as one of "the least," the truck driver responds to the news of Tarwater's drowning of a boy with the flippant question, "Just one?" (458). Like the truck driver, Tarwater still has little apparent regard for Bishop. His primary concern is not that he killed the boy but that, without meaning to, he said words of baptism over him. The plan Tarwater constructs in response to his actions is clear. He is returning to Powderhead, a spot he thinks he never should have left. But, in spite of his momentary lapse, in spite of the spoken words of baptism, he is returning triumphant. He has proven to himself, once again, that he can act. He believes he has burned his great-uncle's body, and now he believes he has drowned Bishop by an act of his will. Readers have known from the start of the novel that Tarwater is mistaken about the first expression of his will. They are about to learn he is at least partially mistaken about the second incident as well.

The truck driver, disappointed that the boy's conversation—even his confession of murder—is not enough to keep him awake, pulls to the shoulder of the road and falls asleep. As Tarwater seems suspended between sleep and wakefulness, O'Connor's narrative voice establishes the context in which a more detailed telling of the incident at the lake will be given:

> The boy sat quietly on his side of the cab. His eyes were open wide without the least look of sleep in them. They seemed not to be able to close but to open forever on some sight that would never leave them. Presently they closed but his body did not relax. He sat rigidly upright, a still alert expression on his face as if under the closed lids an inner eye were watching, piercing out the truth in the distortion of his dream. (461)

O'Connor, I would argue, by using this dream state, is freeing her narrative voice from Tarwater's controlling consciousness. What follows then is as close to an omniscient narrative voice as we experience in her fiction.

While Bishop and Tarwater are alone on the lake, the stranger's presence is made known, "standing like a guide in the boat." The stranger counsels Tarwater to "[b]e a man, . . . be a man. It's only one dimwit you have to drown." But this counsel occurs only after Bishop has taken the initial action leading to his drowning and baptism. "Bishop took off his hat and threw it over the side where it floated right-side-up, black on the surface of the lake." Under the stranger's counsel, Tarwater, "edged the boat toward the dark clump of bushes and tied it. Then he removed his shoes, put the contents of his pockets into his hat and put the hat into one shoe, while all the time the grey eyes [of Bishop] were fixed on him as if they were waiting serenely for a struggle already determined" (462). Removing his shoes is simply a practical matter for Tarwater, but in this story of God and prophets, we must not forget the command God gives to Moses when Moses confronts the burning bush.[7] Apparently, the business about to be enacted here is holy in some way, and Bishop is described as serenely awaiting the outcome.

The next paragraph gives us as much as we can know about what happened on the lake between these two cousins:

The water slid out from the bank like a broad black tongue. He climbed out of the boat and stood still, feeling the mud between his toes and the wet clinging around his legs. The sky dotted with fixed tranquil eyes like the spread tail of some celestial night bird. While he stood there gazing, for the moment lost, the child in the boat stood up, caught him around the neck and climbed onto his back. He clung there like a large crab to a twig and the startled boy felt himself sinking backwards into the water as if the whole bank were pulling him down. (462)

Tarwater wakes in the cab of the truck with a start. But, we are told, "He might have been Jonah clinging wildly to the whale's tongue" (462). That is, he might have been a prophet still resisting the call of God, hoping to remain in the belly of the whale. Following as it does the account of the drowning/baptism, the scene indicates Tarwater's resistance not to the world of his great-uncle, Mason, but to the world of suffering associated with Bishop.

Bishop's agency in this key scene is striking. It is Bishop who throws his hat onto the water, Bishop, when Tarwater is gazing in wonder at the beauty of the natural world, who climbs out of the boat and onto Tarwater's back, catching him around the neck. Just as she does earlier when she uses a direct simile to describe the hand of God resting on Bishop's head, O'Connor here rejects her "as if" construction for a simile, a powerful image of Bishop's agency. Bishop, not simply like a crab on a twig, "but like a large crab to a twig," clings to Tarwater's back. In this configuration, the two boys are pulled down into the water. But it is Bishop who is placed in the position traditionally held by the ordained minister or priest, the position of one guiding Tarwater into the water.

Without question Tarwater drowns Bishop and speaks the words of baptism. Nevertheless, we should not under-appreciate the agency of Bishop in this moment. In a very real sense, Bishop baptizes Tarwater; Bishop leads Tarwater into a country he knows quite well, a country of suffering and pain and often unacknowledged love from others. Bishop opens Tarwater's eyes "forever on some sight that would never leave them" (461). Bishop accomplishes his own needed baptism as well. If Bishop indeed has agency at this time, he is asserting his humanity, asserting that he too needs to be ushered into the messianic kingdom. Remarkably, he takes Tarwater with him into that kingdom, giving him the vulnerability to accept such a kingdom. Tarwater's helplessness in his encounter with the rapist in chapter eleven places him in the vulnerable world that Bishop has always inhabited, the world John the Baptist experiences when he is imprisoned and eventually beheaded.

The novel's final chapter, recounting Tarwater's return to Powderhead, is infused with images of the messianic kingdom taken primarily from Matthew's gospel. After encountering Buford Munson and learning that Mason has been buried and not burned, Tarwater has a vision of a multitude filling the field that Buford has just crossed.[8] The field, "it seemed to him," was "no longer empty but peopled with a multitude. Everywhere, he saw dim figures seated on the slope and as he gazed he saw that from a single basket the throng was being fed" (477). In the gospel, Matthew places the narrative of the feeding of the five thousand directly after the narrative of the death of John the Baptist and the final end of the prophetic paradigm (Matthew 14:13–21). In addition, only Matthew and Mark tell of two crowds being fed. Matthew places the two narratives close to each other (the feeding of the four thousand is related in 15:32–39). It is the feeding of the hungry multitude that Matthew associates with the paradigm shift from the time of John the Baptist to the time of Jesus. The images O'Connor employs are thus appropriate to signal Tarwater's movement from the prophetic paradigm associated with John the Baptist to the paradigm of the kingdom of heaven.

But Tarwater is not satisfied with the vision he sees of the multitude being fed until he can find Mason within it. "His eyes searched the crowd for a long time as if he could not find the one he was looking for. Then he saw him. The old man was lowering himself to the ground. When he was down and his bulk had settled, he leaned forward, his face turned toward the basket, impatiently following the progress toward him" (*CW* 477–78). This is a new image of Mason. He is no longer the prophet of God raging against humanity. He is now one of the multitude waiting to be fed by Jesus—even if he is waiting impatiently. It would be a mistake to read this scene as Tarwater's return to the paradigm of his great-uncle. Rather, the striking images of the messianic kingdom suggest that, like his great-nephew, Mason has been ushered into the messianic kingdom, that in his death he has suffered the loss of agency and borne in his body the suffering of the Messiah who died and was raised to life again.

Burning the woods, therefore, becomes emblematic of Tarwater leaving behind Mason's prophetic paradigm (as well as destroying the economic potential of the property so valued by Rayber, who sees in the lumber his economic security). The messianic kingdom, symbolized as a mustard seed in Matthew 13:31–32, has been planted in Tarwater's life. "He threw himself to the ground and with his face against the dirt of the grave, he heard the command GO WARN THE CHILDREN OF GOD OF THE TERRIBLE SPEED OF MERCY" (*CW* 478). Unlike his sometimes violent relatives, Bishop lived his life under this mercy, repeatedly suffering violence—often at the hands of those most closely related to him.[9] In his death, he has managed to help his cousin make the transition from Mason's prophetic kingdom to the messianic kingdom of heaven.

NOTES

1. My reading of the Gospel of Matthew is profoundly shaped by the Rev. Reuben Welch and the Rev. Steve Rodeheaver who led me and others in a close study of the text. I am indebted to both men and to those who participated in the Bible study with me. Of course, I am fully responsible for the reading presented here.

2. Suzanne Morrow Paulson is one example of a critic who downplays Bishop's role. She writes, "An odyssey toward madness rather than salvation, the novel begins with the death of Mason Tarwater and ends with the grotesque 'resurrection' as old Tarwater's will takes over the psyche of his young nephew, Francis" (121). Such an analysis need pay little attention to Bishop. See Paulson 121–38. In contrast, Christina Bieber Lake writes of Bishop, "He is the cause of conflict, the generator of violence, the locus of the sacred. Although criticism has tended to minimize Bishop's importance in the novel by treating Tarwater's call as merely the vestiges of the old man's vision, O'Connor's prose illustrates the clear centrality of the character as one that represents the divine mystery with which Tarwater will have to come to terms before he can begin his ministry" (147).

3. This is not the first time that I have argued for the significance of Bishop in the novel, but the argument has developed over time. See Martin 27–38.

4. Ferris 85–91.

5. This and all subsequent quotations from Matthew are taken from the New American Standard Bible.

6. That O'Connor does not intend Bishop to be seen as a Christ figure is supported by the scene early in the novel in which Bishop is "gnawing on a brown apple core" (*CW* 349) signifying him as among the fallen. In other words, whatever innocence he may possess, it is not the innocence of Adam and Eve before the fall. I am indebted to my colleague Jenny Bangsund for this insight.

7. "Take off your sandals, for the place where you are standing is holy ground" (Exodus 3:5).

8. This is one of several places in the novel where Buford is marked as another of "the least" in the eyes of the other characters, marked as an emblem of the messianic kingdom.

9. For an excellent discussion of the violence of the family, see Ciuba 148–51.

WORKS CITED

Ciuba, Gary M. *Desire, Violence, and Divinity in Modern Southern Fiction.* Baton Rouge: Louisiana State Press, 2007.

Ferris, Summer J. "The Outside and the Inside: Flannery O'Connor's *The Violent Bear It Away.*" *Critical Essays on Flannery O'Connor.* Ed. Melvin J. Friedman and Beverly Lyon Clark. Boston: G. K. Hall, 1985. 85–91.

Giannone, Richard. *Flannery O'Connor and the Mystery of Love.* Urbana: University of Illinois Press, 1989.

———. *Flannery O'Connor, Hermit Novelist.* Urbana: University of Illinois Press, 2000.

Lake, Christina Bieber. *The Incarnational Art of Flannery O'Connor.* Macon, GA: Mercer University Press, 2005.

Martin, Karl. "Bishop's Role in Flannery O'Connor's *The Violent Bear It Away.*" *Literature and Belief* 16.1 (1996): 27–38.

New American Standard Bible. Grand Rapids, MI: Zondervan, 1995.

O'Connor, Flannery. *Collected Works.* Ed. Sally Fitzgerald. New York: Library of America, 1988.

Paulson, Suzanne Morrow. "Apocalypse of Self, Resurrection of the Double: Flannery O'Connor's *The Violent Bear It Away.*" *Flannery O'Connor: New Perspectives.* Ed. Sura P. Rath and Mary Neff Shaw. Athens: University of Georgia Press, 1996. 121–38.

Srigley, Susan. *Flannery O'Connor's Sacramental Art.* Notre Dame, IN: University of Notre Dame Press, 2004.

CHAPTER 9

Asceticism and Abundance

The Communion of Saints in
The Violent Bear It Away

SUSAN SRIGLEY

I came that they may have life, and have it abundantly.

—John 10:10

The old man said that as soon as he died, he would hasten to the banks of the Lake of Galilee to eat the loaves and fishes that the Lord had multiplied.

—Flannery O'Connor, *The Violent Bear It Away*

The Violent Bear It Away opens with the death of Mason Tarwater, and the drama quickly turns to the dilemma of his great-nephew, Francis Marion Tarwater. He has been left with his great-uncle's words ringing in his ears: "[W]hen I die . . . get me in the ground where the dead belong and set up a cross over me to show I'm there" (*VBA* 15). Mason wants a proper Christian burial, and it is up to the young Tarwater to "do it right" (11). However, immediately following this opening sequence focused on Mason's death and his dying wish to Tarwater there appears a recollection of Mason's life, and in particular how he has struggled with his prophetic calling. By framing the story of Mason's life with his death and narrating his ongoing presence with Tarwater after that death, O'Connor foreshadows a major theme for the novel: the relation between life and death, or, more precisely, the *relationships* between the living and the dead and the spiritual ties that bind them. O'Connor would identify this ongoing relation with the Christian notion of the communion of saints, and she took it to be the heart of a truly spiritual community, a community whose essential interdependence reflects the principle that all human beings are created in the image of God. This communion is an affirmation of the body and the soul, of the personal and the communal, both as human beings live together in the present, and in the continuing mystery of the connection of lives beyond death.

For O'Connor, the assertion of personhood within Christianity signals one of the tradition's most remarkable and distinguishing features. She writes to Elizabeth Hester,[1] "The great difference between Christianity and the Eastern religions is the Christian insistence on the fulfillment of the individual person . . ." (*HB* 458). However, this is never an individual fulfillment achieved at the expense of the communal. It must, she recognizes, be *both*. In *The Violent Bear It Away*, O'Connor dramatically portrays this dual emphasis that runs throughout much of her work but is especially apparent in this novel: both the idea of fulfillment for the *person*—namely Tarwater's desire to find his own vocation (independently of Mason's prophecies)—and the *communal* aspect of fulfillment, which must expand to include the desires of others (notably Mason's) as evidenced in his final vision of the messianic banquet.

Tarwater's desire propels him toward the feast that will truly satisfy *his* hunger, but he arrives to a shared communion: a multitude is gathered with enough food to satisify *all*. The eucharistic banquet, or eternal feast, suggests *abundance*,[2] and divine abundance allows for individual and communal fulfillment. The spiritual kinship between the living and the dead reveals the reality of individuals who live with their own desires in relation to the divine and yet who also must live with others. The communal does not negate the personal, but neither does the personal live outside of its obligations to the community. Instead, the personal comes to completion and true fulfillment in the communal, fed by the life-giving gifts of God. In one of her essays, O'Connor reflects on the action of charity, which she describes as "growing invisibly among us, entwining the living and the dead," an image she identifies with the cross at the end of the novel as Tarwater looks at the grave of his great-uncle Mason (*VBA* 240). Notice the description of love: growing, entwining, ever mindful of both the living and the dead. O'Connor defines this expansive action of love as the communion of saints (*MM* 228).

The image of the communion of saints as defined by O'Connor gives us insight into her vision of love, asceticism, and abundance in *The Violent Bear It Away*. It is a vision of love that is necessarily paradoxical. Tarwater's vision at the end of the novel is a feast of bread and fish shared by the living and the dead, the abundance of love flowing from divine plenitude. How can this eucharistic image be reconciled with the rest of the *The Violent Bear It Away*, the very title of which provokes us to think about violence and renunciation? While this final vision suggests abundance and community, a palpable and often violent force persists throughout the novel animating and impinging on each of the characters. Mason experiences raging visions (*VBA* 4–5), wrestles with the Lord (8), and reminds Tarwater that "even the mercy of the Lord burns" (20). Rayber lives a life of "rigid ascetic discipline" (114), unable to "[conquer] the problem of Bishop" (112), and Tarwater violently resists both Mason and Rayber at every turn, kills Bishop, and is himself raped by a stranger.

Rayber's explanation of this propensity for violence is the shared affliction in the family bloodline, which flowed from "some ancient source, some desert prophet or polesitter": "Those it touched were condemned to fight it constantly or be ruled by it. The old man had been ruled by it. He, at the cost of a full life, staved it off. What the boy [Tarwater] would do hung in the balance" (*VBA* 114). Indeed, at the crux of his discernment, Tarwater exemplifies how O'Connor holds these apparently antithetical ideas of abundance and asceticism in tension. If his vision of the abundant feast at the end of *The Violent Bear It Away* is to be interpreted within the context of the whole novel, it must be considered in relation to the violence of the various ascetic practices throughout. Is there a way to see the abundance of love in the midst of the violence of love, which is characterized by O'Connor as requiring an asceticism more severe than John the Baptist's?[3] Can the idea of the communion of saints lead us to a vision of love that is both ascetic and abundant? How does O'Connor reconcile the idea of self-renunciation and the possibility of self-fulfillment? Is there any personal fulfillment for Tarwater as he smears dirt on his forehead and heads toward the city to join the children of God?

I would suggest that O'Connor sees this double movement of re-nunciation and fulfillment as possible only through an expanded vi-sion of both individuality and community that extends from the living to the dead and back again. For Tarwater, finally discovering the object of his spiritual hunger in the shared feast reveals a new model of fulfill-ment that is both personal and communal, one that extends beyond his individual desire through an increased capacity to see himself in rela-tion to others. Throughout the novel, O'Connor highlights the force-fulness of the competing visions of reality that plague Tarwater, visions that seem invariably in tension with each other. Mason's lessons and view of the world represent the pull toward communal responsibility, and Rayber, among others, urges Tarwater to fulfill his individual de-sires first and foremost. Tarwater appears caught between two choices proffered by his two uncles: abandoning himself (and his own desires) to communal interests and responsibility or affirming his independ-ence and autonomy, driven by the selfish will. If we are to take the devil's word for it (assuming for the moment that the voice of the friend is the devil), then the devil sets the terms for this choice: "Jesus or you" (*VBA* 39).[4] Yet there remains another option signaled by the end of the novel, which neither sinks into the isolation of the selfish will nor en-tirely abandons personal desire (something crucial for the recognition of personhood): namely, the recognition of human interdependence, and the willingness to restrain the selfish will for the service of the larger community.

ELIZABETH HESTER, ONE OF O'CONNOR'S CLOSEST FRIENDS and best readers, also wondered about the consistency of self-renunciation and self-fulfillment and raised this issue with O'Connor in their correspondence. How is it possible to satisfy the disciplining of desire and experience its fulfillment at the same time? In response to Hester's letters, O'Connor is often in the position of clarifying her ideas about asceticism, always careful to describe self-sacrifice *not* as an annihilation of the self but as the disciplining of self-interest, done for a greater good. O'Connor writes, "I don't assume that renunciation goes with submission, or even that renunciation is good in itself. Always you renounce a less good for a greater; the opposite is what sin is" (*HB* 126). Renunciation is not equated with submission. Renunciation is not a good in itself. The point, reflects O'Connor, is to renounce a lesser good for a greater good. One can infer from O'Connor's tone in these responses that Hester must have found O'Connor's language of self-renunciation to be limiting and problematic for the individual person's sense of selfhood and personal fulfillment. Arguably Hester would have felt that this was true even more so for women. To take Hester's letters seriously and raise a similar question, one might wonder what O'Connor was at pains to reveal, repeatedly, in these discussions about self-sacrifice and renunciation. What kind of fulfillment *is* possible in the face of certain forms of ascetic discipline? To address this, it is necessary first to consider O'Connor's account of asceticism in relation to *The Violent Bear It Away* and the novel's biblical epigraph.

O'Connor identifies the phrase "the violent bear it away" in the biblical epigraph with asceticism. She says, "This is surely what it means to bear away the kingdom of heaven with violence: the violence is directed inward" (*HB* 486). In an unpublished letter to LaTrelle Blackburn Oliver (14 February 1963), O'Connor suggests that Matthew 11:12 describes "the kind of passion for the things of God which makes asceticism possible."[5] Asceticism often appears (or *feels*) "violent" when it entails the *restraint* of individual, perhaps selfish, desires for the sake of someone or something else. But a *passion* (for God) is ultimately what drives it. What she calls the "violence of love," therefore, is a violence that is absorbed into or by the self, an ascetic disciplining of the will that is grounded in the Christian idea of *agape* (love that serves the other).[6]

Such ascetic self-discipline does not mean erasing the self. O'Connor is not a Manichean dualist, and this is not a matter of sacrificing the physical *for* the spiritual. As Robert H. Brinkmeyer Jr. rightly notes, "O'Connor believed otherwise, asserting that in approaching the ideal, artist and believer must remain firmly engaged with the world and the body, enduring *and* celebrating humanity's trials with an asceticism of temptation and resistance" (182). In the language of the gospels, self-sacrificial love is a dying to self, or as O'Connor puts it, "self-abandonment"—not to be confused with self-torture or the refusal to be oneself, but instead a "forgetting" of self for the sake of another (*HB* 457–58). O'Connor affirms both the abandonment of self and the fulfillment of that same self in one letter; she argues that a truer form of self-fulfillment is found when one gets beyond the constraints of selfish desire. To get beyond the constraints of the ego affords a freedom to more truly be oneself. Self-sacrifice is not meant to destroy, it is meant to facilitate love, and that in turn is always in relation to others. As Richard Giannone notes of those ancient Christian ascetics whose ideas continue to live in O'Connor's fiction, "The desert ascesis of dying to oneself aims for a rebirth of love of others in God" (*Hermit* 165). Selfish love bars the way to really being able to love the other, hindered as it is by personal interest and individual needs. What orders the asceticism, therefore, makes all the difference for the outcome of its action.

In *The Violent Bear It Away,* the ascetic practices of each character are a response to the madness of divine love that lives in the inherited Tarwater blood: for Tarwater, the spiritual hunger for the bread of life that plagues him, and for Rayber, the mystical love that threatens to throw him down in an act of idiot praise (*VBA* 113). In order to fight these impulses, what kind of asceticism is required? Tarwater wants to "see no more than what was in front of his face and to let his eyes stop at the surface of that," thereby avoiding the "threatened intimacy of creation" (21–22). Ultimately, he rejects any form of spiritual or earthly communion and he fights his hunger assiduously. Rayber's "ascetic" life is intended to discipline himself against his love of Bishop, essentially not to feel anything that may overwhelm his self-control; thus, he too rejects the possibility of spiritual communion. When asceticism is lived in isolation and directed against love, as in the case of Rayber, it ends up being closer to self-torture and annihilation than does asceticism done out of love. By contrast, O'Connor dramatizes how Tarwater's struggle *evolves* as he moves toward finding a meaningful connection between his individual desires and the curbing of those desires for the sake of others.

For both Rayber and Tarwater, Mason is the dead man remembered throughout the narrative, and the conjoining of his life, death and the Eucharist are foreshadowed as he lies in his pine coffin, his large stomach raised above the top, "like over-leavened bread" (13): the bread of life in abundance brimming over the reality of death. O'Connor brings the Eucharist and death together, in agreement with a Catholic theologian familiar to her, Karl Rahner, who in his *Foundations of Christian Faith* describes the Last Supper this way: "The idea of death is of decisive importance: Jesus accepts his fate consciously and connects it with the central content of his preaching. Moreover, Jesus understands this meal in an eschatological way as an anticipation of the joy of the final and definitive banquet" (qtd. in Dych 120). O'Connor would be conscious of this theological understanding, and the eucharistic themes culminating in the vision of the final messianic banquet of *The Violent Bear It Away* are its literary illustration. To Ted Spivey she wrote, "You miss a great deal of what is in my book, my feeling for the old man particularly, because the Eucharist does not mean the same to you as it does to me" (*HB* 387). Herein she is very clearly connecting her feeling for Mason directly to the Eucharist, and she elaborates the point by suggesting that "[t]here are two main symbols in the book—water and the bread that Christ is. The whole action of the novel is Tarwater's selfish will against all that the little lake (the baptismal font) and the bread stand for. This book is a very minor hymn to the Eucharist" (387).

The communion of saints is made possible by love, facilitated by the ascetic impulse and based on the recognition that human beings are capable of sharing the suffering and joy of others. Why else would someone take on the suffering of others, and burden themselves with this suffering, except out of love? The communion of saints, O'Connor says, "has something to do with the fact that the burdens we bear *because* of someone else, we can also bear *for* someone else" (178). There is a mutual sharing of responsibility within the spiritual community, and O'Connor affirms that while human beings can suffer by the will of another, they can, by the same token, also share in the sufferings on behalf of another or for others.

When O'Connor is the sponsor for Elizabeth Hester's entry into the Church she makes this spiritual communion clear through their mutual participation in the Eucharist one Sunday morning at their respective churches: "you will know that your being where you are increases me and the other way around" (150). While this may be a more positive example of sharing in spiritual communion, she also makes the same claim in response to Hester's (unpublished) letter of the grief and difficulty she has had in her life as a closeted lesbian. O'Connor assures her in a letter of 31 October 1956: "I have a tendency to dismiss other people's torments out of hand and this one, being yours, will have to be partly mine too," and further, "If in any sense my knowing your burden can make your burden lighter, then I am doubly glad I know it."[7] For O'Connor, then, love is the reality that joins the personal and the communal; it supports the burden of responsibility for others in their suffering and their joy. At the heart of the idea of the communion of saints is the value of the *individual person,* held and sustained by God's love. So too this spiritual sustenance fosters the *communion* of all relationships. The abundance of divine love feeds a spiritual kinship that extends to the living and the dead, unlimited by human categories and irrespective of physical or intellectual ability.

A WORLD TRANSFIGURED: MASON

> I believe and the Church teaches that God is as present in the idiot boy as in the genius.
> —Flannery O'Connor, *The Habit of Being*

There is no question that O'Connor creates the character of Bishop in *The Violent Bear It Away* in order to express the radical nature of her vision of spiritual communion. The spiritual value of the idiot child is equal to the spiritual value of the genius, she avers and even more radi-cally perhaps, the spiritual value of the dead is inseparable from and equal to the spiritual value of the living. The lessons of Mason to Ray-ber and Tarwater find their essence in this realization. O'Connor was clear about Mason's significant role as teacher and the alternative vision of reality he offered: "People are depressed by the ending of *The Violent Bear It Away* because they think: poor Tarwater, his mind has been warped by that old man and he's off to make a fool or martyr of himself. They forget that the old man has taught him the truth and that now he's doing what is right, however crazy" (*HB* 536).[8] Mason has the audacity to suggest that the communion of saints is real, that what binds human beings spiritually in life also binds them in death, and that all will be sustained by an abundance of bread and fish without end: "Forever, the old man said" (*VBA* 21). Spiritual communion is held and sustained through love, continues beyond death, and it is threatened only by the violence of the selfish will, which seeks its own desire over the good of others.

Mason himself is well versed in the taming of selfish and violent desires. Early in his prophetic career he sought the destruction of "a world that had abandoned its Savior," confident as he was in his own purity and entitlement. Instead of the destruction of others, Mason's "own blood had been burned dry and not the blood of the world" (5–6). Mason learns by fire and this purifying experience shows up his selfishly motivated desires by the light of a broader view of himself and others. Tarwater describes how Mason would disappear into the woods for days where he "thrashed out his peace with the Lord" and return "bedraggled and hungry" (8). Mason learns to redirect the violence of his religious vision inward instead of outward, as a means of learning humility, for himself as much as for the sake of others. This redirection is his asceticism. It is a disciplining of his spiritual hunger, taking care to prevent his extreme zealousness and the pursuit of individual desires over service to the needs of others. Mason instructs Tarwater in his own lessons of purification, as a means of showing him how to live with his own particular desires, especially when he sees Tarwater's similar propensity for grandiose visions of what he expects as God's personal instructions: "It's no part of your job to think for the Lord" (10).

The violence of the novel, read spiritually, begins with Mason's vision of a world transfigured and his insistence on the human responsibility for the living and the dead. Death is central to Mason's understanding of life. Lying in his coffin, Mason reminds Tarwater, "This is the end of us all" (14). Death permeates all that he teaches and it is the beginning of his spiritual lessons on responsibility: "Burying the dead right may be the only honor you ever do yourself" (15). Mason's religious vision certainly charges the resistance of both Tarwater and Rayber: each of their particular spiritual disciplines are formed and practiced in reaction to Mason, and the "seeds" of his vision that have "dropped" into their blood. As O'Connor describes in a letter to Alfred Corn, "Rayber and Tarwater are really fighting the same current in themselves" (*HB* 484–85). Both Tarwater and Rayber experience Mason's effect on them as a kind of violation of self and they actively resist what they take to be the assertion of his will over them. Tarwater, for example, simply denies Mason's influence, declaring to Rayber, "He ain't had no effect on me" (*VBA* 103). Similarly outraged by his spiritual inheritance, Rayber must perpetually struggle against his own internalization of Mason's voice: "You infected me with your idiot hopes, your foolish violence" (73). The "violence" of Mason's religious vision seemingly causes further violence, in the form of resistance, by Tarwater and Rayber.

In teaching Tarwater (to his dread) about "the sweat and stink of the cross, of being born again to die, and of spending eternity eating the bread of life" (8)—ideas which are none too appealing to the fourteen-year-old Tarwater—Mason is implicitly teaching the communion of saints. His idea of the interconnectedness of human beings through life and death fuels his belief in an order of love that runs counter to the commonly justified vision of love that is solely directed towards a self-serving life. His eyes penetrate the truth of human responsibility enacted as spiritual kinship, appearing "*violent* with their *impossible vision* of a *world transfigured*" (114, emphasis mine). This radical insight extends beyond the surface of things to a deeper spiritual vision: "Msgr. Romano Guardini has written that the roots of the eye are in the heart. In any case, for the Catholic they stretch far and away into those depths of mystery . . ." (*MM* 144–45). And ultimately it is *not* a vision of violence, but rather a vision that in its seeming impossibility, in its transfiguring effects, in its radical nature, is *perceived* as violent. Mason's transfiguring vision of the world can be read as O'Connor's dramatic rendering of the communion of saints, a seemingly impossible vision of reality in which a spiritual communion breaks down the barriers that human beings uphold as markers of their independence and autonomy, continuing even beyond death.

Mason's emphasis on spiritual communion is expressed acutely in his desire that Tarwater bury him properly, implicitly assuming that death is never an end to human obligation. The spiritually ordered world that Mason lives in is not limited by the boundary experience of death. This attention to what is beyond death should not be mistaken for an otherworldly preoccupation; Mason's emphasis on a spiritually ordered reality that allows for the communion of the living and the dead suggests their fundamental relation in the present, and in this world. Only when the spiritual is entirely relegated to another realm, or an afterlife, does it risk becoming irrelevant to the present. Mason reclaims the spiritual as that which brings the living and the dead together, joining rather than severing the idea of the after*life* from life. In a letter to Elizabeth Hester on 24 August 1956, O'Connor describes her response to a book she is reading by Jean Guitton on the subject of eternity: "He says that eternity *begins in time* and that we must stop thinking of it as something that follows time. It's all very instructive and I recommend it" (*HB* 171, emphasis mine).

The mistaken assumptions about the dead espoused by the living are part of Mason's curriculum for Tarwater, and his revealing insights often leave the young boy in a minor state of shock: "The world was made for the dead. Think of all the dead there are . . . . There's a million times more dead than living and the dead are dead a million times longer than the living are alive . . ." (*VBA* 16). With a noticeable quiver, Tarwater reveals how deeply he is affected by the magnitude of this idea. The reader witnesses its lasting impact through Tarwater's ongoing interior dialogue with the stranger. The stranger's approach to the dead, which becomes Tarwater's own preoccupation, is to sever the ties of spirit and matter, by which the unique and particular instance of body and soul that is a *person* is rendered meaningless in death. But personhood for O'Connor is a spiritual category and so does not disappear when someone dies. Yet the fourteen-year-old Tarwater resists

Mason's idea of spiritual and physical kinship, and he meets enough people to confirm him in this opinion (namely Meeks, Rayber, and the stranger/friend).

Unlike Mason, these characters argue that death is the *end* of obligation. Meeks, the copper flue salesman, suggests that the dead are the ones for whom we are finally *not* responsible: "And I say thank God when they're dead . . . that's one less to remember" (51).[9] When Tarwater asks Rayber whether the dead will rise again, he answers flatly, "'No . . . they won't rise again.' There was a profound finality to his tone" (110). Rayber also denies the dead any place in life: "A dead man is not going to do you any good . . ." (104). Death acts as the great divide into oblivion: the soul flies off, the body decays. Both are effectively removed from the concern of the living according to the stranger: "His soul is off this mortal earth now and his body is not going to feel the pinch, of fire or anything else" (36). Mason by contrast, wants Tarwater to remember the dead in their particularity and life, and the fact that the novel begins with his death and ends with an image of his resurrected life is central to its eucharistic structure.

VIOLENCE, LOVE, FAMINE: RAYBER

Rayber's rejection of the meaningful relation that continues between the dead and the living is his rejection of the communion of saints. There is no abundance for Rayber, only the poverty of his narrow definition of life, constituted entirely through the lens of the intellect. Rayber's evaluation of the life of Bishop, his mentally challenged son, is frightening, and clearly without any acknowledgement of spiritual equality: "In a hundred years people may have learned enough to put them to sleep when they're born" (*VBA* 168). This negation of Bishop's life as meaningfully lived obviously flies in the face of the communal and spiritual kinship argued by Mason. But how does Rayber actually live out this response in his daily life? By rejecting the idea of a spiritual community, limiting his responsibility to "the duties of a good citizen" (108), Rayber chooses the individual at the expense of the communal. But to do this he must forge his own brand of asceticism against love.

We can learn something of the power of divine abundance by observing the intellectual gymnastics required to repress its rising tide.

O'Connor argues, "I think the strongest of Rayber's psychological pulls are in the direction that *he does not ultimately choose . . .*" (*HB* 488, emphasis mine), suggesting the need for an asceticism of epic proportions. Rayber resists the abundance of divine love for the sake of his own self-control. His psychological condition is one of violent struggle against a love that perpetually threatens to take him over. Rayber both rejects and, at times, succumbs to the legacy of Mason's ideas. He relentlessly disciplines himself *against* love, a love "so outrageous that he would be left shocked and depressed for days, and trembling for his sanity" (*VBA* 113). When Rayber experiences his overwhelming love for Bishop, which for him is only the beginning of an even more encompassing love, he feels that it extends to "everything his reason hated" (114). In these moments of the rush of love, he actually *longs* for the old man's "violent" eyes to be "turned on him once again" (114). He feels, and even desires, the tempting pull of madness in his own blood, but he chooses to act against it according to the strictures of his self-imposed reason. In so doing, he disciplines himself against whatever spiritual legacy he inherited from the old man. Rather than risk surrendering to an overpowering love, he chooses to resist Mason's spiritual lessons "at the cost of a full life" (114).

There are a number of similar conflicts that are narrated about Rayber's willful choices in life and that reveal his ascetic discipline to be a kind of pseudo-asceticism. During Tarwater's visit, he admits to feeling the tension of his violent and rational self dividing him in two (139): he would rather throttle Tarwater than put up with his surly behavior, but his rational concern to "stretch the boy's mind" forces him to quell his desire and discipline his urge to be rid of him. As for Bishop, the only means for managing the mystical love he feels (*HB* 484) is to, as Giannone so eloquently observes, "use love against love."[10] Rayber's technique in relation to the intense love he actually feels for Bishop is to contain it, "by limiting his responsibility to loving only his child, and then caring only for the boy's physical needs" (*Mystery* 133). O'Connor describes this in a letter to Alfred Corn where she writes, "[I]f Bishop were gone, there would be nothing to contain it [mystical love] and he would then love everything and specifically Christ" (*HB* 484).

The threat of mystical love is its expansiveness. The communion of saints and the mystical body of Christ provide the parameters for Mason's understanding of love. He announces that "[t]he world was made for the dead!" (*VBA* 16). How could that not feel as though it were a violation of all normal expectations and assumptions? So too is the love that threatens to overtake Rayber: "a morbid surge of love that terrified him—powerful enough to throw him completely to the ground in an act of idiot praise" (113). In his rejection of the love that violates his rationality, Rayber chooses emptiness over what he takes to be the risk of madness (115). In this choice against the madness of love, the divine mania that animates Mason, Rayber is the most overtly "ascetic" character in the novel; his world is rigidly ordered, sparse, controlled and disciplined, described explicitly by the narrator as an "ascetic discipline" wherein "he denied his senses unnecessary satisfactions. He slept in a narrow iron bed, worked sitting in a straight-backed chair, ate frugally, spoke little, and cultivated the dullest for friends" (114). By these means, Rayber disciplines himself against love, and in his asceticism he also seeks to save young Tarwater from what he perceives as the madness of Mason's blood. His asceticism does not countenance sacrificial or other-serving love, forms of love that he considers "senseless": "I'm no fool. I don't believe in senseless sacrifice" (104).

But love is extreme, a lesson well taught by Mason. It emboldens Rayber when he listens to Lucette Carmody, and in response to her statement that "Jesus grew up and raised the dead," Rayber has a surge of *feeling*, "his spirit [is] borne aloft" and "he [has] a vision of himself moving like an avenging angel through the world, gathering up all the children that the Lord, not Herod, had slain" (132). Or witness Rayber's terrifying love that if not focused on Bishop would encompass the whole world: surely this is the communion of saints. If anything were to happen to Bishop, Rayber realizes that "the whole world would become his idiot child," and this is because the expansive love that threatens him is a love that "appeared to exist only to be itself, imperious and all-demanding . . ." (113). His weaknesses in the face of his ascetic heroism are his love for Bishop, as well as his abiding love for Mason and his memories of Powderhead.

Although Rayber describes one of his last visits to Powderhead as a moment of insanity (201), the experience of the scene of the burnt house matches detail for detail the one witnessed by Tarwater in his final vision, and further illuminates the transfiguring effects of Mason on each of them. He haunts them in different but parallel ways. The reader is left to glean the meaning of the variations in their responses. To dramatize this, O'Connor creates two sets of parallel scenes or views and connects them: the fountain scene in the park, which is the same scene narrated twice, and then two different scenes from the same vantage point, experienced by Rayber and Tarwater approaching Powderhead after Mason's death.[11] The near baptism of Bishop in the city park is presented as one scene from the perspective of both Rayber and Tarwater, separated by sixteen pages (140–47; 163–67).[12] The two scenes of the burnt house at Powderhead occur on either side of Bishop's actual baptism/drowning. For both characters, these scenes powerfully invoke Mason.

In his experience of the park scene, Rayber is reminded of Mason's presence by observing how the place affects Tarwater, who can palpably feel Powderhead among this rare showing of trees in the middle of the otherwise treeless suburbs. What Tarwater "sees" in his imagination, in fact, is the burnt down house between the two chimneys (163). Rayber's primary struggle in this episode is against the love he feels for Bishop: "Without warning his hated love gripped him . . . . he looked as if he might have been nailed to the bench" (141). Thus nailed to his cross of suffering love, Rayber is reminded of the time he nearly sacrificed Bishop, but realized in horror that without him, his love would truly have no containment (141). Instead Rayber enacts his own ambiguous "baptism" of Bishop on that clear day when the witnessing sky was "not quite blue, not quite white" (142), and his image is captured in the newspaper as the overjoyed father who sees his son "revived" (143).

In this relived experience of his near baptism/drowning of Bishop, Rayber awakens to see that the same compulsion is pulling Tarwater toward Bishop in the fountain's pool. The dual pull on Tarwater is visible: "He seemed to be drawn toward the child in the water but to be pulling back, exerting an almost equal pressure away from what attracted him" (145). The same experience of a double pull is narrated by Tarwater pages later: when he feels the old man's lurking presence drawing him toward an act of baptism, the powerful influence of the stranger draws him back, suggesting that he drown Bishop instead

(164–65). He does neither. After Tarwater leaves the park, Rayber has a revelation of his own: "The words the old man had scrawled on the back of the journal rose before him: THE PROPHET I RAISE UP OUT OF THIS BOY WILL BURN YOUR EYES CLEAN. The sentence was like a challenge renewed" (147). Rayber sees his own salvation tied to his ability to "save" Tarwater from Mason's influence: "his mind turned to the problem of Tarwater as if his own and not only the boy's salvation depended on his solving it" (187).

Rayber meets this challenge by revisiting the place Mason still haunts (183–87). While staying at the Cherokee Lodge, Rayber finds himself back at Powderhead with Bishop, and he immediately becomes angry for somehow arriving there. Rayber experiences the same oscillating draw and resistance he witnessed in Tarwater at the park. The pull of the place and its familiarity are immediately destabilizing for Rayber, and once again, Bishop adds to this instability. At first sight of the blackberry bushes Bishop runs gleefully toward them; Rayber protects him from the wasps and picks one for him, handing it to Bishop: "The little boy studied it and then, with his fallen smile, returned it to him as if they were performing a ceremony" (184). This ritual exchange and Bishop's gift of the berry is thrown away by Rayber, who will do what he can to resist any acknowledgment of the sacrality of the place. Nonetheless, it persists, "[t]he forest rose about him, mysterious and alien," the only sound, "[s]omewhere below them out of the silence a bird sounded four crystal notes" (184). When Rayber realizes the property is legally his, his first feeling is one of wonder at the trees rising around him, "majestic and aloof, as if they belonged to an order that had never changed from its first allegiance in the days of creation" (185); his heart beats out of control and he restrains the feeling, reducing the forest instead to board feet for Tarwater's college degree (185). He looks out, *expressionless,* forcing his desire *not to feel* upon himself, yet seeing the two chimneys, "separated by a black space of rubble," his heart is wrenched despite himself (186).

Mason represents the love that Rayber resists; Bishop connects him to it: "He felt a pressure on his hand and glanced down, continuing to see the same expression and barely noting that it was Bishop he was looking at now" (186). In the face of the love that overwhelms and terrifies, Rayber has trained himself to recoil. He knows that he can only flee. The loss he feels, which is compounded by Bishop looking at the scene as he holds him up, forces Rayber to recognize that he cannot stay an instant longer (187). His response is to shut down in the face of the love that threatens. Asceticism against abundant love, in Rayber's experience, lives by the rejection of spiritual communion. To enter into that communion would mean letting loose his contained love for Bishop, extending it, as it were, to the whole communion of saints: "He would have with one supreme effort to resist the recognition [of the whole world as his idiot child]; with every nerve and muscle and thought, he would have to resist feeling anything at all, thinking anything at all" (182). Rayber is left in a spiritual desert, alone and sunk more deeply into the false safety of his illusion that he needs no one beyond himself.

HUNGER, FIRE, FEAST: TARWATER

> I have a sentence in mind to end some story that I am going to write. The character all through it will have been hungry and, at the end, he is so hungry that "he could have eaten all the loaves and fishes, after they were multiplied."
> —Flannery O'Connor, *The Habit of Being*

Rather than simply accept Mason's exhortations about spiritual community undigested or resist them with ascetic rigor like Rayber, Tarwater charts a different course. O'Connor notes in a letter the difference between the two characters this way: "Tarwater wrestles with the Lord and Rayber wins" (*HB* 488). Another version of this idea comes in a different letter to the same correspondent: "Rayber achieves his own will, and Tarwater submits to his vocation" (485). Phrased another way, we might say that Rayber chooses his individual will over and against communal obligation, whereas Tarwater submits finally to a desire that is deeply written in his body and spirit; namely, he comes to terms with his spiritual hunger and its source.

Tarwater's asceticism can be mapped out as resistance to his hunger, which is challenged perpetually by the various desires of his will. Rather than assume that this creates an either/or choice between his individual desire for autonomy or freedom and an acceptance of Mason's ideas about spiritual communion, the novel reveals the possibility that Tarwater moves steadily toward an experience of both/and. Rayber fasts against love, and Tarwater fasts against his spiritual hunger. Love and food are offered to them in abundance at the end of the novel—O'Connor's eucharistic hymn—but only one of them is able to receive. The personal and communal cohabit in the shared meal of the banquet: Tarwater finds the spiritual sustenance for which he has been hungering, but it is a desire fulfilled that he shares in the company of others. O'Connor highlights how in Rayber's and Tarwater's struggles against divine reality, Rayber's ability to shut down is matched by Tarwater's ability to open up. To open is to be able to receive.

When Tarwater returns to Powderhead—after he has been raped, and after baptizing/drowning Bishop—we see the same scene witnessed earlier by Rayber, but through Tarwater's different, now changed eyes (*VBA* 235–38). Tarwater pauses at the same place Rayber did, his glance passing quickly over the ripening berries, a brief reminder of Bishop's continued presence. He hears the same bird: "Somewhere in the wood a woodthrush called and as if the sound were a key turned in the boy's heart, his throat began to tighten" (236). Tarwater gazes at the rubble of the burnt house, where the "two chimneys stood like grieving figures" (236). At this same sight Rayber's heart wrenched in his chest but he closes himself, refuses to feel it and flees (187); Tarwater, on the other hand, feels a key turning in his heart and moves on toward the rubble, toward the two grieving figures, perhaps symbolizing the towering influence of both Mason and Rayber. Tarwater, this passage seems to suggest, has come into his own. But unlike Rayber, he is not alone. The communion of saints appears as he gazes out over the field of his new home: "It seemed to him no longer empty but peopled with a multitude" (241).

Throughout the novel, rather than simply having to choose between the mentorship of Mason and Rayber, Tarwater has his own desires to contend with. What is it that keeps him searching and hungry? And where is he led by this desire? In light of O'Connor's significant use of food symbolism and in particular her ongoing referencing of hunger as a metaphor for spiritual longing, how might we then understand this relationship between hunger, desire, asceticism, and the communion of saints? The spiritual hunger that Tarwater experiences is largely painful, often resisted, sometimes violent in its intensity, but ultimately rooted in a desire that seeks fulfillment, that seeks God in abundance. Yet hunger also suggests a lack. Focusing on Tarwater's hunger, we can direct our attention to the vision beheld by Tarwater at the end of the novel: fulfillment that is both personal—the human desire for the bread of life—and yet communal—the messianic feast of abundance. The living and the dead come together, the personal and the communal are entwined, all separations are dissolved and yet the individual person comes to completion. To find himself able to *receive* the gift offered to him, the gift that will truly and fully satisfy his hunger, Tarwater has to recognize that he needs others and that he alone is incapable of providing his own satisfaction.

O'Connor's reading of the mystic St. Catherine of Genoa may offer further insight into this idea of spiritual hunger and its relationship to the Eucharist for our interpretation of Tarwater's desire. We know O'Connor was reading St. Catherine's *Treatise on Purgatory* around the time that she was writing *The Violent Bear It Away*.[13] And we know that the *Treatise* is saturated with references to purification via the metaphors of bread and fire. It seems reasonable then to suggest that O'Connor's imagery in *The Violent Bear It Away* is drawing heavily on her reading of the saint.[14] For instance, St. Catherine describes the soul's approach to and desire for God as hunger; O'Connor describes Tarwater as in a constant state of unsatisfied hunger. In the *Treatise,* St. Catherine depicts her vision of the soul's longing for God as something that is like a seed sown in us all at the moment of creation. While no single metaphor or image can capture this idea, she uses hunger as an apt description of this desire: "Let us imagine that in the whole world there was but *one bread* and that it could satisfy the hunger of *all*" (*Purgatory* 76, emphasis mine).[15]

St. Catherine is giving an account of her vision of purgatory, which is not so much about a place but a condition of the soul, where the desire for God is mixed with an acute suffering as the soul recognizes its lack. According to her vision, the souls in purgatory are full of hunger, and "the closer they come to this bread, the more they are aware that they do not as yet have it. Their yearning for this bread increases . . ." (76). For St. Catherine, this experience of yearning is felt by all, sown into human desire, as it were, from creation. And so, while each human being experiences it singly, it is nonetheless a desire that is *shared*. The abundance of the feast, however, does not disappoint: the miraculous multiplication of the loaves and fish implies that there is plenty for all and that no individual desire will interfere with the satisfaction of another's. Thus the desire, or hunger, is both individually and communally shared. St. Catherine's vision of purgatory suggests that the suffering of purgatory is the suffering of this hunger that ultimately leads all souls toward their "true joy": "the true bread and the true God . . . [t]his, then, is their suffering, the waiting for the bread that will take away their hunger" (76–77).

Tarwater's spiritual journey is one marked by hunger. Indeed, O'Connor first conceived of the novel as one in which the protagonist was so hungry he could consume the miracle of the bread and fish multiplied. Food pervades the inner and outer worlds of Tarwater's resistance to his prophetic vocation, a vocation that could also be characterized in terms of his resistance to the bread of life, despite a crippling hunger for it. With Mason, Tarwater is always in the presence of an abundance of food, enough to make him not want it. As soon as Tarwater reaches the city, however, his hunger makes itself felt more forcefully: "The first day in the city he had become conscious of the strangeness in his stomach, a peculiar hunger" (*VBA* 161). While the interior voice of the friend continually refuses to allow Tarwater to entertain this hunger as a "sign," it is nonetheless a force: "Since the breakfast he had finished sitting in the presence of his uncle's corpse, he had not been satisfied by food, and his hunger had become like an insistent silent force inside him . . ." (162). Clearly, if ironically, Tarwater's spiritual desire seems to become more present to him when he is deprived of his great-uncle's company.

Throughout the novel, food is powerfully symbolic of the spiritual challenge that the novel stages. Indeed, the novel begins with an image of abundant food as Mason and Tarwater sit down to a vast breakfast, a meal that will turn out to be Mason's last supper, for he dies at its conclusion. Breakfasts at Rayber's, by contrast, are pale in comparison, and the absence of abundant food is clearly intended to signal Rayber's spiritual impoverishment as well:

The city food only weakened him. He and his great-uncle had eaten well. If the old man *had done nothing else for him,* he had heaped his plate. Never a morning he had not awakened to the smell of fatback frying. The schoolteacher *paid scarce attention to what he put inside him.* For breakfast, he poured a bowl of shavings out of a cardboard box; in the middle of the day he made sandwiches out of light bread; and at night he took them to a restaurant. (161–62, emphasis mine)

Tarwater's relationship to his hunger has been deeply affected by Mason, and his distaste for Rayber's food, coupled with his inability to eat it, is a significant part of his struggle to work out his experience of his two uncles and their varying degrees of influence. Tarwater does not want to acknowledge that his hunger has anything to do with Jesus, desiring instead his spiritual freedom. But he eventually comes to acknowledge that he hungers for something more than bread alone.

For Mason, the bread of life—that for which he and Tarwater hunger spiritually—is found in Jesus. The bread of life, however, especially tied to Jesus, was an appalling thought to the young man: "in the darkest, most private part of his soul, hanging upside down like a sleeping bat, was the certain, undeniable knowledge that he was not hungry for the bread of life" (21). The madness that Tarwater identifies with Mason and fears in himself is his spiritual hunger: "this was the heart of his great-uncle's madness, this hunger" (21). Tarwater has an early vision of his inherited hunger/madness listening to the old man talk: "The boy would have a hideous vision of himself sitting forever with his great-uncle on a green bank, full and sick, staring at a broken fish and a multiplied loaf" (62). In the eucharistic image foreshadowed in this scene, we see that Tarwater does everything in his power to resist the vision. Yet it is precisely to this scene that he returns at the conclusion of the novel.

In the city, Rayber uses food as a lesson plan in multiculturalism: "at night he took them to a restaurant, a different one every night run by a different color of foreigner so that he would learn, he said, how other nationalities ate" (162). But the food never satisfies and Tarwater only feels monetarily indebted to Rayber for the dinners. At each restaurant he would write the approximate value of the meal down on a piece of paper, insistent that "he would pay back the total sum . . . as he did not intend to be beholden" (116). Food shared with Rayber becomes part of an implicit debt economy in which Tarwater feels, without ever being told, that he *owes* Rayber. The food neither sustains nor interests him: "He was a finicky eater, pushing the food around on his plate before he ate it and putting each forkful in his mouth as if he suspected it was poisoned" (116).

At the Cherokee Lodge after Tarwater binges on buns and barbeque, which Rayber reads as originating in some kind of clinically compulsive behavior, the two go fishing. The sight of the water has already weakened Tarwater, who is unnerved by that lake and baptismal font. The combined effects of talking, fishing, and eating too much barbeque conspire like a rising column in Tarwater's stomach and he loses his lunch over the side of the boat. Rayber immediately sees this purgation as a moment of vulnerability and his comment here comes remarkably close to the idea of the communion of saints, but in modified form and with Rayber claiming his absolute status as savior/father confessor: "It's just as much relief," his uncle said, pressing his advantage, "to get something off your mind as off your stomach. When you tell somebody else your troubles, then they don't bother you so much. . . . Somebody else shares the weight" (174). Rayber's assent to the idea of sharing the burden of another's suffering is here simply used to *his own advantage*. Rayber wants to "save" Tarwater from Mason's ideas, only to replace them with his own. Rayber tells him, "you need help. You need to be saved right here now from the old man and everything he stands for. And I'm the one who can save you." (174). It is clear that for Rayber, Tarwater is an idea: "He gazed through the actual insignificant boy before him to an image of him that he held firmly developed in his mind" (90). There is no real sense of the individual that Tarwater is. He is only a receptacle that Rayber can fill with his own ideas and a smattering of cultural content via foreign morsels of food.

But as Tarwater discovers, Rayber's "guts are in his head" (172). With such a relocation of the passions, hunger is effectively displaced and ultimately controlled by the brain's logic; Rayber's asceticism is not driven by desire but rigidly monitored by the intellect. By contrast it is

Tarwater's spiritual hunger that finally propels him beyond Rayber's grasp and returns him home to Powderhead. The night he sees the bread in the store window, Rayber thinks that he has found something that he can buy for Tarwater, something that will finally satisfy him, but Tarwater is in the grip of something else, a hunger that cannot be easily assuaged with a new purchase: "It looked to him like the face of someone starving who sees a meal he can't reach laid out before him. At last, something he *wants*" (122). St. Catherine describes the experience thus:

> That bread is what a healthy man, with an appetite, would seek; and when he could not find it or eat it, his hunger would increase indefinitely. Aware that that bread alone could assuage his hunger, he would also know that without it his hunger could never abate. Such is the hell of the hungry who, the closer they come to this bread, the more they are aware that they do not as yet have it. Their yearning for that bread increases, because that is their joy. (*Purgatory* 76)

Despite all of his protestations to the contrary, Tarwater seeks this bread, and his spiritual longing is lived through the embodied experience of hunger. He had undeniably been nourished by Mason both physically and spiritually, and bereft of his care, the pseudo-ascetic Rayber offers meager sustenance. Tarwater must move beyond and away from Rayber because despite his interest in Rayber's claim to autonomy, something that he also seeks, the resulting isolation (imaged repeatedly in the novel by his hearing aid) results in stagnant emptiness: Tarwater notes, "He can't do nothing. All he can do is figure it out. He's got this wired head. There's an electric cord runs into his ear" (*VBA* 212). Tarwater understands that while Rayber can simply "shut off" the outside world by shutting off his hearing aid, nonetheless he is ultimately ruled by it, and thus not free.

Increasingly aware that there is something about Rayber's expression of his autonomy that is actually a form of impotence, Tarwater is challenged to live his autonomy differently. Here the subtle influence of "his friend" takes over. Rayber shows Tarwater how dispensable Bishop is, and his friend directs him on how to *act that idea out* by drowning him. It is precisely in response to the driving hunger and Rayber's inability to act that the friend suggests to Tarwater that he drown Bishop. Mason's spiritual presence and Rayber's autonomy and self-styled salvation merge in the disembodied voice of the friend. The voice mocks that hunger and in the face of it, knowing it to be the real spiritual force that lives in Tarwater, tries to persuade Tarwater that the experience itself is a physical manifestation of illness: "as for that strangeness in your gut, that comes from you, not the Lord. When you were a child you had worms. As likely as not you have them again" (161). Tarwater's unease, precipitated by the spectre of lake at the Cherokee Lodge, and his abiding nausea/hunger elicits further guidance from the so-called friend: "Steady, his friend said, everywhere you go you'll find water. It wasn't invented yesterday. But remember: water is made for more than one thing. Hasn't the time come? Don't you have to do something at last, one thing to prove you ain't going to do another?" (167).

The dismissal of Tarwater's hunger echoes the dismissal of baptism as the gift that comes from God. The friend wants Tarwater to reject the gift and use it to his own advantage. Tarwater, however, is still receptive, and while he drowns Bishop, the baptism is received by both. Tarwater's starkest rejection of the bread of life is his murder of Bishop. But the drowning draws him into a baptism, and what happens then is an introduction to a new landscape, peopled with those who witness both the baptism and the murder. He feels as though Bishop's death initiated him into the company of the dead. Remembering the moment, he felt "bodiless as if he were nothing but a head full of air, about to tackle *all the dead*" (215). In his memory, he is no longer simply killing Bishop alone; with this act, the community enlarges. The communion of saints cannot be willed away, and so they are present at Bishop's death and new life in baptism.

On his return trip back to Powderhead to claim his uncle's land as his own, Tarwater begins walking, "violently hungry and disappointed" (219). He has assumed that his arrival home will officially mark his full autonomy and freedom, "where he could begin to live his life as he elected it" (218). Tarwater has his own ascetic practice to work out by the end of *The Violent Bear It Away*. He is contending with the devil—who purposely takes himself out of the equation—to force Tarwater into an extreme choice between himself and spiritual community. But the devil gets it wrong. Mason has taught Tarwater the importance of personal human freedom: "I saved you to be free, your own self!" (16), affirming the notion of personhood. The devil, then, forces Tarwater to work against his own desires, his own hunger that would take him to a place that is both an affirmation of personal fulfillment/freedom *and* communal responsibility.

Tarwater's hunger takes on explicit Christian imagery: "his hunger and his thirst combined in a pain that shot up and down him and across from shoulder to shoulder" (222). Deeper movements are happening in Tarwater's soul; the cross of his hunger marks him indelibly. It also begins to include others—he hungers not just for food: "He hungered now for companionship as much as food and water" (226). The companionship he finds with the "old-looking young man" in the panama hat, however, is not what he truly desires. Tarwater's exclamations in the car sound false and forced as he downs the proffered liquor: "It's better than the Bread of Life!" and his hunger is only momentarily relaxed by the drugs and alcohol to create the (again false) impression that he is "*pleasantly deprived of responsibility* or of the need for any effort to justify his actions" (230, emphasis mine). The same impression is of course espoused by the stranger. When Tarwater emerges from the woods after he is raped, the devil is still at his heels and the push to be autonomous and independent still proffers its tempting discourse: "Go down and take it, his friend whispered. It's ours. We've won it. Ever since you first begun to dig the grave, I've stood by you, never left your side, and now we can take it over together, just you and me. You're never going to be alone again" (237). But these are only more lies from the devil. Tarwater resists this pseudo-companionship, painfully aware already of its effects.

Instead, he feels pulled toward the land, and as he draws closer, he finds Buford Munson. His first thought is that "[h]e would go home with him and eat" (239). Tarwater arrives to find Mason already buried, and when he looks at the cross on Mason's grave it is the extended community of saints we see. Tarwater's eyes—with their expanded spiritual vision—"stared downward at the cross as if they followed below the surface of the earth to where its roots encircled all the dead." The empty field was "peopled with a multitude," and "he saw from a single basket . . . a throng being fed" (240). John Desmond describes the meaning of this same vision in *Risen Sons:* "Tarwater's vision of the multitude sharing in the food of life conveys O'Connor's understanding of the mystical community composed of all the living and the dead, who are bonded together by one central act—the Incarnation and Resurrection of Christ" (64).[16] In the landscape are now others who share his hunger, and in this moment of communion, Tarwater's self-understanding, rather than diminished, is increased and deepened by their presence. Tarwater sees the fulfillment of his hunger in the loaves and fishes multiplied, *shared* among the living and the dead.

The freedom and autonomy that Tarwater has sought since the death of Mason has come full circle, and he arrives at a place of communion rather than isolation. No longer imposing the free reign of his selfish will, he is himself enlarged by the community that surrounds him. He joins the living and the dead and the feast is *abundant.* He embodies a desire for something larger than himself, his hunger is no longer painful but like a "tide," "rising in himself through time and darkness, rising through the centuries . . ." (242). By finding the fulfillment of his hunger, the source of his spiritual desire, Tarwater learns that this abundance feeds without diminishing, no matter how many are at the feast. The communion of saints is real. Bread and fish without end.

NOTES

1. Elizabeth Hester is the correspondent initially identified as "A" in Sally Fitzgerald's edition of O'Connor's collected letters, *The Habit of Being.* Hester and O'Connor became friends after Hester wrote to the writer, and they carried on an intense correspondence for the rest of O'Connor's life.

2. This notion of abundance has come primarily from my colleague Sal Renshaw, whose work on abundant love has influenced my discussion here. See Renshaw.

3. "That this is the violence of love, of giving more than the law demands, of an asceticism like John the Baptist's . . ." (*HB* 382).

4. See O'Connor's letter to John Hawkes, 26 December 1959: "I certainly do mean Tarwater's friend to be the Devil" (*HB* 367).

5. Manuscript, Archives, and Rare Book Library, Emory University. Manuscript Collection, number 59, box 2, item 15.

6. For additional attempts to understand the meaning of O'Connor's "violence of love," see Srigley, *Flannery O'Connor's Sacramental Art* (98–105); and Srigley, "The Violence of Love." Several scholars have written with insight on this issue of asceticism in O'Connor clarifying the inward orientation of the violence; see, for example, Giannone, *Mystery;* Giannone, *Hermit Novelist;* Desmond; and Brinkmeyer.

7. Emory University Archives, Flannery O'Connor/Elizabeth Hester Correspondence, collection 1064, box 1, ff. 2.

8. She says further, "A good many Catholics are put off because they think the old man, being a Protestant prophet, so to speak, has no hold on the truth. They look at everything in a confessional way . . ." (*HB* 536).

9. This ultimately reflects the Gnostic position O'Connor repeatedly resisted. The "stranger's" suggestion that the soul is off the mortal earth now, leaving the useless body behind, is just one more example of the separation of the physical and spiritual. See Peters, "The Source." For an interesting discussion of Gnosticism in Wendell Berry, which has remarkable parallels with O'Connor's anti-Manicheism, see Peters, "Wendell Berry's Vindication."

10. For the most illuminating study on love in O'Connor see Giannone, *Flannery O'Connor and the Mystery of Love.*

11. There are other scenes that the reader witnesses from different perspectives, for example the different angles from which Rayber and Tarwater view Lucette Carmody's performance. My intention here is not to address all of these episodes in the novel but to focus on the link between the scene in the park and the experience at Powderhead as instances of Mason's presence and how Tarwater and Rayber react to that presence.

12. For other scholars who address these parallel scenes in detail, see Christina Bieber Lake, Karl Martin, and Richard Giannone.

13. O'Connor first mentions reading St. Catherine of Genoa's treatise on purgatory in a letter to Elizabeth Hester, 30 October 1955, a year before her letter to Hester about a character (Tarwater) who is hungry for the bread and fish (24 March 1956).

14. See Srigley, *Flannery O'Connor's Sacramental Art* 135–59, where I suggest that O'Connor's idea for Ruby Turpin's purgatorial vision in her story "Revelation" comes from St. Catherine's *Treatise on Purgatory.*

15. "Because there is one bread, we who are many are one body, for we all partake of the one bread" (1 Corinthians 17).

16. "I think that the Church is the only thing that is going to make the terrible world we are coming to endurable; *the only thing that makes the Church endurable is that it is somehow the body of Christ and that on this we are fed*" (*HB* 90, emphasis mine).

WORKS CITED

Brinkmeyer, Robert H., Jr. "Asceticism and the Imaginative Vision of Flannery O'Connor." *Flannery O'Connor: New Perspectives*. Ed. Sura P. Rath and Mary Neff Shaw. Athens: University of Georgia Press, 1996. 169–82.

Desmond, John F. *Risen Sons: Flannery O'Connor's Vision of History*. Athens: University of Georgia Press, 1987.

———. "Violence and the Christian Mystery: A Way to Read Flannery O'Connor." *Literature and Belief* 17 (1997): 129–47.

Dych, William V. *Karl Rahner*. Collegeville, MN: Liturgical Press, 1992.

Giannone, Richard. *Flannery O'Connor and the Mystery of Love*. Urbana: University of Illinois Press, 1989.

———. *Flannery O'Connor, Hermit Novelist*. Urbana: University of Illinois Press, 2000.

Lake, Christina Bieber. *The Incarnational Art of Flannery O'Connor*. Macon, GA: Mercer University Press, 2005.

O'Connor, Flannery. *The Habit of Being: Letters of Flannery O'Connor*. Ed. Sally Fitzgerald. New York: Farrar, Straus and Giroux, 1979.

———. *Mystery and Manners: Occasional Prose*. Ed. Sally Fitzgerald and Robert Fitzgerald. New York: Farrar, Straus and Giroux, 1969.

———. *The Violent Bear It Away*. New York: Farrar, Straus and Giroux, 1960.

Peters, Jason. "The Source of Flannery O'Connor's 'Flung' Fish in *The Violent Bear It Away*." *American Notes and Queries* 18.4 (Fall 2005): 48–53.

———. "Wendell Berry's Vindication of the Flesh." *Christianity and Literature* 56.2 (Winter 2007): 317–32.

Renshaw, Sal. *The Subject of Love: Hélène Cixous and the Feminine Divine*. Manchester: Manchester University Press, 2009.

Srigley, Susan. *Flannery O'Connor's Sacramental Art*. Notre Dame, IN: University of Notre Dame Press, 2004.

———. "The Violence of Love: Reflections on Self-Sacrifice through Flannery O'Connor and René Girard." *Religion and Literature* 39.3 (2007): 1–15.

St. Catherine of Genoa. [*Treatise on Purgatory*]. *Classics of Western Spirituality: Purgation and Purgatory and the Spiritual Dialogue*. Trans. Serge Hughes. Mahwah, NJ: Paulist Press, 1979. 71–87.

CONTRIBUTORS

GARY M. CIUBA is the author of *Walker Percy: Books of Revelations* (University of Georgia Press) and *Desire, Violence, and Divinity in Modern Southern Fiction: Katherine Anne Porter, Flannery O'Connor, Cormac McCarthy, and Walker Percy* (Louisiana State University Press). He is a member of the editorial board of the *Flannery O'Connor Review*, where he has published articles and reviewed books on O'Connor. His other articles on southern literature have appeared in *African American Review, American Literature, Mississippi Quarterly, South Atlantic Review, Southern Literary Journal,* and *Southern Quarterly* as well as in book-length collections of essays on Percy, McCarthy, and southern literary culture. Ciuba is Professor of English at Kent State University.

JOHN F. DESMOND is the Mary A. Denny Professor Emeritus of English, Whitman College. He is author of *Risen Sons: Flannery O'Connor's Vision of History* (University of Georgia Press), *At the Crossroads: Ethical and Religious Themes in the Writings of Walker Percy* (Whitston Publishing Co.), and *Walker Percy's Search for Community* (University of Georgia Press). He has published more than fifty essays on O'Connor, Faulkner, Twain, James, Percy, Malamud, Graham Greene, Seamus Heaney, and Eudora Welty.

RICHARD GIANNONE is Professor Emeritus of English, Fordham University. He is the author of *Music in Willa Cather's Fiction, Vonnegut: A Preface to his Novels, Flannery O'Connor and the Mystery of Love,* and *Flannery O'Connor, Hermit Novelist.* In spring 2012, Fordham University Press will publish his new book *Hidden: Reflections on Gay Life, AIDS, and Spiritual Desire.*

SCOTT HUELIN is Associate Professor of English and Director of the Honors Community at Union University. His research interests include the history of Christian theology, ethics, and spirituality; classical, medieval, and early modern literature; and the twentieth-century Catholic literary renaissance. His published essays and book reviews have appeared in *Religion and Literature, Christian Scholar's Review,* the *Journal of Religion, Christian Reflection,* the *Cresset,* and the *Journal of the National Collegiate Honors Council.* He has recently completed a manuscript on the ethics of literary interpretation entitled "The Hermeneutics of Hospitality."

RUTHANN KNECHEL JOHANSEN is Emerita Professor at the University of Notre Dame. Since 2007 she has been president of Bethany Theological Seminary in Richmond, Indiana. She is the author of *The Narrative Secret of Flannery O'Connor: The Trickster as Interpreter* (University of Alabama Press) and *Listening in the Silence, Seeing in the Dark: Reconstructing Life after Brain Injury* (University of California Press).

P. TRAVIS KROEKER, Professor of Religious Studies at McMaster University, is the author of *Christian Ethics and Political Economy in North America* (McGill-Queen's University Press) and co-author of *Remembering the End: Dostoevsky as Prophet of Modernity* (Westview Press). Kroeker's current research interests include apocalyptic literature and political theology and the relationship between immortality, ethics, and political judgment in selected ancient and modern theologies.

KARL E. MARTIN is Professor of Literature in the Department of Literature, Journalism, and Modern Languages at Point Loma Nazarene University. Martin has published scholarship regarding O'Connor in *The Flannery O'Connor Bulletin, Religion and Literature,* and *Literature and Belief.* In addition to his work on O'Connor, Martin has published work and delivered conference papers examining a variety of American religious narratives.

JASON PETERS is Professor of English and the Dorothy J. Parkander Chair in Literature at Augustana College in Rock Island, Illinois. His work has appeared in *Sewanee Review, South Atlantic Quarterly, English Language Notes, Explicator, American Notes and Queries, Christianity and Literature, The Review of Politics,* and *Journal of Religion and Society.* He is also the editor of *Wendell Berry: Life and Work* (University Press of Kentucky).

SUSAN SRIGLEY is Associate Professor of Religions and Cultures at Nipissing University in North Bay, Ontario, Canada. She is the author of *Flannery O'Connor's Sacramental Art* (University of Notre Dame Press). Her primary area of research is religious ethics and literature, focusing on the interplay between ancient spiritual thinkers and traditions and their dramatic representation in modern literary texts.

INDEX

Nietzsche, Friedrich, 12, 30, 123
nihilism, 11, 13, 16, 20, 30

"Parker's Back" (O'Connor), 31, 87, 89
Percy, Walker, 41
Plato, 119, 132, 133n18, 148
prophecy, 68, 110, 143, 154n4, 158, 169
prophet, 23, 90, 108–9, 113–15, 153, 154n4, 158, 187, 200
    Isaiah as, 113, 165
    John the Baptist as, 136
    Jonah as, 145, 181
    Mason as, 65, 69, 71, 75, 77, 81, 106, 162–63, 182, 211n8
    Tarwater as, 11, 28, 70, 77, 89, 137, 169, 174, 176
    the Misfit as, 22
prophetic vision, 137, 142

Rahner, Karl, 191
rationalism
    in Rayber, 35, 40–41, 44–46, 51, 54, 54n4, 122, 138
reason, 18–19, 21, 27, 40, 42, 44, 50, 55, 114, 119, 121, 142, 144, 151, 197
    See also *imago Dei;* love: without reason
responsibility, 9, 27, 37, 154, 194
    communal, 188, 192, 194
    moral, 22, 37, 106
    Rayber's, 37, 41, 196–97
    Tarwater's, 22, 24, 80, 209
revelation, 11, 37, 144, 147, 154, 169–71, 200
    Christian, 14
"Revelation" (O'Connor), 211n14

sacramental, 136–37, 145–46, 152–53
sacramentum, 138
sacrifice, 20, 73, 198
    Jesus', 18, 47
    self-, 159, 189–90
    See also under love
Sartre, Jean-Paul, 9
Shengold, Leonard, 79
Sheol, 23
sin, 9, 27, 54n4, 129, 149, 189
    Augustine's teachings on, 128
    incurvatus in se, 128
    Rayber's, 51–52, 128
    Tarwater's parents', 67
    the Misfit's, 21
Surin, Kenneth, 44, 48

"The Artificial Nigger" (O'Connor), 29, 60
"The Displaced Person" (O'Connor), 29, 105
The Habit of Being (O'Connor), 7, 148, 192, 201
"The Lame Shall Enter First" (O'Connor), 8, 60, 62, 83n2
"The River" (O'Connor), 32, 36, 60
theodicy, 43–44
Trinity, the, 89, 133n7, 169

Verrier, Nancy Newton, 65–66, 83n7

Weil, Simone, 104–12, 114–15, 127, 130
Welty, Eudora, 50
Wise Blood (O'Connor), 8–11, 13, 15–16, 29, 60
World War II, 7, 9, 27, 30

SUSAN SRIGLEY

is associate professor in the department of religions

and cultures at Nipissing University.

She is the author of *Flannery O'Connor's Sacramental Art*

(University of Notre Dame Press, 2005).